PENGUIN BOOKS

HOW TO RUN A GOVERNMENT

Sir Michael Barber is the co-founder of Delivery Associates and Chief Education Advisor at Pearson. Over the last two decades he has worked on government and public service reform in more than fifty countries. From 2001 to 2005 he was the first Head of the Prime Minister's Delivery Unit in the UK. His previous books include *Instruction to Deliver: Fighting to Transform Britain's Public Services*.

MICHAEL BARBER

How to Run a Government

So that Citizens Benefit and
Taxpayers Don't Go Crazy

PENGUIN BOOKS

PENGUIN BOOKS

UK | USA | Canada | Ireland | Australia
India | New Zealand | South Africa

Penguin Books is part of the Penguin Random House group of companies
whose addresses can be found at global.penguinrandomhouse.com.

First published by Allen Lane 2015
Published in Penguin Books 2016
009

Copyright © Michael Barber, 2015

The moral right of the author has been asserted

Set in 9.24/12.44 pt Sabon LT Std
Typeset by Jouve (UK), Milton Keynes
Printed and bound in Italy by Grafica Veneta S.p.A.

A CIP catalogue record for this book is available from the British Library

ISBN: 978–0–141–97958–8

For Karen

Between the idea
And the reality
Between the motion
And the act
Falls the Shadow

– T. S. Eliot,
'The Hollow Men'

Contents

Conclusion: The Future of Delivery

In which some emerging themes destined to reshape and strengthen
government approaches to delivery in future are predicted.

Preface

Why do we need a book about how to run a government? Isn't the world already flooded with books about government? Aren't there columnists in every serious newspaper – and now a host of bloggers too – churning out more political commentary, much of it excellent, every hour?

Well, yes there are, but surprisingly very few of the books and very little of the commentary focus on how to run a government so that it delivers the change it has promised. In fact, there is a gaping hole where this should be.

Governments' errors, needless to say, attract plenty of attention (as they should); as does the practice of politics – how to win and lose elections, how to gain and lose power – which is endlessly fascinating; the fortunes of individual politicians as their ambitions are fulfilled or (more often) dashed are an endless soap opera; and, as thinking about government and politics advances, ideas are debated too, sometimes even at a rarefied level. But for some reason the practices of governments that succeed in making real improvements to the lives of their citizens attract very little attention.

Perhaps at first glance this is due to the way outcomes for citizens are ground out (and they usually are ground out), which looks a little dull compared to the gossip or the commentary or the controversy about a big idea. But in this book I aim to show that this is a totally false conception. The reality is that the process by which governments deliver results is not just fascinating, but also vitally important.

Why? Because, while what the president of the World Bank Jim Yong Kim calls the 'science of delivery' – the growing knowledge base about how governments can successfully deliver – is new and a phenomenon of the past decade or so, governments across every time zone are wrestling with the challenge of delivery on a daily basis. Across continents, their problems are remarkably similar as well as remarkably soluble, as the chapters that follow set out. In these pages there are stories and examples from every continent (except Antarctica), and every stage of development, which indicate practically how governments could massively increase their chances of success. As Jennifer Gold points out, 'For all the differences in the way various centres of government are approaching the task of improving implementation ... across government, there are also important similarities.'[1]

Furthermore, history provides many examples of leaders of governments – kings and emperors, as well as presidents and prime ministers – who sought to improve the lives of their citizens and sometimes succeeded. As they did so, they weren't aware that one day they'd provide the historical evidence for an emerging science of delivery; nor, generally speaking, were the historians and biographers who wrote about them. Yet by sifting through the stories of, for example, Theodore Roosevelt, Horatio Nelson, Mohandas K. Gandhi and Henry VII, king of England, all of whom appear in these pages, one finds there, among the debris of historical writing, just as an archaeologist does among ruins, artefacts which, once assembled, provide insight into how governments of the future can get things done, often against the odds.

Understanding how to run a government effectively is important because the success or otherwise of governments is fundamental to the prosperity and well-being of all of us, wherever we live. There is a tendency in the West, especially in the US, to see government as the problem, not least because a lot of the time government is hapless or worse. Government can be a problem, but you only have to look at what life is like when it breaks down to realize how important good government is.

Also, we fool ourselves if we set up a false dichotomy between markets and governments, since the functioning of one depends absolutely on the other. Whether government is big or small is a political choice that countries can make but, whatever your politics, the effectiveness (or lack of it) of government is immensely important. As Theodore

Roosevelt pointed out over a century ago, there is much more risk to markets from power being insufficiently concentrated than from its concentration in 'responsible and accountable hands'.[2] His successor but one, Woodrow Wilson, made a similar point, in the process summarizing a very modern American argument: 'The English race ... has long and successfully studied the art of curbing executive power to the constant neglect of the art of perfecting executive methods.'[3]

In short, the process of delivery is important to politics since democracy is threatened if politicians repeatedly make promises they don't then deliver; it is also important to citizens regardless of politics, because if government fails, their daily lives – education, health, safety, travel and parks, for example, not to mention the effective regulation of markets – are materially threatened. And it matters to the success of economies, at both national and global levels, because even where government is small, it takes up over 20 per cent of GDP. In many countries it is 40 or 50 per cent, and if it is unproductive it is a huge drag on economic growth. Moreover, as Matthew d'Ancona has argued, successful political leadership is becoming increasingly challenging as leaders face 'higher expectations of government, raised standards of accountability and media scrutiny more intense and unrelenting than at any time in history'. The challenge is acute as these leaders attempt to reconcile citizens to 'the thunderous forces unleashed by globalisation'.[4]

The perspective of the book throughout is from the centre of government looking out. The aim is to convey to the reader what it feels like to be in there looking at the world beyond and trying desperately to get something done so that the citizen benefits. From the outside, people at the heart of government look all-powerful; on the inside, they often feel helpless, stretched to and beyond breaking point by the weight of expectations on the one hand and the sheer complexity and difficulty of meeting them on the other.

Political leaders of both talent and genuine goodwill, of which there are many more around the world than public commentary would have you believe, find themselves struggling to deliver their promises. Huge public bureaucracies, which is what government departments are, should in theory enable these political leaders to deliver outcomes for citizens; in practice they sometimes become barriers to implementation. It is in the interests of both transparency and understanding to describe, not just to experts but also to interested citizens, what these challenges are and how they might be overcome. This is the purpose of this book.

As we all know, habits are hard to change. In governments, with deeply ingrained cultures and in the full glare of constant media attention, changing culture is harder still. But if our governments and public services are to provide the services and regulation on which our prosperity as individuals and as a global community depends, their cultures and processes will have to change. The chapters in this book describe the challenge governments face and the vital processes which, if adopted by governments around the world, would make a huge difference to all of us. They are the foundations of a science of delivery.

Spread across the chapters are 57 Rules to follow. They are a summary of the main practical points in the book, and are gathered together, by chapter for ease of reference, in the Appendix.

Introduction:
The Missing Science of Delivery

FOUR CHARACTERS: ONE PROBLEM

Viktor Chernomyrdin was the prime minister of Russia in those heady, rollercoaster years of the 1990s after Communism had collapsed and before Putin imposed his steadily tightening stranglehold. Throughout the ups and downs of his time in power, Chernomyrdin somehow kept his sense of humour, remarking on one occasion: 'We keep trying to invent new organizations, but they all turn out to be the Communist Party of the Soviet Union' and on another: 'It's never been this way before and now it's exactly the same again.' In spite of the hardships they endured, therefore, the Russian people had an affection for him that none of his predecessors or successors has enjoyed (or deserved, one might add).

But his most famous saying of all is about the frustration of governing: 'We tried to do better,' he said, 'but everything turned out as usual.'[1]

Charles I was king of England, Scotland and Ireland from 1625. The Van Dyck portraits show the long hair, the wide and curling moustache, the epitome cavalier look, but nevertheless Charles was not one of royalty's great successes. Between 1638 and 1649, he managed to provoke separate but overlapping civil wars in all three of his kingdoms, ran out of money, upset the Parliament in England by trying (but failing) to arrest some of its members, steadily lost friends, and ended up losing a civil war. Finally, on 30 January 1649, a cold morning in Whitehall, he lost his head.

Part way through this catalogue of error and ultimately disaster, he had a moment of deep insight. 'There's more to the doing,' he realized, 'than bidding it be done.'[2]

Thomas Phillip O'Neill, known as Tip after a baseball player with the same surname, served as Speaker of the US House of Representatives from 1977 to 1987, and remains the only speaker to serve for five consecutive congressional terms. With his swept-over shock of white hair and his unrivalled grasp of political wheeling and dealing, he was both a match and a foil for Ronald Reagan, whom he once described as 'the most ignorant man who ever occupied the White House'. Part of O'Neill's genius was to be able to maintain cordial relations with the president in spite of such remarks. On a later occasion, he said affectionately, 'I've known personally every President since Jack Kennedy and I can honestly say that Ronald Reagan was the worst. But he would have made a helluva king!' O'Neill had first been elected to the House of Representatives as long ago as 1952, and his razor-sharp mind had time to absorb and distil the central challenges of governing. 'It is easier to run *for* office than to run *the* office,' he once said.

Interviewed at the end of his long career by the Harvard political scientist Derek Bok, O'Neill was asked to comment on how politics had changed over the course of his career. 'The quality [of the people] is clearly much better,' he commented. 'But the results are definitely worse.'[3]

Paul Corrigan is a good friend and was a close colleague and collaborator during my time in No. 10 Downing Street, when he was the special adviser to successive health secretaries. A quick phone conversation with Paul would result in a decision and action that, had they been pursued through the normal civil service channels, would have taken weeks and thousands of words in formal submissions.

Paul's most memorable comment to me related to the quaint British custom under which whoever has won an election takes power right away. After the election on 1 May 1997, John Major, having lost, vacated No. 10 by the back door in the early afternoon of 2 May (and memorably went to watch cricket), while Blair and his entourage came in through the front door. 'It's funny,' commented Paul. 'You do the second most difficult thing in politics – which is to win an election – and then, without time even for a good night's sleep, you start to do the most difficult thing in politics, which is to run a country.'

Four people, separated by time and space, with senior (in some cases very senior) roles in government, and all in different ways commenting on the difficulty of getting things done.

THE EMERGING SCIENCE

There are countless books and manuals on every aspect of elections and campaigns, on policy and policymaking and on ideas and shaping public opinion, but on how to get things done in government there is almost nothing. No manuals. Virtually no academic literature. Surveying the academic literature on the subject of political science, I once explored the field known as implementation studies. There are worthwhile academic debates there which I have nothing against, but almost no guidance on the practical implications, and if you summed up the entire field – which no doubt rightly comes from a critical perspective – in a single sentence, it would be 'Nothing works.' Viktor Chernomyrdin all over again.

There are plenty of business books on 'execution', but their messages don't necessarily translate into the context of government, and in any case they are often written with an underlying contempt for public officials. Fortunately, in the past decade or so, a new field has begun to emerge, partly I'm glad to say in response to the establishment of the Prime Minister's Delivery Unit (PMDU), which I founded in Tony Blair's second term (2001–5). The PMDU has both its supporters and detractors, as you might expect, but there's real value in the debate. More importantly, the PMDU also has its emulators – delivery units or their equivalent have sprung up in many countries at different levels in political systems. In North America, the mayor of Los Angeles, Antonio Villaraigosa, was one of the first to follow the path. Martin O'Malley, governor of Maryland, was another. So too did Dalton McGuinty, premier of Ontario from 2003 to 2013. In Europe, the Dutch government of Jan Peter Balkenende sought to learn from the PMDU experience and adapt the approach.

David Cameron's Conservative Party in Britain dismissed some of the Delivery Unit's experience, but soon after being elected found itself establishing an Implementation Unit. In part this may have been a result of a conversation I had with the brilliant Steve Hilton about six months after Cameron, with Steve as his chief 'blue skies' thinker, had moved into No. 10. 'I know we disparaged targets and delivery and all that when we were in Opposition,' Steve began, 'but now we've been here a while, we have a question: How did you do it?' He had learned Paul Corrigan's lesson. 'You've learned fast,' I replied. 'It took Blair four years to learn the same thing.' In 2014, with the experience of four hard years governing, Cameron moved to further strengthen his Implementation Unit, appointing the excellent Simon Case to run it.

It is not only in North America and Europe that there is emulation. Malaysian Prime Minister Najib Razak created Pemandu (Malay for 'driver') on the PMDU model. Chief Minister Shahbaz Sharif has applied the approach to education and health in Punjab, Pakistan. Sierra Leone's President Koroma has used a delivery approach to drive health outcomes, while in Chile, Colombia and some states of Brazil, there have been experiments along these lines. In the Middle East, Kuwait established a delivery unit too. Melanie Walker, head of the President's Delivery Unit at the World Bank, claims to have counted fifty-eight delivery units or equivalent around the world.

Not all of these attempts at emulation have worked. The Malaysian and Ontarian efforts referred to have been outstandingly successful; the one in Kuwait much less so. The point is, though, that each of these attempts at establishing units whose primary focus is delivery or implementation, rather than policy or strategy, has enabled us to learn much more about what works and what doesn't. From this perspective, the failures are as valuable as the successes. As a result, we are beginning to have a much deeper understanding of the issues. Political scientists such as Steve Kelman at Harvard, Paul C. Light at New York University and Gwyn Bevan at the London School of Economics, some of whom had been beavering away for years on related subjects, have put delivery or implementation at the centre of their work. The towering figure of political science, Francis Fukuyama, has told me he plans to make the capacity of a state to implement central to the next phase of his work. A field is at last beginning to emerge.

After I had left the Blair administration in 2005, I wrote the story of the establishment and impact of the PMDU in an attempt to interest a wider audience both in the riveting ups and downs of four years at the heart of government and in the challenges of getting things done. Shortly after that book, *Instruction to Deliver*, was published, my friends in the US education reform movement urged me to bring this thinking across the Atlantic to assist with improving the outcomes of America's schools. Joel Klein seized the ideas and applied them in his heroic and remarkably successful drive to improve New York City's schools. Similarly, Paul Pastorek and Paul Vallas drew on this thinking in creating the Recovery School District in New Orleans. With the help of my friends, I then founded the US Education Delivery Institute, which has been assisting more than a dozen US states by applying delivery thinking to their education systems. As part of this work, I wrote, with colleagues, the first practical guide to driving delivery, specifically aimed at US education, though the techniques it describes are generally applicable to government. We called the book *Deliverology 101*.

'Deliverology' originated as a term of gentle abuse in the UK Treasury as shorthand to describe the work and techniques of the PMDU. Just as in the past 'Whig' and 'Tory' had transmuted from being insults to badges of honour, so we decided to adopt deliverology as our rallying cry. The implication of the -ology suffix was that something akin to a science was emerging. And indeed that is what I believe.

More importantly, a health academic who had become president of Dartmouth College was beginning to believe it too. During his tenure at Dartmouth, Jim Yong Kim took to carrying *Deliverology 101* around with him – or so he told me when we met. Its rigour appealed to him as someone who in his work as an academic had tried to change the facts on the ground, rather than simply write about them. Along with Paul Farmer, he founded Partners in Health which, in places such as Haiti and Peru, had enormously beneficial effects for hundreds of thousands of people.

In some ways, Jim Kim was an unlikely candidate to be president of the World Bank. In the book he co-edited, *Dying for Growth*, published in 2000, he and his colleagues had questioned the conventional wisdom of the World Bank and other global institutions. They pointed out that, 'while the proportion of people in good health may be greater than 50 years ago, the absolute number of people suffering from preventable diseases with little or no access to healthcare has risen dramatically in the same period'.[4]

Maybe it was this iconoclasm that recommended Jim Kim to President Obama who, in March 2012, nominated him the next President of the World Bank, a post he took up in July 2012. *Deliverology 101* went with him and, not long into his tenure, he made a speech in Korea, the country from which his parents had emigrated, in which he set out the case for a new science, 'the Science of Delivery'. Some months later, writing in *Voices on Society*, he put the case in plain terms:

> Over the past few centuries, evidence-based delivery systems have revolutionised our lives. They have shown us what can work. The problem is that we still lack a framework for systematically understanding what does work in a given time and place, and for holding officials accountable to that standard. Now development agencies can fulfil their public trust by creating a science of delivery that will compile global delivery knowledge and mobilise it for practice.[5]

This is a bold and timely vision. Indeed I would say it is extremely urgent. It is not simply that in too many countries development policies are clearly not working and governance is demonstrably poor; it is also evidently the case that even in relatively well-governed countries, government is often both inefficient and ineffective. This has a massive economic effect which, especially in a time of austerity, is highly problematic. Worse still, it leads citizens to question the value of paying taxes, to be sceptical of government in general and in the worst cases to doubt the value of democracy. In America, frustration with federal government has rarely, if ever, been greater, so much so that Paul Volcker, the distinguished former Chairman of the Federal Reserve, has (in his late eighties) dedicated the next phase of his career to 'working for effective government'.

A readable summary of what we know – a first sketch of a science of delivery – then, is needed not just for the developing world as Jim Kim suggests, but globally. And the sooner the better. There is another reason why it is needed. Delivery units have become fashionable: the words are regularly used, but few people know the secrets that distinguish those that succeed from those that don't.

This book is an attempt to summarize, on the basis of both my direct experience and the growing evidence, what works in delivery. I certainly don't pretend it provides all the answers, not least because we don't yet have all the necessary knowledge. The science is far from complete and, based on human relationships as politics and government inevitably are, it never will be. However good the science becomes, the art involved will remain significant.

Nevertheless, I will make two claims. First, this book will help to map the territory, setting the agenda for those in government who want to deliver, for those in universities who want to research delivery and for those citizens who would like to see governments succeed. Second, if the agenda set out in chapters 1 to 7 were systematically applied by governments around the world, outcomes across a range of services such as policing, health and education would improve dramatically, the value realized from taxpayers' money would be substantially increased and citizens would have much more confidence in government than they currently do. Chapter 8 – about effective use of public money – is just as important, but so far the territory it covers is less well understood or applied. To sum it up, the application of the delivery knowledge we already have would make the world a better place.

If this knowledge had been readily available to Viktor Chernomyrdin, he might have ended his career somewhat more optimistically . . . and maybe if he'd had it too, Charles I would not have lost his head.

THE VALUE OF GOOD GOVERNANCE

In 2013, one of the great global debates in political and economic science was about the future of India, a country where close to one in five of the world's population lives. Two leading Indian intellectuals took up the cudgels for radically opposing views on the way forward.

Jagdish Bhagwati, a towering Indian-American scholar based at Columbia University, teamed up with Arvind Panagariya to write *Why Growth Matters*. Their basic argument was that economic growth in India only really took off after the 1991 deregulatory pro-market reforms; before that it had been far too slow to meet the needs of the growing Indian population. Further, they argued that poverty reduction, far from being set back by these liberalizing reforms, has actually been enhanced. In effect, they claimed, unless you grow the cake, you have no chance of giving the poor a significantly bigger slice. Finally, they argue that the need of the present time is to further extend those liberalizing pro-market reforms including bringing quasi-market pressures into traditional public sector areas through measures such as the use of vouchers in the school system.

Ranged against this case was the equally towering figure of Amartya Sen, the Nobel Prize-winning economist who, in collaboration with Jean Drèze, published *An Uncertain Glory: India and Its Contradictions*. Their analysis and prescription are very different. They argue that while, yes, there has been impressive growth since the early 1990s, the major problem is that the benefits of this have been unevenly distributed. They are frustrated that the debate about India's future, especially in the media, is one in which the wealthy are talking among themselves about themselves. 'What is remarkable,' they say, 'is not the media's interest in growth rates [which have declined recently], but its near-silence about the fact that the growth process is so biased, making the country look more and more like islands of California in a sea of sub-Saharan Africa.'[6]

Their solutions are much greater empowerment of the poor, especially women, so that they seize a much bigger voice in public debate, and reform of the public sector, which is necessary, they argue, because 'the general state of public services in India remains absolutely dismal, and the country's health and education systems have been severely messed up'.[7] Above all, they urge a much more equitable distribution of power.

While prescriptions in the two books are very different and this battle of titans enlivened the pages of academic and popular papers as well as the airwaves, the truth is there is quite a lot they agree on:

- Current growth rates are too low.
- There is a great deal of inequality.
- Public services are 'messed up'.

There is then a legitimate political debate, which is the classic one around the world, not just in India, about whether to depend largely on the market and 'the hidden hand' to solve these problems, or whether to rely on an extension of the public and social sectors (as in Bangladesh) to address them. There is no right answer here – it is exactly the kind of debate that should take place in a democracy.

Crucially, though – and this is my central point at the start of this book – neither Bhagwati's solutions nor Sen's will succeed unless government in India, at federal and state levels, becomes much more effective than it currently is. Even with the more limited role that Bhagwati would recommend for the state, its effectiveness is critical, for example, to enforce property rights, regulate markets or fund and oversee – if not always provide – health and education services. From Sen's perspective, government effectiveness is more important still. Following India's 2014 election, we will see how Narendra Modi, the new prime minister, fares. The *Economist* says he is 'a strong-willed moderniser' who likes setting targets and that 'measurably better performance' is what excites him.[8] If so, the chapters that follow should excite him too.

This is the point of the emerging science of delivery. Whether your political preference is for a minimalist state or a much larger one, you have an interest in government being effective at what it does. As William Easterly puts it, 'The debate about market versus government is ... the wrong debate.'[9] Both are essential. After all, we live in an era where demonstrating outcomes, whether you are a business or a government, is increasingly important, and the science of delivery will help make that possible.

The argument in this book applies both to democratic countries (such as Canada, whose province of Ontario appears later in the book), and more generally to countries committed to the rule of law and the accountability of government. In some cases, democracy might not fully be in place, and indeed the prospects may be uncertain but, at the time of writing, I have taken the view that the direction of travel is right. The importance of delivery to emerging democracies – and the risks of failing – are brilliantly captured by Ryszard Kapuściński's description of the tragedy of 'the honest and patriotic post-colonial leader' who faces the:

> ... terrible *material resistance* that each one encounters on taking his first, second and third steps up the summit of power. Each one wants to do something good and begins to do it and then sees, after a month, after a year, after three years, that it just isn't happening, that it is slipping away, that it is bogged down in the sand ... The politician begins to push too hard. He looks for a way out through dictatorship. The dictatorship then fathers an opposition. The opposition organises a coup.
>
> And the cycle begins anew.[10]

The path to accountable government is that much easier to walk if governments succeed in delivering at least some of what they have promised. I am not recommending the content here to blatant autocracies or 'extractive' regimes interested purely in enriching themselves, though of course I can't be sure that some of them won't read the words.

This is important because my belief is that the case made in the book has a moral purpose. More people are more likely to lead more fulfilled lives if they live in countries with effective accountable governments which can enforce basic individual rights and deliver effective public good. As Daron Acemoglu and James Robinson argue in *Why Nations Fail*, their monumental analysis of why some nations succeed and others don't, effective and accountable governance is the key difference between those countries that pursue inclusive growth strategies and those that use the state as a means of enriching the elite.

Meanwhile, Francis Fukuyama points out, in *The Origins of Political Order*, that for countries to break out of 'dysfunctional equilibrium' requires either a radical change in economic and social circumstances or great leadership, or both. Shahbaz Sharif, chief minister of Punjab – who appears a number of times in this book – is a good example of someone contemporary seeking to provide precisely that kind of leadership.

In *Political Order and Political Decay*, which builds on his previous volume, Fukuyama takes the argument a stage further. While the state, rule of law and accountable government are prerequisites of success, they are not enough, especially as citizens' expectations rise. As he says, referring to Turkey and Brazil but in an argument that applies more generally, 'Government actually had to deliver better results if it was to be regarded as legitimate.'[11]

A common criticism of deliverology in its brief life is that it is necessarily top-down and therefore in some way encourages government to become overbearing. This is emphatically not the case, and is a theme that will emerge throughout the chapters that follow. Of course, this book is written from the perspective of people at the centre of governments – whether federal, national, provincial or local – but it is a mistake to deduce that because it takes that perspective it must necessarily lead to top-down or centralizing reform. Indeed, if a government was elected with the sole purpose of empowering local communities and reducing its own influence, the science of delivery would help it succeed.

Crucially, by applying what we know, the capacity of government to deliver inclusive growth will be significantly enhanced. That is because the contents of this book are not a policy prescription but elements of a process by which a government can massively enhance its capacity to deliver outcomes for citizens, by learning rapidly as implementation occurs and adjusting its approach in the light of that learning. 'Governing is messy and complicated and difficult and no system of government can change that,' says Daniel Finkelstein, but he adds, crucially, that 'politics can be improved and of course change is possible'.[12]

Planning and targets, both of which are examined and recommended in later chapters, got a bad name from Stalin's five-year plans because in that infamous case the targets were unashamedly top-down and those involved in implementation manipulated the data to fit the plan and distorted the truth to (appear to) succeed. The science of delivery – recommended here – is not just distinct from this; it is the polar opposite. It says get started, learn fast from the real world, understand the messy reality and adjust the plan accordingly.

In summary, the science of delivery sees the world from inside government looking out and is:

- Valuable whether you want a smaller or larger state.
- Either top-down or bottom-up, or something in between, according to choice.
- A disciplined process rather than a policy prescription.
- An important ingredient in the future of accountable government.

With that context set out, we are ready.

I

Priorities

THE CHALLENGE OF GOVERNMENT

Robert Arthur Talbot Gascoyne-Cecil, Third Marquess of Salisbury, was the British prime minister on three occasions, and for a total of over thirteen years. It was under his leadership that Britain saw in the twentieth century. The portraits reveal a broad forehead, shrewd, dark eyes and a very large, classically Victorian, beard. His appearance exudes stability. Given that his era witnessed Britain at the height of its imperial power and Queen Victoria's diamond jubilee, stability was exactly what Salisbury set out to provide. He summarized his beliefs in a sentence which, as a definition of true conservatism, has never been bettered. 'Whatever happens,' he said, 'will be for the worse, and therefore it is in our interest that as little should happen as possible.'[1]

Salisbury was by no means the only leader back then who aspired to do very little. William Evarts, secretary of state in the administration of US President Rutherford B. Hayes (1877–81), admonished him once by saying, 'You don't sufficiently realise, Mr President, the great truth that almost any question will settle itself if you only let it alone long enough.'[2]

Fifty years later, the Americans elected another president who preferred to let things alone. Calvin Coolidge, Silent Cal as he became known, made his case clear, long before he became president, in a letter to his father: 'It is much more important to kill bad bills than to pass good ones.'[3] As his biographer, Amity Shlaes, puts it, 'Congress always says "Do". Coolidge replied, "Do not do", or at least, "Do less".'[4]

For these leaders, for whom success is doing as little as possible, understanding the science of delivery is less important (though it wouldn't have done them any harm and, we shall see later, Coolidge was actually an exponent of parts of the delivery approach). For every other kind of leader in government, it is central. They have an agenda, a set of commitments, beliefs about how they would like the world to be different, but they are not necessarily equipped with the knowledge, skills and understanding to get the job done. As Margaret Thatcher cried in exasperation to her advisers just before she was elected prime minister, 'Don't tell me what. I know what. Tell me how.'

In the modern world where the pace of change is unrelenting and the demands of the electorate are insistent, the Lord Salisbury philosophy looks increasingly anachronistic. Citizens expect immeasurably more of government than they did a century ago, and they (or the media on their behalf) are only too quick to complain if, as often happens, those expectations are dashed. And when the world changes, especially in a crisis, they turn to government. As Keith Joseph, Margaret Thatcher's mentor, so memorably put it: 'The first words a baby learns in this country are "What's the government going to do about it?"'

In short, delivery matters. And the first question political leaders have to ask themselves is what exactly do they want to do. It's one thing to have a broad agenda or view of the world; it's quite another to turn that into a practical programme for government.

> **RULE 1**
> HAVE AN AGENDA
> (even if, like Lord Salisbury, it is to do nothing)

PRIORITIES

Every successful business leader will tell you that unless a business is clear about its priorities it will struggle to succeed. The same is true for a government. As the mid-twentieth-century firebrand Labour minister Aneurin Bevan memorably put it, 'The language of priorities is the religion of socialism.'[5] Actually, not just of socialism. Prioritization is easy to advocate but difficult to do. It requires great discipline, not least because – by definition – establishing what the priorities are also means establishing what they are not.

The model leader in this respect in my experience is Najib Razak, who became prime minister of Malaysia in 2009 and was returned in an election in 2013. He had told me before the election that business as usual would not be good enough; he wanted transformation. Once he became prime minister, he engaged in a consultative process with his cabinet to arrive at six national priorities (or National Key Results Areas – NKRAs – as they became known). They included rural basic infrastructure, crime reduction and education – but not health. From that collective decision, through to the election in 2013, the government genuinely prioritized the six NKRAs with time, energy and commitment.

Not prioritizing something doesn't mean not doing anything at all. As Tony Blair used to say to me, 'There are priorities, and things you just have to do.' This is one of the differences between government and business. A business can choose a focus and close down or sell off the parts of the business that don't relate to that focus, but Najib Razak could not sell off his health department because that is clearly a function of modern government. In the non-priority areas, the function still needs oversight and management. There was – and still is – a health minister and budget in Malaysia, of course, and the minister was encouraged, as were all the ministers, to set departmental priorities. Twice a year the prime minister holds each minister, priority or not, to account for what they've done. Similarly, in Britain under Blair, while literacy and numeracy at primary level were priorities for the government, that did not mean that science or arts teaching stopped or that no one paid attention to the wider agenda.

When Gordon Brown became prime minister in the summer of 2007, it soon became evident that, in spite of having spent many years aspiring to the top job, he did not establish clear priorities. He was, it is true, soon overwhelmed by the worldwide financial and economic crises in which he played a vital global role, but by then the absence of clarity about his priorities had left him, in Bob Dylan's words, 'condemned to drift or else be kept from drifting'.

By contrast, by 2001 when Blair set up the Delivery Unit, he had become very clear about his priorities. With No. 10 Policy Unit colleagues, I went to him in my first week in the job with a selected list of goals or targets. Sitting in the sunshine outside the Cabinet Room, Blair took a pen and put a line through numerous suggestions, leaving a few: 'I want the Delivery Unit focused on issues of real salience ... for example, in transport, I only want Michael to sort out the railways.'[6] With the frustrating experience of his first term behind him, he knew how much focus it would take to get some tough things done. (And 'only sorting out the railways' took three years or more of unremitting effort!) Moreover, because he had just returned from the election campaign, he also knew what was uppermost in the minds of the British people.

If anything, Margaret Thatcher was clearer sooner about her priorities than Blair, and more determined to make progress on them in her first term. As one of her more radical ministers, Nicholas Ridley, put it: 'She was adamant she would not start down this sort of road [welfare reform] at the beginning. There was enough to do sorting out industry, the economy, taxation and the trade unions.' Her own summary was even more succinct: 'The supply side must come first.'[7] So, for her first and second terms, the priorities were set. Welfare, health and education reform had to wait. Her judgement seems to have been vindicated by history – those supply-side reforms have not been reversed and without doubt changed Britain for the better.

> **RULE 2**
> **DECIDE ON YOUR PRIORITIES**
> (really decide)

AMBITION AND A MAP OF DELIVERY

It is one thing to decide your priorities; it is another to decide how ambitious you want to be about them. How much change do you want, and how fast?

In political circles, a favourite phrase is 'underpromise and overdeliver' and of course there is a point to this. It implies managing expectations, setting some achievable, modest goals and then doing better than expected – the idea being that the electorate will be duly impressed. In times of rising prosperity and broad goodwill towards government, this is a plausible scenario. It was the approach taken by the government of Steve Bracks, premier of Victoria, Australia early in the twenty-first century: his White Paper *Growing Victoria Together* was an agenda for steady progress towards modest targets. The boat wasn't rocked and Victoria advanced. Similarly, a decade or more after the Second World War was over, the British government of Harold Macmillan was claiming 'You've never had it so good.'

But in tough times – such as the present era of austerity – or in the case of a government with a radical reforming agenda and a leader who aspires to transformation (and perhaps a place in history), underpromising and overdelivering is too cautious an approach. Historical perspective suggests that in the 1950s Macmillan might (I would argue should) have done more to tackle the underlying structural weaknesses of the British economy which were brutally exposed in the 1960s and 70s. Sometimes the situation demands clear priorities and bold ambition. This is one reason why history judges war leaders as great. Lincoln's commitment to saving the Union and (ultimately) ending slavery provided a clear mission and called for unwavering ambition – literally whatever it took. The same is true of Churchill's determination first to save the island nation and then to defeat the scourge of Nazism.

In peacetime, though, the degree of ambition depends in part on the situation and in part on the courage of the political leader. Margaret Thatcher's case combined both. She was elected at a moment of economic and social crisis, but when the worst of it was past and many of her ministers were urging her to take a softer line, she said famously, 'You turn if you want to. The lady's not for turning.' Similarly, in his second term, Blair was determined to bring about irreversible structural reforms of both health and education, and hence set ambitious goals for the Delivery Unit. Najib Razak in Malaysia opted for transformation rather than a quiet life. A leading influence on Najib Razak has been Idris Jala, whom we shall meet several times later in this book. He argues that unless targets 'really, really stretch', they are not worth getting out of bed for. 'Set goals you yourself think you cannot meet,' he told me, disarmingly.

The degree of ambition also depends to an extent on political calculation. President Obama chose to give high priority to healthcare reform and was prepared to pay a heavy political price to get it through (and did!). Getting the law passed was very difficult, but turning the legislation into real gains on the ground proved harder still. The dilemma for political leaders in the twenty-first century is that people are impatient for results. If they don't come, the pressure from the people (and the media) intensifies, and political support can crumble. Thus, for reforming political leaders, the paradox is that they have to have a long-term strategy if they are to secure irreversible reform; but unless they deliver short-term results, no one believes them. On the horns of this dilemma some politicians (and in the developing world, donor agencies) revert to announcing 'initiatives', which they hope will convey an impression of activity but which do not result in transformation. (I have spent much of the past ten years trying unsuccessfully to abolish this sense of the word 'initiative'.)

The Map of Delivery, which I originally drew for the Blair cabinet in 2002, is meant to assist with deciding the degree of ambition for a whole government, a leader or an individual minister.

Map of Delivery

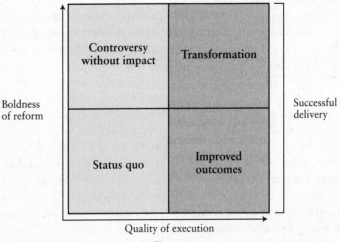

Figure 1

6

The vertical axis deals with the staple of political debate in most political systems – how bold or radical do we want to be? Some politicians and their advisers are bold by nature, others more cautious. When John F. Kennedy made his famous commitment that the US would land a man on the moon by the end of the 1960s, it captured people's imagination around the world – but most of his advisers had counselled against it. In fact, a relatively junior official had inserted the proposal into a draft at the last minute, and it was by luck that this draft got to Kennedy without it being deleted by one adviser or another. Kennedy, of course, loved the ambition!

Often the debate between boldness and caution is played out between politicians on the one hand and career civil servants on the other. Part of the value of career civil servants, after all, is that they have seen it all before. While politicians come and go, they are permanent. So the sight of a naïve – in their view – politician making an unreasonable – in their view – commitment is grist to their mill. Their ingrained cynicism often leads them to advise a more cautious approach (which is also incidentally likely to be less work). They avoid the 'controversy without impact' in the top left corner of the map by retreating down the vertical axis. The writers of the BBC programme *Yes, Minister* created an entire, and memorable, comedy series from precisely this dilemma.

Perhaps a pilot study instead of a full-scale rollout? Maybe some more research first? Or slow down the timetable for phasing it in? In the old days in Britain, there was always another option too – perhaps we could try it out in Scotland first?

Evidence-based policymaking, while obviously a good thing on the face of it, plays into the case for caution too because, by definition, the evidence relates to the past and often recounts numerous failures. Too often it is used to justify incrementalism or delay. As one of the characters in Boris Pasternak's classic, *Doctor Zhivago*, concludes, 'Yuri Andreevich was in too much of a hurry to establish ahead of time the failure of the efforts he made, announcing too confidently and almost with satisfaction the uselessness of any further attempts.'[8]

And, by definition too, the research is never complete and cannot tell you whether an innovation will succeed or not. This is not an argument for ignoring the evidence. On the contrary, it should always be taken into account, but it does not and cannot replace the need for judgement (which is what we elect politicians to exercise).

In any case, the Map of Delivery only really comes into its own when the horizontal axis is brought into play. The picture looks different now; it becomes possible to break out of the old debate. A cautious idea, implemented well, might provide exactly those short-term results that a transformative political leader needs in order to show that he or she is on the right track. Meanwhile, for a bold idea, the map asks the insistent question: How will you get it done? In addition, it enables a government or an individual minister to think strategically. Anything on the left of the map needs to be moved, over time, across to the right. You might like to have a 'controversy without impact' on the way because, as Blair used to say, a good row provides definition and engages people, but in the end you want to ensure you deliver outcomes.

However, even the boldest politician won't want everything in the 'transformation' box if he or she is wise, because the risks would be too great. Similarly, if everything is in the 'improved outcomes' box then the programme would be too incremental. Prioritization again. And sequencing. Both are vital to effective delivery.

In the Blair health reforms, getting waiting times for routine surgery down delivered the short-term results that built confidence, while introducing patient choice to a state-owned monopoly over time was truly transformational. Similarly, Joel Klein as Chancellor of New York City Schools delivered rapid early improvements in elementary school test scores, which built public confidence in his programme, before embarking on much more radical, quasi-market reforms which have become irreversible.

In the end, though, no amount of analysis can replace the need for political courage. Sometimes what Margaret Thatcher called the 'calculated bounce' is what is required. I discovered this myself once when, the day before I appeared in front of a parliamentary committee, Tony Blair announced on television that we would halve the number of illegal asylum seekers within six months. He was responding to sustained public and media pressure and decided to 'bounce' the system (and me). When I told him later that day that I had had to tell the committee that I had not known his announcement was coming, he replied simply: 'I don't know how you could have known; I didn't know myself until I said it.' (We hit the target six months later, incidentally.)

Sometimes it's not so much a matter of a bounce, as of a leader setting a big, impossible-looking goal in order to transform expectations. Not all politics is 'the art of the possible', R. A. Butler's famous phrase; the pursuit of the impossible matters too. Kennedy and the moon landing has already been cited; eradicating smallpox also looked impossible once; and, at a more mundane level, no one believed Shahbaz Sharif, chief minister of Punjab, when he announced in 2011 that he aimed to achieve universal primary enrolment in time for the 2015 Millennium Development Goal. It remains to be seen whether he will, but progress since the announcement has been remarkable.

In part it is a question of initiative; and one public servant said to my friend and colleague Simon Rea, 'You can sit and watch the garden grow or you can get out there and be the gardener.' George Bernard Shaw made the point best: 'The reasonable man adapts himself to the conditions that surround him . . . The unreasonable man adapts the surrounding conditions to himself . . . All progress depends on the unreasonable man.' Like it or not, we need unreasonable political leaders sometimes.

> **RULE 3**
> BE UNREASONABLE (sometimes) AND USE THE MAP OF DELIVERY

TARGETS

Priorities and ambition are necessary for transformation, but not sufficient. It is also necessary to define more precisely what outcome is intended. This is where targets come in. I shouldn't have been surprised, I suppose, given the role I had in the Blair administration, but I hadn't expected to become so personally identified with targets and governments setting them. In some corners of the media I was even called 'Mr Targets'. In others, the criticism was sharper still. After I had made a presentation at one of Tony Blair's press conferences, the then *Times* columnist Simon Jenkins, never one to moderate his tone, described me as 'a control freak's control freak ... a Great War general sitting in a chateau counting "targets" as they go over the top and then counting them back'.[9]

The comment reveals just how controversial the targets had become. People who for years had demanded that governments make specific promises (i.e. set targets) and then make transparent whether progress towards them is being made (i.e. publish data), suddenly found that targets were 'top-down', 'imposed' and 'distortionary'. In the end, though, unless a government aspires to do very little (like Lord Salisbury), it needs to set some clear goals. To use Delivery Unit jargon, it needs to make clear 'what success looks like'. This enables a government to make a case in terms people can understand and also, just as importantly, enables it to be held to account.

That definition of success does not need to be called a target – there are plenty of other words available, such as 'goal' or 'objective' – but in practical terms that is what it is. If the definition of success is not clear, many of the same people who are critical of targets would accuse the government of lacking clarity or, worse, of obfuscation. In any case, governments set targets all the time, even when they claim to oppose the idea. Within months of being elected and having specifically criticized targets, David Cameron said he wanted Britain to be a top-five destination for tourists. You don't have to call that a target, but that is what it is. After three years in office, he didn't feel the need to pretend any more. In Prime Minister's Questions (on health service performance) on 6 November 2013, he responded to the critics by asserting 'we are hitting our targets'.

Since governments, whether they like them or not, are going to set targets, we might as well have the real debate about them, which is about how to use them – and how to avoid the pitfalls (about which I learned a lot in the Blair years).

Consistent with the emphasis on priorities, the first point to make about targets is that you don't want too many of them. As we have seen, Najib Razak in Malaysia chose six areas. Dalton McGuinty, the education premier of Ontario, set three for his education system – improved performance in literacy, numeracy and graduation rates; narrowed gaps between disadvantaged groups and the rest; and improved public confidence in the system. Specific, measurable, ambitious, realistic and timebound (SMART, the famous acronym) targets were set for each. It is hard to argue that for an education system in a province of over 15 million people that is too many. Similarly, in the Punjab education and health reforms, the chief minister has set a handful of measurable goals.

By contrast, in the early phase of the Blair administration, there *were* too many, and it did cause confusion. Moreover, some of those targets exemplified another pitfall. They were badly set – unmeasurable, for example, or broad, uninformed guesses plucked out of the air as part of a political deal on the spending review. On one occasion, when I proposed that we might get from 80 to 82 per cent of eleven-year-olds achieving the literacy standard, I was told that was too detailed and the percentage had to end in a nought or a five. (We set it at 85 per cent and hit 82.) Other targets had been set without thinking about how the data would be collected. The worst example was on road congestion, where we had an incomprehensible target measured by a bizarre process. (See p. 133 below for an explanation.)

David Cameron may have started out as a target sceptic, but he set a very high profile 'net immigration' target – the idea was to ensure that in any given year more people emigrated than immigrated. If achieved, the prime minister thought, it would prove that he had immigration, a major political issue, under control. The problem with the target is that achieving it depends on much that the PM cannot influence. He has no influence on how many people choose to emigrate and minimal influence on immigration from within the European Union. All he can influence, therefore, is immigration from elsewhere, but however much you tighten up here (at whatever cost), the other factors still dominate the outcomes. As the *Evening Standard* front page put it when the 2013 net migration figure revealed 212,000 more entering Britain than leaving it, 'PM's IMMIGRATION PLEDGE IN TATTERS'.[10] Set the wrong target and even if you make progress, as Cameron has, you risk political defeat.

The ministers in the Blair government would sometimes wobble on the subject of targets, perhaps confusing the problem of bad targets with the wider question of targets in general. Occasionally I'd think that even the prime minister himself was wobbling – but in the end he always came through. He says exactly this in his memoirs.

> . . . in domestic policy, changing public service systems inevitably meant getting into the details of delivery and performance management in a radically more granular way. Increasingly, prime ministers are like CEOs or chairmen of major companies. They have to set a policy direction; they have to see it is followed; they have to get data on whether it is; they have to measure outcomes.

Any political leader who ignores this advice does so at his or her peril. Crucially, Blair adds:

> There was . . . a lot of exaggerated nonsense about targets . . . some criticism was valid. Targets can be too numerous . . . Sometimes different targets conflict . . . Sometimes they are too prescriptive . . .
>
> However, as I used to say to ministers and civil servants, if that is true, cut them down to their essentials, unwind any conflicts, grant a sensible discretion on how they should be met – but don't think for an instant that in any other walk of life you would spend these sums of money without demanding a measurable output.[11]

In a nutshell, that is all there is to it.

For those who want to delve more deeply into the details – not everyone does – there are crucial decisions to make about the nature of the target itself. You can set a floor target – a standard below which performance is deemed unacceptable, as Michael Gove, the Secretary of State for Education from 2010 to 2014 in the Cameron government, did for school performance in England. You can set a percentage target – 90 per cent of trains to arrive on time, for instance. You can set a 100 per cent target too: this has the attraction of being able to tell people the impact will be universal; but it has the disadvantage that the last 1 or 2 per cent of anything often represents exceptional cases which either end up being very expensive to change or turn out to be genuine exceptions to the rule. We found this with the target for Accident & Emergency departments that no one should wait more than four hours to be seen and treated and either sent home or admitted to hospital. This was clear and plain for the vast majority, but for the exceptional spinal injury where the patient could not be moved, not appropriate. In these cases we always insisted that the target itself wasn't the point; it was the service standard the target represented that mattered. We agreed that there would and should be clinical exceptions – the professionals told us these would never be more than 1 or 2 per cent. The target was met on time in December 2004, and rarely missed for almost a decade until the NHS was, absurdly, allowed to stop paying attention.

> **RULE 4**
> SET A SMALL NUMBER OF WELL-DESIGNED TARGETS (but don't call them targets if you don't want to!)

BENCHMARKING

Once the priority is settled and the kind of target established, there is science in target-setting. Of course there will (hopefully) always be 'unreasonable' politicians who set 'unreasonable' targets, but for them too, being informed by the science can only help. The best way into it is through benchmarking, of which, as aficionados will know, there are five types (see Table 1). Each of the five, or a combination of them, can be used.

Often governments, systems or people want to exceed past performance; benchmarking against history provides real insight, which is why athletes pay so much attention to their personal best. This is the first type of benchmarking. I remember discovering once, when we were debating road congestion in London and what to do about it, that when Lord Salisbury was prime minister, he was able to get from King's Cross (where his train from Hatfield arrived) to the Foreign Office (where he liked to work) in seventeen minutes ... in a coach and four. Yet 100 years later, with all the improvements in transport, that was completely impossible except perhaps for a prime minister with motorcycle outriders. Ironic really, because having rushed to the office, Salisbury, as we've seen, aspired to do 'as little as possible' when he got there.

Meanwhile, countries could set targets to be as good at education as some other countries in the international comparisons that are

Benchmarking . . .

1. against history	What levels of performance have we achieved in the past?
2. against the world	What levels of performance are achieved in systems like this elsewhere in the world?
3. against other similar systems	How do we compare to other systems like ours (e.g. among Australian provinces or German *länder*)?
4. within the system	What levels of performance are achieved by the best-performing units in the system (e.g. a hospital, a school, a police force)?
5. against organizations that are altogether different but have some similar relevant functions	What can we learn from them about how they do that?

Table 1

now published regularly. For example, in the 1990 Goals 2000 Act, the US set out to become the best in the world at maths and science by the year 2000, but apart from asserting this in legislation, they did nothing about it and failed to achieve it. This is benchmarking against the world, the second type.

To take another example, US states are able to compare their performance in education by looking at the long run of data collected every two years through the National Assessment of Educational Progress. Massachusetts usually comes top and Louisiana bottom. A state could set a target to be as good as the top 10 per cent or the top

25 per cent of states by a certain date, the former being much more ambitious than the latter. This would be using the third type of benchmarking.

Benchmarking within a system, the fourth type, is often the most useful of all. There are forty-three police forces in England and Wales, and comparing the different levels of crime among them provides real insight into what the system as a whole might achieve. Suppose every police force achieved the levels of crime reduction achieved by the top ten, or just the top half. Targets based on these kinds of assumptions are not only soundly based; they are hard to argue against. The Manchester constabulary could argue that being asked to match the performance of Devon and Cornwall's would be unfair because one is urban and the other rural, but it would be hard for it to justify not matching the top half of all forces in England or the best five large urban forces. Similarly, each of the thirty-six districts in Punjab is able to see monthly how its performance compares with the other thirty-five.

Sometimes best-in-class performance at a level of specificity is not to be found in the expected places, which is where the fifth type of benchmarking applies. The best example I came across was a top-brand hotel chain which wanted to further improve its arrival and check-in process. They broke this down into sixteen steps and then sought best practice for each one. So, who was best in the world at opening the door of the taxi or limousine and welcoming the guest by name? Not another hotel chain, as it happens, but the people who run the Oscars ceremony. They are brilliant at it and a lot could be learned from them.

Another way to approach target-setting is to estimate the effects of different policy actions by making good, plausible, informed guesses of what impact they might have. Assemble a dozen or more people with a stake in the system and work on the estimates, perhaps both a cautious one and an ambitious one, and see where they come out. I've been involved in workshops along these lines in Pakistan, America, Russia and the UK and always found them helpful. (See also chapter 4, on Data and Trajectories.)

Table 2 is an example worked up for the National Literacy Strategy in England. The starting point was 63 per cent achieving high standards

The UK National Literacy Strategy, 1997–2002

	1997	1998	1999	2000	2001	2002
Increased focus and priority	NA	+1	+2	+1	0	0
Increased test preparation	NA	+1	+1	0	0	0
Improved materials	NA	0	+1	+1	0	0
School improvement strategy	NA	0	+1	+1	+2	+1
Improved quality of teaching	NA	0	0	+2	+1	+1
Total	63	65	70	75	78	80

- In 1997, the Blair government announced an 80 per cent literacy target

- Despite the limited data available, the team in the Department for Education made a rough estimate of the potential impact of a series of interventions

- In fact, these estimates were very close to the actual improvements the system made until the last year

Table 2

in literacy; the goal was 80 per cent five years later. We estimated the gain year-on-year from five key aspects of the strategy. Our predictions made in 1997 came out close to reality for the years 1998 to 2000, but turned out to be too optimistic for 2001.

In the end, precisely where the target is set is still a judgement about how ambitious to be, but a target based on this combination of benchmarking and policy impact analysis is likely to be better informed.

RULE 5
APPLY THE SCIENCE
TO TARGET-SETTING
(but don't depend on it)

As a codicil, let me come back to Blair's calculated bounce on illegal asylum applications mentioned on page 8 above. No one had planned a new target, not even Blair, but a day or so before he made his new promise on *Newsnight*, he had seen the outcome of some benchmarking and impact analysis we had done on this theme, which showed halving over six months to be within the realms of the possible. My guess is that this analysis had lodged itself somewhere in the prime ministerial brain; so although he was guessing, at least it was an informed guess. The bureaucracy was furious of course, but the target was achieved.

UNINTENDED CONSEQUENCES

A further question about targets relates to perverse or unintended consequences. These are real risks, and all the time you have to keep reminding yourself and all those involved that there is a moral purpose behind every target (or there should be) – and it's the moral purpose that really matters, not the target. Lose sight of the moral purpose and the edifice begins to crumble. So if a given target has perverse or unintended consequences which might defeat the wider moral purpose, it's a genuine problem.

For some, this becomes an argument for not having targets at all, but then you risk all the problems outlined at the start of this chapter – lack of clarity about priorities, lack of clear definitions of success and ultimately lack of accountability. There is one approach that avoids the pitfalls of targets but maintains accountability, and that is the one pursued by Mayor Rudolph Giuliani in New York City and carried on by his successor. This involves choosing priorities, ensuring good, close-to-real-time data on key indicators such as major types of crime, publishing the data regularly and using rigorous benchmarking among, for example, precincts in the New York City Police Department, to drive up performance. All the evidence is that this works – and it works because it has all the elements of the target-setting approach, but here without actually specifying a goal other than, for example again, continuous crime reduction.

However, this approach is as likely to have perverse or unintended consequences as one that formally sets targets, which still leaves that problem to be resolved. There are only three things you can do. One is to make sure the target, or in the Giuliani approach, the chosen metric, is well designed. One of the health targets we pursued in the Delivery Unit days was clearly flawed, and the flaw had consequences. The goal was that you should not have to wait more than forty-eight hours to see your GP – the moral purpose was to make it easier for people to see their doctor quickly and to end the common complaint at the time that, in some cases, it was very hard to make an appointment. Some GPs chose to interpret the new target narrowly, so that you could *only* get an appointment within the next forty-eight hours, which meant that if you called to make a routine appointment, say for your day off work the following week, you'd be told that was not possible. Interpreted in this way, the target caused as many problems as it solved; a case of a badly designed target (and some block-headed GPs) leading to a perverse consequence.

The second thing you can do is work with the key people in a given sector to try to anticipate as many of the perverse or unintended consequences as possible, consider these in the design of the target and then, as the plan unfolds, check whether they happen or not. When we persuaded the police in England's big cities to focus on cutting muggings – there was an epidemic of them in 2001–2 – they reluctantly agreed, but said that as they moved police officers from other duties onto this agenda, other crime types would get worse. Their assumption was, at least implicitly, that they were working at maximum efficiency, so prioritizing one crime would adversely affect others. There was no reason to believe this was true. After all, at the time, a police officer in London made on average only five arrests a year. In any case, we agreed to check.

Nothing of the sort happened. The good news was, in the places where mugging fell fastest, other crime types fell too. The Chief of the Metropolitan Police at the time commented that we had achieved more for collaborative working in those few weeks than had been managed in the previous twenty years. Good policing is good policing, so if it is put in place for one crime, it is likely to bring benefits in relation to others too. We saw this pattern again and again. For example, if you train primary teachers to be better at teaching maths, they are quite likely to get better at teaching other subjects, simply because they are learning to teach better.

That is not to say there are never perverse consequences – the key though is to explode the urban myths and take the battle into the media. You have to remember that any time you want to bring change to a major public service, those who don't want a given target will argue that it will have perverse or unintended consequences – most of which will never occur. If you don't battle this out on the airwaves, your critics will fill the vacuum. Where the perverse or unintended consequences do happen, you have a choice: adjust the policy or decide that the price is worth paying. Better to be a prophet armed than a prophet unarmed – in this case armed with facts.

The third and final thing you can and should do is to review periodically the data-collection process to check for abuses or unintended negative consequences. In the Punjab Education Roadmap we have employed independent people to review the effectiveness of the data-collection process and then the accuracy of the data. We found that in some cases the people checking the headcount of students – crucial for measuring progress on student attendance – were going by the attendance register rather than actually counting the children in classrooms, yet we knew that attendance registers were often inaccurate. While the review confirmed that most of the data we relied on was acceptable and that these abuses were relatively few, we were now able to correct the problem.

Similarly, on the four-hour A&E wait target, there were stories of ambulances waiting outside an A&E Department with an injured patient because the clock for the target technically started ticking only when the patient came through the door. This kind of thing did happen, but we knew from our data checks that it didn't happen very often. One wonders at the professional ethics of the staff involved in such an abuse – a classic case of losing sight of the moral purpose.

> **RULE 6**
> CHECK FOR
> PERVERSE OR
> UNINTENDED
> CONSEQUENCES
> (they may not happen)

A simple but essential point needs to be made briefly here and will emerge again in chapter 4. Whatever dataset you choose to base your target on, make sure there is an alternative dataset, ideally beyond reach of government's and public servants' control, that covers broadly the same theme. Use survey data as well as recorded crime figures to understand crime trends, for example. This will provide triangulation – confirmation or otherwise from another source – that movements in your target dataset are real and not manipulated. It will also provide you with a stronger foundation when you need to communicate your success (or failure).

CONSULTATION

Given that targets help define priorities, and priorities, by definition, are important, a further question that arises is how much to consult on them. After all, there is no point in a target that is established by government – such as the US Goals 2000 Act – but not taken up by the system.

In Malaysia, the government went out of its way to consult the Rakyat (as the citizens of Malaysia are known). They did major surveys. Then they hired an exhibition hall in downtown Kuala Lumpur and invited the Rakyat, the opposition and the media – including the country's vibrant blogger community – to come and comment on the targets and the plans for implementing them. This was bold and imaginative. (It also put pressure on those producing the plans to do a good job.)

Our process in the Blair administration was much less open than this, although the original delivery targets were set in the immediate aftermath of an election campaign in which many of the issues to which they related had been debated vigorously. Over time, we became much more consultative about targets, encouraging – even requiring – the departments responsible to consult their stakeholders.

However, standard government consultation exercises – unlike the bolder and more imaginative Malaysian approach – while essential, have their limitations. Yes, they are necessary, in terms of natural justice in a democracy. And yes, it makes sense to consult those who will be involved in implementation; they may well spot practical flaws in what is proposed, and with luck they will take greater ownership of the targets once they are set. Also, at the very least, dividing lines become clearer and the nature of future public debate is laid bare.

But there are limitations in the nature of the exercise itself. The stakeholders with whom a government department regularly interacts, and therefore consults on targets (or anything else), inevitably represent the producer interest and/or the most powerful lobby groups. These groups tend either to have a vested interest in the status quo or to adopt standard positions that are regularly repeated and well known. They are therefore likely to err on the side of caution rather than ambition when it comes to setting a target because, as the producer interest, they'll have significant responsibility for implementation. In short, they are likely to aim to trim the unreasonable.

Meanwhile, the voice of the potential beneficiaries – call them citizens or customers or both – is less likely to be heard because they are less likely to be organized and often include the powerless and voiceless. This is why from time to time politicians claim to be representing 'the silent majority' or 'the little platoons'; this may sound pretentious or arrogant out of some mouths, but is often a fair point.

Thus, when the chief minister of Punjab decided he wanted an Education Roadmap and a serious approach to delivery, he didn't consult on the targets at all. He simply asserted that he wanted 100 per cent enrolment, improved attendance and much higher quality. Our team then turned these aspirations into real numbers. Needless to say, some of the officials thought the level of ambition bordered on madness, but there was never any doubt that the goals were ones that parents across Punjab would have wanted. Their only doubt at the time would have been about whether anything would actually get done – after all, they had heard empty promises many times before.

This leads to the final point about targets, which is this: in big systems, such as the school system in Punjab or the National Health Service in England, the targets need to be cascaded out. How did we do that in Punjab? We took the provincial-level targets and then asked ourselves what each of the thirty-six districts would have to achieve for the province as a whole to reach its targets. We had some (rudimentary but good enough) data from the past which enabled us to set different starting points for districts according to their social composition, and therefore the degree of challenge they faced. Led by the outstanding Secretary – Schools of the time, Aslam Kamboh, we then summoned the district leaders to Lahore in April 2011 and shared their targets with them. There was some bewilderment; few had even heard of the Roadmap at that point, and fewer still believed that any attempt at reform would work. At that time, even the secretary was of the view that this was just another of the countless donor initiatives that came and went. It is worth noting that some powerful organizations in the province thought the targets were far too challenging. One leading representative of the World Bank accused us at the time of being too ambitious and going too fast. We readily agreed we were guilty on both counts. By 2013, though, the province and almost all of the districts had met or exceeded the targets set that day.

In short, we could not have been more top-down if we had tried. 'Top-down' is often hurled as a term of abuse, but there are circumstances when it is the best approach – and a massively under-performing school system is a case in point. It is also often said that top-down can't work, which is simply inaccurate, as the Punjab education reform and many other successful changes around the world make clear.

However, it is by no means the only approach to cascading out targets nor the best in all circumstances. An alternative is to consult the frontline units – a hospital, a police force or whatever – and ask them to state what they think they might achieve. In my experience, often (but not always) this will result in less ambition, but on the plus side ensures a greater sense of ownership.

The third way is to have a negotiating process. This is what we did with the original National Literacy Strategy in 1997–8. The national target had already been set and made public. Department for Education statisticians then produced a range for each of the 150 local authorities within which they would have to come out for us to achieve the national target. In the days before ubiquitous email, these ranges were handed in brown envelopes to representatives of the local authorities at a conference in London, and they were asked to come back to us a week or two later with their view on what they could achieve. All but one readily came back with targets within the range we had proposed.* Then each year, as the actual results came in, we engaged in a data-informed dialogue with them

> **RULE 7**
> CONSULT WITHOUT CONCEDING ON AMBITION
> (opposition is inevitable)

---

* The exception was County Durham. When I called the chief education officer and told him he was the only exception and that I would have to point this out to the prime minister, whose constituency was in County Durham, he reluctantly came into line too.

about progress towards the target. The targets were seen as exceptionally ambitious, yet within two years even the lowest-performing local authority had exceeded the national average we had at the outset. Further evidence of the power of ambition itself to drive progress.

MORAL PURPOSE

The art of prediction or forecasting is a subtle one, and when you set a target, make no mistake, that is what you are doing. In a political system this has its risks. David Blunkett famously said back in 1998 that if the government didn't meet its literacy target for 2002, his 'head was on the block'. When I said to him I thought that was a rash statement, he replied with some cutting edge, 'It is important that everyone takes responsibility, including me. And, by the way, if I go down, you're coming with me.'

In other words, reputations are at risk. But David's point was right; if you want thousands of public servants to take responsibility for their part in achieving a goal, you need to make it clear that you take your responsibility seriously too.

Nate Silver, in his magisterial survey of 'the art and science of prediction', *The Signal and the Noise*, urges us to think probabilistically when we forecast: rather than 'it's going to rain tomorrow', 'there is a 90 per cent chance of rain tomorrow'. This is, of course, the right way to think analytically when a target is being discussed. He also makes another crucial point – that it's dangerous to depend purely on the data. His discussion of major league baseball led to vigorous debate about whether data analytics or the judgement of scouts gave better predictions of future success. He concludes firmly that a combination of the two is most effective. Statistical inferences are much stronger when backed up by theory and judgement or at least some deeper thinking about their root causes. As the economist Jan Hatzius (whom Silver quotes) says, you need a story. Data on its own is not enough.

As if to confirm this, 2013 saw a young Norwegian, Magnus Carlsen, crowned world chess champion after he comfortably defeated the Indian Viswanathan Anand. Carlsen beats computers too, even though, as long ago as 1997, a computer, Deep Blue, had defeated his esteemed predecessor as world champion, Garry Kasparov. Given all the multiple increases in computer power (not to mention many more chess games to be fed into the analysis), how come, all these years later, the best computers can't beat the Norwegian upstart? It seems the answer is that the computer analysis has helped Magnus Carlsen too – he can absorb all that massive insight from a computer and then apply human judgement on top of that. The computer, of course, cannot do the latter. The eagle of computer analysis soars to a great height, and then the wren of human judgement, sitting on the eagle's back, can fly that little bit higher.

Having a story is important, not just to ensure the best possible prediction, but because for a target to have real impact on the ground it has to be motivational, it has to have that moral purpose. Without this, however good the analysis, the benchmarking and the probabilistic thinking, none of it will cut ice. Someone – ideally the leader – has to tell a good story. Imagine Henry V on the eve of the battle of Agincourt making his speech, 'We happy few, we band of brothers . . .' and going on to argue that, with the odds stacked against us, we have a 10 per cent chance of victory, or that in seven of the past ten battles such as this, the army on home soil has won.

This is not the speech Shakespeare wrote. Instead, he had Henry V tell a powerful story – that the events of the day ahead will become legendary.

More prosaically, when I led the Prime Minister's Delivery Unit, we had to tell a story about each target and about its moral purpose. The way I explained it to Britain's top civil servants in 2002 – in language that I admit fell well short of Shakespearean – was this:

> [Delivery] demands consistent focus on the targets and the data . . . But the targets, however good, and the data, however clear, are only imperfect representations of something even more important: that is, the real world outcomes that matter to citizens.

Yes, it's important that no one waits more than four hours to be seen and treated in an Accident & Emergency Department, but that is not the point – the point is that patients should get high-quality treatment rapidly (and go home thinking that the service is a good use of taxpayers' money). Similarly, a certain percentage passing a literacy test at age eleven is worthwhile too – but it's not the point. The point is that children should leave primary education able to read and write well because those skills are essential in the modern world – and because being able to do so will change their lives.

So the last rule about targets is to come back constantly to the moral purpose. Even Lord Salisbury, with whom the chapter began, had a clear priority and an implicit target – that Britain's dominant place in the world should be maintained. (The British navy of the time had a target too – that it should be bigger than the next two largest navies in the world combined.) This may not seem like a moral purpose all these years later, but no doubt at the time that was how it was perceived (at least in Britain). Sadly for him (but not so sadly for many others), rather a lot did happen in the twentieth century – in spite of Lord Salisbury – and his target was not achieved.

RULE 8
TARGETS ARE
IMPORTANT BUT
NOT THE POINT
(state and restate the story
about the moral purpose)

2

Organization

So now you know what you want to do. That's a good start, of course. But do you know how? To repeat: 'Don't tell me what! I know what. Tell me how!' How indeed ... There will need to be a strategy and some planning; we will come to those in the next two chapters. First you need an organization capable of delivering the priorities you've set. It is hard to exaggerate the importance of thinking this through, and this chapter is intended to make that possible.

For a newly elected government in particular, there is so much to learn, and often the most talented politicians find that the campaigning skills which propelled them to government are absolutely not the skills they need now that they find themselves governing.

In May 1997 in the Blair administration, there was a huge sense of euphoria after a spectacular, once-in-a-generation election victory, but the degree of ignorance once we were in government was vast. In No. 10 they were much more focused on 'the message' than on getting things done, because for the years in opposition 'the message' was all there was. The message still matters in government of course, but it is by no means everything. Here's my account of those first days:

The first few weeks were utterly chaotic but incredibly productive. Throughout there was an air of unreality and above all a confidence ... that for a while defied gravity ... Both the confidence and chaos were in evidence on the Thursday of that first week. I bumped into [Conor] Ryan in the foyer of the department and he asked me if I was ready for that morning's meeting with the PM at No. 10. 'What meeting?' I asked. Shortly afterwards I found myself in the Cabinet Room, gulping for air as Blair asked whether we were sure we would meet the 80% target [for literacy] and everyone went silent and looked at me.[1]

From his more exalted position, Blair was discovering the harsh realities too, as his own account makes clear.

The instincts were by and large spot on. The knowledge, the experience, the in-depth understanding that grappling over time induces – these qualities were missing. There was a political confidence, even swagger about us; but it was born of our popularity with the country, not our fitness to change it . . .[2]

Since those years, I've watched governments – the Sarkozy administration in France, the Cameron government in Britain, or the recently elected Nawaz Sharif government in Pakistan – go through the learning process of answering the 'How?' question . . . as waves of hope crash on unforgiving rocks.

Politics is an unforgiving business, and no one seems to think that a PM, a president or a minister needs to learn their way into the job, whereas in fact they are just like everyone else. And when you ask what it takes to become expert in a highly skilled role, the answer is surprisingly clear – it takes 10,000 hours of deliberate practice. This means not just 10,000 hours of doing something, but systematically working on the skills required in a conscious way. The starting point, therefore, is self-knowledge – being able to admit you are not an expert already (which means ruling out those political leaders, no small number, who suffer from hubris). Work this out for a PM who has this self-knowledge: 300 days per year at ten hours a day gives you 3,000 hours work a year. He or she may do more than that, but take it as a starting point. On this basis, if things went well, you would be expert roughly as you moved from your third to your fourth year in power.

Remarkably, that is precisely when Blair himself says he became fully competent in the 'How?' skills of government. Reflecting on 1998, just a year after becoming PM, he says, '. . . something was missing, some dimension barely glimpsed . . . Now of course, I know what was wrong. But then I was seeing as through a cloud.'[3] Another two years later, with maybe the 10,000 hours clocked up, the cloud had cleared: 'For me, the process [of putting together the ten-year plan for reform of the health service] was extraordinarily revealing and educative ... I stopped thinking of it as a gamble ... and started realising it was a clear mission whose challenge lay in ... how it was carried through.'[4]

People had been telling him from the beginning that he'd need to get a grip on the civil service machine, but at first he hadn't had the depth of knowledge to recognize how important that was. He had mastered politics, but not government – until the end of that third year in office.

With many terms of office lasting three, four or five years, depending on the constitution of the country, it becomes abundantly clear why so many leaders find their first terms so frustrating. And if they don't get another term, all too often they look back on their time in office much as Viktor Chernomyrdin did.

A newly elected leader without experience of government should be thinking: Who am I going to learn from? How can I get the necessary learning in faster than 10,000 hours? The answers come in part from building a team, which we'll come to later in the chapter.

DELIVERY CAPACITY

A good place to start, however, is to ask right away: Is the government machine capable of delivering our agenda? We asked this in the education department in 1997. The answer, we knew, was 'No'. We decided to set up the Standards and Effectiveness Unit – my first taste of dealing with implementation – precisely in response to the gaps in delivery capacity we had seen from outside before the election. We brought in leaders from the education field to work alongside civil servants, we employed experienced local government officials to strengthen the dialogue with their former colleagues across the country, we brought statisticians and researchers into the heart of the policy process, we had plans and checked progress ... and (although by no means perfectly) it worked! There was a wonderful moment on my first day when I was negotiating my terms of employment. I argued that I would like my compensation to be tied to the performance of eleven-year-olds in literacy and numeracy tests. Eyebrows were raised to the skies. I'm afraid that would be impossible, came the reply. Accountability for performance in the civil service? Certainly not!

At the beginning of his second term, Blair asked me to set up the Delivery Unit, again as a direct response to an evident capacity gap at the centre of government. In Ontario, soon after he was elected, Dalton McGuinty, learning from our experience, set up a Literacy and Numeracy Secretariat in his education department to drive teacher development – before then the teachers felt the civil servants were not capable of a deep enough dialogue about teaching and learning. In Malaysia, Najib Razak made the training of his top civil servants a key early task because he knew he would be unable to deliver unless he did. At the same time, he established Pemandu, modelled on the Delivery Unit, to drive his agenda forward. Each of these leaders realized sooner or later that, too often, the civil servants they inherit suffer from what has been called 'strategic atrophy', under which 'established assumptions' inhibit the formulation of 'new visions' and 'discount anything that challenges' the status quo.[5]

On the basis of experiences such as these, some colleagues and I developed a review process we call a Delivery Capacity Review, designed explicitly to answer the 'How?' question. The review has a rubric divided into five sections and fifteen modules. The five headings are:

- Develop a foundation for delivery
- Understand the delivery challenge
- Plan for delivery
- Drive delivery
- Create an irreversible delivery culture.*

The rubric simply asks a set of questions under each of the five sections, such as (under 'Plan for delivery'): Do plans track relevant performance metrics, leading indicators and implementation indicators for each intervention?

That is hardly a question designed to set the pulse racing, but the point of the rubric is not to emulate a good thriller, but to be

---

* See *Deliverology 101* for a much more detailed explanation

thorough, to make sure, in the classic phrase, that no stone is left unturned in checking out whether a government machine or an individual department is ready to deliver or not.

The rubric then offers best-case and worst-case options to help those responsible answer the questions for themselves. Again, thorough rather than exciting – but then a lot of government is about just that, thoroughness, which is why Mario Cuomo claimed to campaign in poetry but govern in prose.

On each of the fifteen modules, a team responsible can score itself from Red (not remotely ready) to Green (ready to go), with Amber-Red and Amber-Green in between. This may be the moment to introduce the four-point scale and traffic lights. A *Guardian* profile of me once said, 'He must dream in four-point scales.' This was meant to be a joke, but the sad truth is that I have dreamt about four-point scales. In the Delivery Unit, we took the three colours of a traffic light and split the middle one because we could see that, unless we did that, people making judgements would too easily be able to opt for the middle. With the four-point scale, we all had to decide – was it basically green or basically red and, since these colours then drove follow-up action, that was important. In the case of the Delivery Capacity Review, you end up with a chart of your system which you can put on the wall – it may be a sea of red or (more rarely) a field of green, or something in between. Either way, it will tell you exactly where your delivery capacity challenges are so that you can begin to address them (see Table 3).

There is one problem with almost all review processes in government – they take far too long and are therefore far too slow to have an impact. Often they start with someone setting up a committee or a task force or a working group. It meets periodically, but everyone involved has a day job, so very little gets done between meetings ... meanwhile, the real world changes in unexpected ways, which is what always happens with real worlds ... and so it goes on. The British Audit Commission, before its sudden demise in 2010, used to spend two years producing its excellent reports. I once asked one of the authors of these reports how long after starting on one did they know 90 per cent of what was in the final version. 'A month,' he replied. Since then, I've overseen the production of a number of review

Capacity Review Summary

	On target
G	
AG	
AR	
R	Off target

1. Develop a foundation for delivery	2. Understand the delivery challenge	3. Plan for delivery	4. Drive delivery	5. Create an irreversible delivery culture
(AG) Define your aspiration	(AG) Review past and present performance	(AG) Develop a reform strategy	(R) Establish routines	(AR) Build capacity
(AR) Review current state	(AR) Understand the drivers of performance	(AR) Review current state	(R) Review current state	(R) Review current state
(AR) Build the unit		(R) Build the unit	(AR) Build the unit	(AG) Build the unit
(G) Create a guiding coalition				

Table 3

processes that take a month, tell you 90 per cent of what you need to know, and then drive action.

The Delivery Capacity Review is based on that lesson. It is action-oriented. Following a brief pre-meeting a few weeks in advance, and having read a lot of materials (none of them produced specifically for the review), my team and I were able to do a pretty accurate Delivery Capacity Review for the State Department of Education in Massachusetts or Tennessee inside three days. The key is to make it interactive and to draw on the knowledge, often implicit, that the people who work there already have.

This is how it works. At the start of day one, armed with the knowledge you have from reading the documents, you run a three-hour workshop with the senior management team of the organization – but without the boss, so that people feel more freedom to tell it how it is. You get them to score themselves on the five sections and fifteen modules – Red, Amber-Red, Amber-Green or Green. You create an atmosphere in which people feel it is safe to confront the facts, however brutal they might be. A key aspect of this is to make clear that judging something Red isn't necessarily a comment on any individual's performance. Rather, it is a judgement about the future: are we equipped to deliver the new goals we've taken on? In the case of Massachusetts, for example, these were the goals they had committed to for the 'Race to the Top' grant they won from the federal government.

The debate goes back and forth. Those involved really enjoy it – it's practical, it's sometimes edgy and it's always productive. At some point they (nearly always) tell you that they've never done this kind of thing before and they now wish they had. By the end of the workshop, you have their picture of themselves, usually, incidentally, very honest. Also you, the review team, have learned a lot. Newly knowledgeable, you then interview or run focus groups with many stakeholders from every level in the system. You ask them what they think the department at the centre of the system does well, what it does badly and what advice they have about how it could achieve its goals. Once you get beyond the standard rhetorical stances and people relax, they too tell you what they really think – and your picture of where the organization is and how it needs to change becomes ever sharper. A key interview in this part of the process is a good hour alone with the boss – top official, minister or both – of the system. He or she will often, perhaps surprisingly, ask you to focus on the weaknesses, as this helps them drive actions which they know are necessary but haven't yet had the time or courage to take on.

On the penultimate evening (the evening of day two), the review team meets without others present and reaches its own judgements on each of the fifteen modules, debating as it does so what the management team's perspective has been, whether it tallies with what has been learned since, what weight to give to strongly held views of particular individuals . . . Someone has to manage time and maintain momentum otherwise any one of the debates could go on and on. There's always someone who threatens to 'die in the ditch' for a specific viewpoint, but come the end of the meeting they remain alive, and not in a ditch. The conversation may be a couple of hours in total. The review team now has its judgements on each of the fifteen modules on the four-point scale and can compare them with those reached by the management team the day before.

Now for the final morning. The review team and the management team, again without the boss, debate their differences and seek to agree. Usually, the differences are few, maybe on four or five judgements out of the fifteen, and usually only one shade apart. The beauty of this process is that the management team always knows much more about their organization, while the review team always knows much more about what 'good' (or 'bad') looks like in other, similar organizations. Once agreement is reached, as it almost always is (the head of the review is the ultimate tiebreaker), participants can move on to the even more important task of deciding what should be done to address the problems identified. What can be done in one month? Three months? And beyond? As a result of the preceding debates, the actions are easy to identify. They almost always literally fall out of the process. So in this meeting the key is to clarify precisely what the action is, who should be responsible and when it should be done.

Then, in the final act of the Delivery Capacity Review, the two teams together report to the leader; here's the picture of our capacity to deliver the goals we've set and here's what we suggest should be done about it. The leader is often stunned by the accuracy of the picture – like a mirror held up to them – and impressed by the action plan. I can still remember the look on the face of the Tennessee Schools Commissioner when he heard the report – challenging, real and, above all, action-oriented.

There is one key piece of sensitivity required before the final act. If there are personnel issues – it might have become clear that one senior manager is part of the problem – they need to be raised separately and confidentially. If the leader is part of the problem, it is more complex still, but you are undoubtedly better off than you were, as you now have an evidence base. If these personnel issues are a major barrier to making progress towards the goals, then they have to be addressed, however uncomfortable that might be.

This process is quick and effective and can be applied to any large public system. Why wouldn't any minister with a sense of purpose ask for this to be done in the

> **RULE 9**
> REVIEW THE CAPACITY OF YOUR SYSTEM TO DELIVER THE AGREED GOALS
> (and do it quickly)

first couple of months in office? Will the picture that emerges be perfect? Of course not. Will it be a lot better than the picture formed from rumour and counter-rumour which is the stuff of large bureaucracies? You bet it will.

A DELIVERY UNIT

Your priorities and goals are clear, you know how well (or not) your organization is set up to succeed, and you know what you need to do to strengthen its capacity to deliver. Now you need to know which part of the centre of your organization – whether it's a single department or an entire government – will make sure that delivery happens. And in this book, remember, delivery means that the citizens actually see and feel the difference, not just that a policy is announced or a law passed.

Responsibility for delivery lies with the relevant department – hospitals with health, schools with education and so on – but who at the centre of the system will track progress for the political leader and make sure that focus is sustained, draw attention to problems and help solve them as necessary? Or play the equivalent role within a department, which itself will have numerous sections or branches and perhaps several associated agencies?

A common response to this question is to say, if the leader appoints good ministers to lead the various departments, why would he or she need such a function? Or the equivalent at departmental level?

Well, in theory, if all the ministers were highly competent and loyal to the president or prime minister this might be OK, but ministers are often appointed on the basis of the political faction they represent or for some other reason not directly related to competence. There is nothing wrong with this – it is how politics works – but it does mean that it is unlikely that all ministers will be excellent. In any case, as we've seen, being good at politics is not the same as being good at governing. And, of course, there's still the centre of government to consider. First, a delivery function there can make sure that small amounts of the leader's time can be applied systematically and routinely to the identified priorities. Second, if there is no delivery or implementation function there, then the centre is likely to focus on politics, strategy and policy, and not take implementation seriously enough. In Blair's first term, people from No. 10 used to come and see me in the education department. Always a pleasure. And the question they asked was, 'Have you got any more ideas?' Of course I had ideas but, I used to reply to them, how come you never ask me whether we've implemented the ideas we've already had?

Third, a delivery unit can ensure that all the relevant departments and agencies contribute to achieving a government goal, thus overcoming the lack of collaboration between departments or agencies (the silo effect) that is so strong in most democracies. Fourth, a delivery function can become a centre of expertise on delivery and implementation; it can learn lessons which might apply to several departments or to the entire government machine, which simply can't be learned otherwise. In the twenty-first century, this capacity to learn rapidly and effectively is not just desirable, it is necessary.

Indeed, this learning is fundamental to building delivery capacity. The truth is that in the modern world success is not achieved by the standard model people have in their heads, which looks like Figure 2.

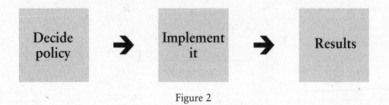

Figure 2

Actually, in politicians' heads it is often more like Figure 3.

Figure 3

The Implementation Cycle

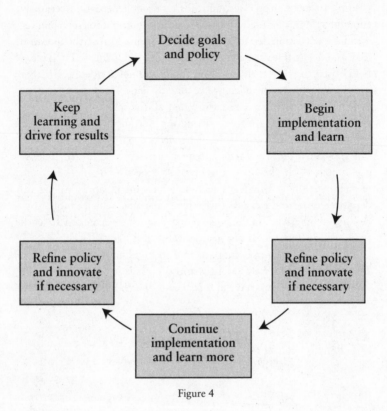

Figure 4

(Hence my consistent advice to politicians: policy is 10 per cent and implementation 90 per cent.)

But, given the scale of the challenges ambitious governments take on and the pace of change, it's not just a question of the relationship between policy and implementation, it's about the nature of that relationship. And it should look more like Figure 4.

I didn't realize at the time, but Blair had clearly understood this, as his memoirs made clear:

> We established a Delivery Unit ... It was an innovation that was much resisted, but utterly invaluable ... It would focus like a laser on an

issue, draw up a plan to resolve it, working with the department concerned, and then performance manage it to a solution ... often it became clear that the problem was systemic requiring wholesale change to the way a public service worked, rather than a centrally or bureaucratically driven edict.[6]

In most cases where an ambitious goal is set, you cannot know enough at the beginning to be sure of success; you have to learn as you go. The establishment of a delivery function makes that possible, not just in relation to each goal, but across all the goals. In government capacity terms, this is massive.

Some governments – Australia's, for instance – have responded to these demands by setting up a Strategy and Delivery Unit or a Policy and Delivery Unit. I would not say that can't work; I would say that it is less likely to work for the simple reason that, in political systems such as governments, strategy and policy usually trump implementation and delivery. It is always tempting to pitch into any one of the range of debates going on in government about future strategy – they are absolutely riveting and they are at the core of what politicians love, their essence even. Meanwhile, tracking implementation, checking actions have been taken across a system, exploring data sets for evidence of progress ... these tasks,

> **RULE 10**
> SET UP A DELIVERY
> UNIT (call it what you
> like, but separate it from
> strategy and policy)

however essential they might be, are (unless you are a sad graph-lover like me) fundamentally dull. For this reason, my advice is to separate delivery from strategy so as to ensure there is a senior person whose sole focus is delivery, as mine was in the original Delivery Unit and as Idris Jala's has been in Pemandu in Malaysia.

What should a delivery unit look like? That's the next question. It should be small in relation to the overall task and focused solely on the priorities. At the beginning of the original Delivery Unit, we debated designing it to track everything. I opposed this because I thought the last thing we needed was a new, big bureaucracy to track a set of old, big bureaucracies. Blair, in any case, didn't give the idea

How Units Fail

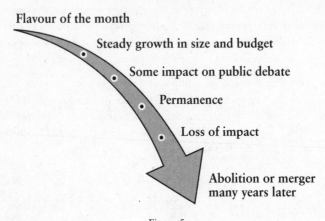

Figure 5

the time of day. It was the start of his second term, he wanted a legacy of reformed public services, and had learned to prioritize.

How small? In the Louisiana Department of Education, a delivery unit of three or four people drove big changes in outcomes, especially graduation rates from high school. In the original PMDU we had around forty people pursuing twenty or so priorities across four major departments. I had learned from studying previous newly established units at the centre of government that their traditional trajectory went roughly as in Figure 5.

I chose to do the opposite from the outset; putting a cap on size and budget (in that first year, I returned some of our budget to the Treasury early, saying I didn't need it – the entire institution nearly fell off its collective chair: that had never happened before!) and promising to abolish it after three years unless there was strong demand for it from top civil servants and politicians.

Forty was enough for us. Pemandu in Malaysia has around 100 people to drive the six NKRAs and an economic reform agenda. Idris Jala, its leader, emphasizes the importance of 'having a small team, lean, to go and deliver'.[7] One way to look at size is these total numbers. Another is to consider the leverage ratio. We worked out once that for every pound spent on the Delivery Unit, we influenced roughly £50,000 of public expenditure. Once people saw the value we added, this began to look like a very good deal indeed. It is also a daunting and empowering thought for delivery unit staff.

Focus on the priorities, keep it small and ensure it is well led. The person responsible for the delivery unit needs a distinctive set of characteristics. Get the wrong person and its influence will rapidly wither; get it right and everything else will follow. What are those characteristics?

I prepared a list for the chief minister of Punjab, Shahbaz Sharif, setting out the attributes required to lead a delivery unit (see Table 4).

There are people with this set of characteristics, but not that many in any given system. The first requirement alone rules out plenty of otherwise qualified people. I was lucky; I had got to know Blair in opposition by working on speeches and policy documents with him and his team. It's much harder for a PM to establish that level of trust once they are in office and surrounded by people jockeying for position and trying to impress.

Najib Razak found the ideal candidate to lead Pemandu in Idris Jala. Idris had had a stellar career at Shell as a global problem-solver before returning to Malaysia. The PM knew him and respected his track record. Idris is a larger-than-life character with tremendous energy and motivational power, but he did not need or seek political credit; he wasn't interested in the politics at all. What he wanted to do was solve Malaysia's problems, and if the PM and cabinet got the credit, that was fine by him. As he put it, 'they must take the credit and our job is to help them to deliver'.[8]

George Noell, who headed the delivery unit in the Louisiana Department of Education, was a professor seconded from Louisiana State University by the then State Education Chief, Paul Pastorek. George was a master of data and education research, and so leapt at the chance to make a big difference in his adopted state. His most notable characteristic was his integrity – he deeply believed in the mission of improving Louisiana's schools – which he brought to bear on relationships in the fractured political world of the state's education system. Some might have disagreed with George; everyone admired him. While his boss, Paul Pastorek, was a risk-taker and master of the

Characteristic	Reason
Completely trusted by the PM or CM	Has to be able to represent the PM or CM effectively and be the bearer of bad tidings sometimes.
Determined, hardworking and focused	Without these characteristics, delivery is unthinkable.
Optimistic and confident	Belief is a vital ingredient of success. If the head of the delivery unit doesn't believe that success is possible, why should anyone else?
Good at building relationships	There will be many sensitive conversations to be had, especially when things are going wrong. The delivery unit head needs to be a calm, problem-solving influence.
Happy to be out of the limelight, giving credit to others	If there is delivery in health, the minister of health should get the credit... The delivery unit needs to help others succeed and give them the credit (which is the currency of politics).
Have a successful track record in business or government	Essential for credibility, especially at the beginning.

Table 4

cut-throat policy environment of Baton Rouge – at weekends he hunted alligators – George kept the agenda and the data in focus. He insisted on telling Paul the bad news even when sometimes he would rather not have heard it!

Note how in each of these cases it's not just the general personal characteristics that matter, but the specific fit to that leader and that political environment. With delivery leaders such as Idris or George, the potential for success is greatly enhanced.

The delivery unit then requires a structure. This too needs to be specific to the context. In the original PMDU, my first thought was to have four teams. The first were the account managers, one for each department we interacted with. They held the relationship, worked with the department on its plans, checked the data, led progress checks and did the behind-the-scenes work for meetings between the PM and ministers. Second, there was a group of problem-solvers who could be flexibly deployed on problems as they arose, rather like a consultancy, which is where some of them were recruited from. Third, there was a team of data analysts led by the brilliant Tony O'Connor, servicing all the other teams. Fourth, there was a small team of capacity-builders who organized training events for the key officials in departments responsible for delivering the priority outcomes.

It was a good theory, and worked quite well in practice for a while, but it left me holding too many senior departmental relationships with politicians and top officials. Also it exposed my own weaknesses as a manager – I tend to like chaos, often replying 'What's so good about clarity?' when someone demands it. We finally reorganized on a plan produced by my deputy, Peter Thomas, who wanted clarity for himself and everyone else and decided (rightly) that I needed to be pushed. This structure was built around departments – capacity-building was dropped as a separate function, and account management and problem-solving were combined in teams that related to each relevant department. The number-crunchers kept crunching numbers. The huge gain for me was that each departmental team now had senior leadership that could interact with top people in the departments, so it freed up my time. The PMDU was organized by priority (see Fig. 6 overleaf) and it worked.

Figure 7 shows how we were then able to illustrate clearly how we interacted with departments.

The redesign, which had in effect been imposed on me by Peter, worked excellently and was crucial. The 2001–3 model of organization had laid the foundations; his new model unleashed our capacity

Prime Minister's Delivery Unit (PMDU)

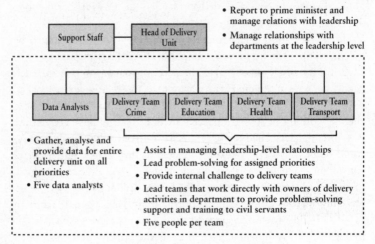

Figure 6

and was responsible for the tremendous success of the years 2003 to 2005. Idris Jala used this as the starting point for Pemandu while at the same time drawing on his own experience at Shell.

With the right leadership and structure, the next question is, what kind of people to staff it with. Given the goals of keeping small and driving a big impact, it is obvious you need a small number of highly dedicated people, driven by the mission.

For the establishment of the Roadmap in Punjab, eventually I recruited a small delivery team of three who worked with the Secretary – Schools to set the ball rolling. At first, there was just one person, Katelyn Donnelly, whose imagination, dedication and persistence, I came to discover, are more than a match for almost any bureaucrat, public or private. Over time, Hiran Embuldeniya and Saad Rizvi spent more and more time in Lahore too. Since I visited once a month for a week, I had to be confident that the team on the ground would be self-organized, self-motivated and would come to me either in our weekly calls or by email if they had a problem. As the team developed, they were brilliant, incredibly hardworking and wonderful at building relationships in the challenging circumstances of a Pakistani bureaucracy. Later, led by the

Collaboration between PMDU and Departments

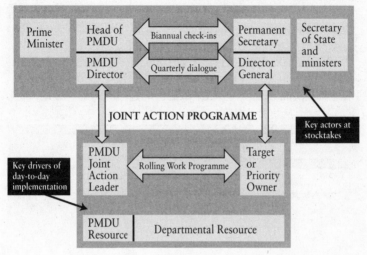

Figure 7

dedicated Fenton Whelan, they recruited young Pakistani talent from the excellent Lahore University of Management Sciences. These young graduates not only worked tremendously hard, but extended our capacity to work at the district level across the province, since they could go where security worries prevented us from going.

In the PMDU and in Pemandu, a virtue was made of combining in the teams some excellent civil servants with others brought in from outside – consultancies, audit organizations and university research departments. The mutual learning that resulted was one of the attractions of working there. This approach also addressed head-on the evident lack of delivery skills in the civil service.

Figure 8 showing the previous roles of the various members of staff gives a flavour of the Delivery Unit in 2004. Rigorous recruitment and selection processes were vital to ensure the necessary relationships and leverage. We did not just want clever consultants – we wanted them to have a passion for the cause and relationship-building skills too. Adrian Masters, who joined PMDU from

Previous Work Locations of PMDU Staff (2004)

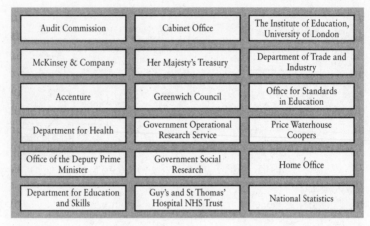

Audit Commission	Cabinet Office	The Institute of Education, University of London
McKinsey & Company	Her Majesty's Treasury	Department of Trade and Industry
Accenture	Greenwich Council	Office for Standards in Education
Department for Health	Government Operational Research Service	Price Waterhouse Coopers
Office of the Deputy Prime Minister	Government Social Research	Home Office
Department for Education and Skills	Guy's and St Thomas' Hospital NHS Trust	National Statistics

Figure 8

McKinsey and has gone on to an outstanding career in the National Health Service, illustrates the point.

In the original PMDU, we built a culture around five key words:

- *Ambition* – No compromise. That's what it takes.
- *Focus* – Never be distracted.
- *Clarity* – Collect and examine the data. Confront the brutal facts and don't be afraid to tell the prime minister.
- *Urgency* – Constantly counteract the tendency of bureaucracies to delay.
- *Irreversibility* – See the change through so it will stay changed.

I repeated the five words, like a mantra, whenever I got the chance.

There was one other central idea that underpinned our work – simplicity. Government is genuinely complicated, and on top of that there are some people in bureaucracies who seem to relish adding further complexity, perhaps because they believe if they (and only they) understand the state of affairs, it adds to their sense of power. If things are to get done, if delivery is to happen, there has to be a countervailing drive for simplicity. This is what we aimed to provide. In the end, we said, there are only five questions that matter, and we're

The Five Key Questions

(1) What are you trying to do?	• Clear priorities • Specific, measurable goals	
(2) How are you trying to do it?	• Clear practical plans which are used regularly and updated	
(3) How, at any given moment, will you know whether you are on track?	• Good, steady, close to real-time data on key indicators • Monitoring routines (such as stocktake meetings) with all key players involved	
(4) If you are not on track, what are you going to do about it?	• Agreed actions, followed up, tested in practice and refined if necessary • Always try something. Never neglect a problem once identified	
(5) Can we help?	• Constant ambition, refusal to give up • Focus on goals, no distractions • Maintaining the routines • Analysis and problem-solving where required • Bringing to bear lessons from elsewhere	

Table 5

going to keep asking them, calmly and persistently, until we get answers.

Simple. Really simple. The difficulty is the sheer discipline and persistence required to keep it this simple. To this day, if I find myself in conversation with a prime minister, president or minister, these five questions set an ideal agenda.

The final piece of putting a delivery unit in place is to think through the different relationships it needs and how to ensure they work effectively. I saw many potential pitfalls in this respect when I took on the Delivery Unit role. There was the looming presence of Gordon Brown and the Treasury wondering how to deal with a new part of the Blair machine, seemingly intended to trample on Treasury territory. There were Cabinet ministers, powerful New Labour figures, thinking anything from 'Don't waste my time' to 'Are you Tony's spies?' And there were the permanent secretaries, the mandarin class, made legendary by *Yes, Minister* and without compare in their ability to shrug off any challenge from yet another new unit which might threaten their ordered world.

So, quite early on, we drew up a list of things we knew all these powerful people hated about units at the centre of government and we promised not to be like that. Instead, we said, we'll demonstrate the characteristics you say you would like. And we listed those too. This became our calling card, in effect a contract about how we would work.

OUR WORKING APPROACH SEEKS TO AVOID

- micro-management
- generating bureaucracy or unnecessary work
- getting in the way
- policy wheezes (or gimmicks)
- being driven by headlines
- short-termism
- opinion without evidence
- changing the goalposts

OUR APPROACH EMPHASIZES

- keeping the PM well informed about his key priorities
- consistent pursuit of those priorities
- data and evidence
- plain speaking
- early identification of problems
- imaginative problem-solving
- application of best practice
- recognizing differences as well as similarities between departments
- urgency
- building capacity
- leaving responsibility and credit where they belong
- the expectation of success.

I promised ministers and officials that if they found any of my staff following the 'seeks to avoid' list, I would intervene immediately. Afterwards I summarized on a PowerPoint slide how I'd thought about each of our key relationships (Table 6).

The problems won't be identical in other governments and bureaucracies, but you can guarantee that there will be similar challenges with relationships because, in the end, whatever else government is, it

PMDU: Key Relationships

Getting the key relationships right

- **The Prime Minister:** Whatever you're doing we're focused on your priorities.

- **The Chancellor of the Exchequer:** We'll make sure the money you allocate delivers results.

- **Cabinet ministers:** We'll help you get your bureaucracy to deliver the government's priorities.

- **Top civil servants:** We'll sustain a focus on these priorities and help you solve your problems.

- **Everyone:** However much we contribute you get the credit.

Table 6

is always a soap opera. Rather than simply letting relationships develop, much better to be conscious about fostering the relationships you would like to see.

It is worth emphasizing how subtle and subjective these issues of leadership, selection of staff and relationships are. Now that delivery units have become fashionable, some major consultancies have

RULE 11
THE DELIVERY UNIT
NEEDS TO BE SMALL
AND WELL LED
(and excellent at building
relationships)

become prone to touring the world recommending delivery units as the solution to pretty much any public sector problem. Their cookie-cutter approach misses these key subjective factors, with the result that all too often the delivery unit that looks beautiful on the organization chart fails in practice.

DELIVERY AND THE CENTRE
OF GOVERNMENT

Geoff Mulgan was a colleague of mine in No. 10 Downing Street, responsible for strategy when I was responsible for delivery. Both before and since that experience, Geoff thought deeply and widely about government and how it should operate. He has also learned more about how it worked in different parts of the world than anyone I know. Recently he has turned his attention to the centre of government – the range of functions around a president, PM and/or cabinet – and asked what its role should be and how it should work. He says, 'Current structures usually fail on four counts (there are plenty of other problems – these are just some common ones)':

1. 'They are insufficiently effective at delivering legitimation . . .' In other words, they don't build trust and fall into the gap between expectations and delivery.
2. 'They are poor at making use of the right types of knowledge needed for good decision-making.'
3. 'They are poor at coordination and alignment of the often sprawling government machine . . .'
4. 'Many get timing wrong – it's not just that they do slowly things which should be done fast, but they also default to doing fast things which should be slow.'

My own experience, not just in No. 10, would confirm Mulgan's perspective. The Delivery Unit came in time to ameliorate the problems he lists, but none of us involved believed we had a coherent structure in No. 10 at that time.

Mulgan's answer is to use the metaphor of a brain. The centre of government should have the following capabilities:

- *Observation* – seeing what's happening
- *Attention* – focusing
- *Cognition* – reflecting and analysing
- *Creation* – imagining and designing
- *Memory* – learning and not repeating mistakes
- *Judgement* – discerning and deciding
- *Wisdom* – making sense of complexity and bringing a moral perspective to bear.

With this perspective, Mulgan identifies twelve tasks which he says 'need to be part of someone's job. Indeed a test of coherence of any current centre of government is whether it's clear where responsibility lies for each of these . . .'[9]

1. Make the direction of government explicit . . . and avoid the temptation to generate blizzards of initiatives.

2. Shape and share the strategy for the whole of government – and create capacities to do this.
3. Ensure that the important things happen – and create capacities to keep a sharp focus on the ones that matter most. (This is the role of a delivery unit, as he goes on to say.)
4. Align national, regional and local actions as far as possible.
5. Ensure structures are aligned with purpose – rather than accepting traditional silos.
6. Bring in the right inputs – from open data to citizen experience – to guide experience.
7. Mobilize the best available knowledge and insights to guide decisions.
8. Try to do what works – and leave better evidence behind for your successors.
9. Put money to work – and ensure finance is aligned to strategy.
10. Prepare for the future.
11. Organize the top politicians and officials as a single team with a shared commitment to ends and means. (This is the guiding coalition idea – see next section – at whole-government level.)
12. Take care of the relationship with the public.

It's a fascinating list. Numbers 1 and 12 are essentially tasks of communication. Numbers 2, 4 and 5 are organizational. Tasks 6, 7 and 8 are all about the capacity to learn more and better – a key role for the delivery unit and other parts of the centre. The key point for our purposes is that the delivery function is crucial not just in ensuring the most important things happen but in contributing to the wider agenda of better-informed decision-making.

It is worth testing Mulgan's theoretical perspective against a real example. Soon after he became president in Chile in 2010, Sebastián Piñera decided to reorganize the centre of government, including the establishment of a President's Delivery Unit. Piñera had been a successful businessman and was at home with the idea of priorities and targets. I met him that summer. I remember the breathtaking views of the Andes at dawn as my flight arrived in Santiago, I remember too Piñera's restlessness, speed of thought and the slight twitch of his eye.

Overall, his presidency, which finished in 2014, was mixed. He was considered unlucky, having to deal with not just, like others around the world, an era of financial and economic crisis, but also the famous mining accident, earthquakes and other disasters. He had to face massive student protests against policies which he supported but which originated before his time. It is true that he committed some gaffes as well, including making a particularly offensive remark about women. All this tarnished his reputation.

His story is a cautionary tale for anyone who takes a simplistic view that improving delivery of results will, alone, lead to political success. Of course, delivery helps, but for any leader or government, a lot else – including the 24-hour media churn – affects reputation or credibility.

As a recent report from the Inter-American Development Bank makes clear, on delivery the Piñera administration made real headway. 'We expect Chileans to judge us on our results, not our good intentions,' the president asserted early in his term.[10] His Delivery Unit would check progress on demanding goals in the president's agenda, such as 'Reduce by 25%, by 2013, [criminal] offences committed in public places' or 'Create a million new, quality jobs during the period 2010–14, at the average rate of 200,000 per year'.

These by no means trivial goals were grouped under seven 'pillars' covering everything from economic growth to health and reducing poverty. With ups and downs, the PDU made a significant contribution to progress on these goals, according to the IDB account. It acted vigorously and collaboratively with departments when progress slipped, as in 2013 when there was a crisis in relation to the crime goals. It helped 'to maintain the attention and the focus on the government's goals, irrespective of headlines' and it made 'the government programme more actionable'. Through its daily contact with ministers, it facilitated 'rapid identification of bottlenecks and coordination failures'.[11] Certainly the departments were constantly aware of its existence. 'The PDU is like a fly buzzing in your ear,' said one official.[12]

This commentary suggests that the PDU contributed significantly to the agenda Mulgan sets out, especially to the central task of ensuring the important things get done. In fact, the PDU was one part of a wider reorganization of central government designed to address more comprehensively the kinds of challenge Mulgan identifies: the OECD lists four key functions which encompass most of what he describes. They are strategic planning, coordination, the monitoring of delivery and providing public accountability. The PDU in Chile dealt with the third of these but other reforms addressed the wider agenda. This is illustrated in Figure 9, which places the Delivery Unit in its context. Those planning a delivery unit have to think through its place in the centre, as the Piñera administration did in Chile.

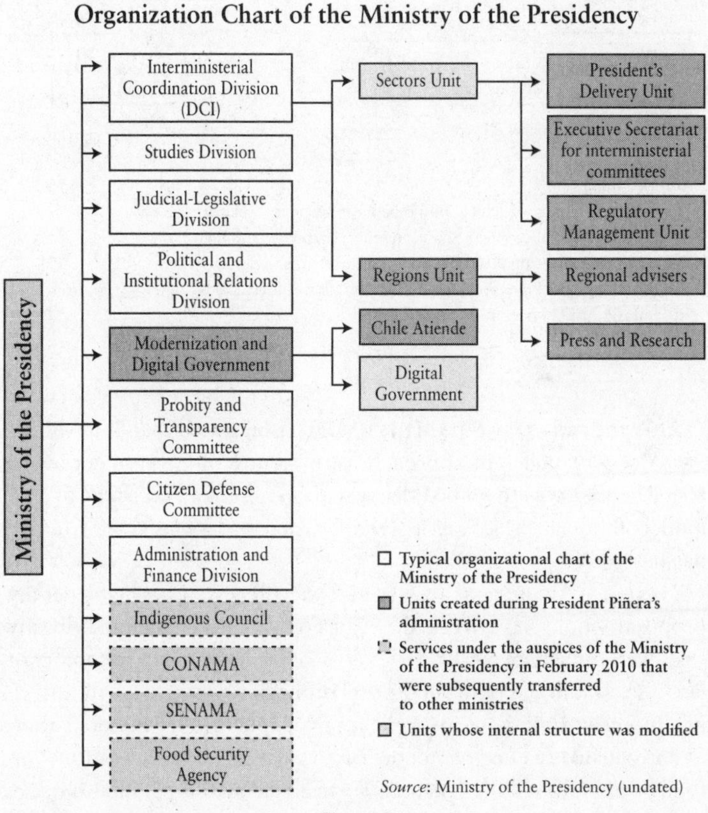

Organization Chart of the Ministry of the Presidency

Figure 9

Source: Ministry of the Presidency (undated)

□ Typical organizational chart of the Ministry of the Presidency

▣ Units created during President Piñera's administration

▨ Services under the auspices of the Ministry of the Presidency in February 2010 that were subsequently transferred to other ministries

□ Units whose internal structure was modified

Coherent Organization at the Centre

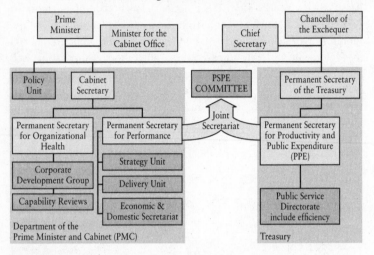

Executive function
- Perm Sec PPE oversees CSR (Comprehensive Spending Review) and efficiency
- Perm Sec Performance oversees and integrates strategy and delivery
- Perm Sec Organizational Health oversees capabilities
- Perm Sec PPE and Perm Sec Performance relationship critical to match integration at PSPE (Public Services and Public Expenditure) Committee

Figure 10

After the end of my time in the PMDU, I suggested that Blair should adopt a more coherent approach to the centre of government in the UK. The idea was to embed delivery thinking into a coherent overall model of the centre (see Fig. 10) that learned the lessons Geoff Mulgan has described.

There is no single right answer, and we will never know whether my proposal would have worked because it was never adopted. In any case everything depends on the quality of leadership and the ability of leaders to build the right kind of relationships, which we will turn to in a moment. In Indiana, as we'll see in chapter 8, they adopted a different but highly effective model of embedding the delivery function firmly within the finance function. There are numerous plausible models.

All in the end depend on the people and their relationships. Mulgan concludes that the centre needs no more than a few hundred people in total, 'highly skilled; highly networked; and well-integrated'. It should, he suggests in a judicious phrase, combine 'clarity with lightness'.[13]

As for Piñera's PDU, the evidence in the IDB report suggests it made a significant difference to outcomes, with over half the president's commitments, some of which were very ambitious, being delivered. It did so largely due to its persistent monitoring. As we've seen, though, successful delivery does not always translate into political success. As the IDB comments drily, such work, even when it changes the experience of citizens significantly, 'may not be a source of political gain'.[14]

THE GUIDING COALITION

The great Admiral Lord Nelson lies dying in the arms of his faithful friend, Thomas Masterman Hardy, on the burning deck of the *Victory*, knowing that the result of the great battle of Trafalgar is assured, but also that he will not live to tell the tale. 'Thank God I have done my duty,' the admiral manages before losing his power of speech and, soon afterwards, drawing his last breath. (Whether he also said 'Kiss me, Hardy' remains a matter of conjecture.)

Trafalgar was a great victory, scotching the threat of a Napoleonic invasion of Britain and laying the foundation for a century of naval dominance. And it was not the only victory Nelson had won – he had been a heroic captain at Cape St Vincent, and a bold, imaginative admiral at the Nile and Copenhagen. What was it that enabled him to achieve this string of spectacular victories?

Everyone agrees that his courage and the way he led by example were vital ingredients. His attention to the health and well-being of the ordinary sailors was exemplary as well. But these were not the game-changing qualities – other admirals could do these things too (and some did, if not to quite the same heroic levels). What made Nelson different was what today we'd call his management style. John Sugden in his brilliant and epic biography explains:

The increasingly large forces deployed in modern warfare made it diffi-cult for generals or admirals to exercise close supervision or control. Communications could easily break down . . . in sprawling, complicated encounters wreathed in smoke. Nelson never dispensed with signals [flags run up a mast to communicate with his captains] . . . but he did reduce his dependence on them by briefing his senior officers before-hand . . . His purpose was to draw them into the spirit and detail of the enterprise and to harness them to his expectations and standards of performance, so that they might use their judgement more effectively.[15]

While the French or Spanish captains were waiting for signals from their admirals, the British captains could exercise judgement and act without waiting because Nelson had built them into a team and trusted them. Far from being less cohesive as a result, the British were more cohesive. Nelson and his captains all understood why they were doing what they were doing, what the battle plan was and how they intended to execute it. Once in battle when, of course, everything does not go according to plan, each of them knew the overarching goal and the principles of the strategy and so each could replan and act on his own initiative. If in doubt, 'get in amongst them' – meaning the French – was the watchword.

Reforming a large public service or implementing a major new government policy may not be quite as demanding as the battle of Trafalgar, but Sugden's words 'Communications could easily break down . . . in sprawling, complicated encounters wreathed in smoke' seem uncannily accurate as a description of life at the heart of govern-ment. Nelson had invented something to which a professor at Harvard Business School has much more recently given a name.

One of the key ideas in *Leading Change*, John Kotter's excellent guide to successful business leadership, is the concept of the guiding coalition. He is referring to transforming businesses, but it struck me as a concept that was perhaps even more relevant in a government environment. The guiding coalition is not the same as a management team; it's a shared understanding among seven to ten people in key positions about what needs to be done and how. Margaret Mead once said famously: 'Never doubt that a small group of thoughtful, com-mitted citizens can change the world. Indeed, it's the only thing that ever has.'[16] In essence, the guiding coalition is the same idea inside a large organization. And it is exactly what Nelson created around him as an admiral.

In government we found that, if you got it right, the guiding coalition idea worked excellently. Yes, there may be a cabinet or a ministerial team, or a cabinet committee, or a departmental board, and each of these might have a function, but each has its limitations when it comes to driving delivery. A guiding coalition is quite different, and if you put it in place the difference it makes is incredible.

When I read John Kotter's book, I was just leaving the Department for Education to set up the Delivery Unit and I realized immediately that one of the reasons for our success in education (relative to other departments) in the first Blair term was that, without even knowing the term, we had a guiding coalition in place. Let me illustrate. One of our goals had been to improve literacy and numeracy in primary schools. We had in fact seen the percentage achieving good standards in literacy rise from 57 to 75 per cent, with a similar improvement in numeracy. In 2001, international comparisons put England third in the world for reading among ten-year-olds; in 2007 England was shown to be the most improved system in the world in primary school mathematics over the previous decade.

The strategy had been good if sometimes controversial, but a key to it had been the shared understanding among a handful of people; the Secretary of State for Education, David Blunkett; his Minister of State, Estelle Morris; myself as head of the Standards and Effectiveness Unit which was responsible for implementation of the strategy; Conor Ryan, David Blunkett's brilliant political/media adviser; Andrew Adonis and David Miliband in No. 10; David Normington, the top civil servant who was Director General of Schools at the time; and (at least until the autumn of 2000) Chris Woodhead, Chief Inspector of Schools. We all thought the strategy was important and the mission vital to the future of the country; we all understood the case for it and how to rebut the critics; and we all understood how it should be implemented. We were like Nelson and his captains; because we shared an understanding, we could act in harmony.

The result was that we could proceed rapidly and effectively without needing endless conversations or meetings. David Blunkett barely mentions the strategy in his memoirs, not because he didn't care – he burned passionately for the cause – but because he knew we were getting on with it and it was working. One of the threats to successful implementation in government in the absence of a guiding coalition is the dissonance that can arise in public statements made by different individuals or the contrast between public and private statements. Rapidly, these are reported as 'rows', and sometimes they reflect real rows, but the biggest problem is the confusion that results in the field. In education, for example, teachers on the receiving end of mixed messages start asking 'What do they want us to do?' and end up shrugging their shoulders and saying 'They haven't a clue.' It is all too easy to slide down this slippery slope.

With our guiding coalition in relation to the literacy and numeracy strategy in the first Blair term we avoided this fate. David Blunkett or Estelle Morris could answer a question in Parliament, Conor Ryan could brief the editorial writer of *The Times*, I could address a head-teacher conference and we'd all say the same thing – without needing to check. Resonance in place of dissonance.

Compare this to the same issue in the Blair second term which featured three secretaries of state for education in four years, none of them as passionate about literacy and numeracy as David Blunkett had been. Some of the officials wanted to add other objectives to the agenda, such as behaviour or information technology because the literacy and numeracy strategies had proved to be such an effective implementation mechanism. As a result, the focus was lost. No one could say any longer, as I had to primary headteachers, that as long as you deliver on literacy and numeracy, everything else will be forgiven. Meanwhile, the department as a whole began to listen to teachers' pleas for less prescription and less pressure. Eventually ministers started talking about 'letting go'. Stephen Twigg, a junior education minister at the time, even said on the *Today* programme that each teacher knows best in their own classroom, precisely the line that had caused the fifty-year plateau from the mid-1940s to the mid-1990s. In No. 10 we were still wedded to the hard-edged (and previously successful) approach but had become just one voice in a cacophony. No guiding coalition there! And very limited improvement in results in the second term compared to the first.

So what is the generalizable lesson for the science of delivery? For each key goal, identify the seven to ten key positions. Seek to make compatible appointments and make time early on to create the shared understanding. Make sure that there is an honest dialogue among this group so that problems of implementation are identified and resolved. It sounds simple, as does so much of the science of delivery, but it is hard to do in practice amid the tumult of government.

Dalton McGuinty achieved it brilliantly as premier of Ontario in relation to education and health. Most of the time he didn't have a separate delivery unit, but he was a master of delivery and consciously built guiding coalitions to lead key priorities. Similarly, even in the political chaos of Washington DC, Arne Duncan, the US Secretary of Education, was able to build and maintain the cross-party guiding coalition that put his ground-breaking Race to the Top programme in place successfully. The results are now coming

> **RULE 12**
> CREATE A GUIDING COALITION FOR EACH PRIORITY
> (to increase clarity and speed)

through. Both these talented political leaders are proof that the philosophy or mindset of delivery is more important than the unit itself.

CIVIL SERVICE REFORM

Sooner or later, a conversation about how to improve delivery capacity in government slides into a more general one about civil service reform. This in turn raises much wider issues about governance – corruption, for example. When a top official in Punjab praises one of his officials, he calls them 'hard-working and honest', which by implication is a negative reflection on many others.

So civil service reform is a vital issue for reasons far beyond delivery capacity. Getting it right is fundamental. As Bismarck, the great (and ruthless) German Chancellor put it, 'With bad laws and good civil servants . . . one can still govern, with bad civil servants even the best laws cannot help.'[17]

But it's also a risk. It is a risk because it can look so overwhelmingly difficult that political leaders give up. The opposite can happen too. They take it on and it becomes all-consuming; the reform of the civil service and the structure of government absorb all the time and energy available and the citizen sees little or no benefit, at least in the short-term. Donor agencies are often to be found proposing huge structural reforms, new agencies and generic capacity-building without ever specifying what goals they are meant to achieve.

This is not a book about civil service reform. The science of delivery lesson here is clear: don't avoid civil service reform, but equally don't let it absorb you and the bureaucracy totally either. Set your goals and focus on delivering them; that is what the citizens will want and what you'll be remembered for. (In 2007, Scotland did just this, abolishing traditional departments and building a unified civil service around five directors general responsible for five broad policy goals, such as Safer Scotland or Smarter Scotland.) Learn the lessons of delivery as you go and from this build an agenda for civil service reform which can be approached in a measured way behind the scenes. Don't ask, 'How should we change the civil service?', ask instead, 'How do we need to change the civil service in order to deliver our goals?' These are two very different questions! Don't depend on generic civil service reform to achieve the outcomes you want; you don't have the time.

> **RULE 13**
> BUILD THE CAPACITY TO DELIVER YOUR AGENDA (civil service reform for its own sake can be an energy drain)

Emmet Regan, a talented MBA student at Warwick Business School, reached a good understanding of what underpinned the success of the PMDU; and the lessons he identified – the 'six Ps' – I would argue, apply generally.

- *Prioritization* – establishing clear, specified goals
- *People* – choosing good people, establishing good relationships
- *Power* – using the power of the prime minister's office wisely to drive action
- *Public spending* – focusing investment on delivering agreed outcomes

- *Politics* – understanding and seeing the value of politics, rather than seeing politics as a problem
- *Performance* – focusing on the actions required to deliver the agreed outcomes.[18]

Each of these topics is addressed in one or more chapters of this book. As a delivery unit comes into place, though, it is worth testing the design of any proposed organization against Regan's checklist. Whatever the country, whatever the context, whatever the agenda, these ingredients are the irreducible core. In fact, if you have them in place, the unit itself is not an essential requirement. In other words, the disciplines of delivery are more important than a unit with the name; an effective unit just makes it more likely that these disciplines will be operational. With them, success is possible. Without, it is not.

The first two chapters have been about realizing that winning an election and governing a country are two very different activities requiring very different skills. The message is clear: in the inevitable hubris following an election victory or an appointment as a minister, remain clear-eyed and humble. Set an agenda (chapter 1), review the current state of the bureaucracy on which you depend to deliver that agenda and establish an organization capable of delivering that agenda (chapter 2). Meanwhile, remember that, unless you already have 10,000 hours of deliberate practice behind you, you have a lot to learn – so make sure you create the circumstances in which you learn fast. As you do, set your strategy, the subject of the next chapter.

3

Strategy

Someone in the meeting suggested that the word 'preference' would be easier to 'sell' to the unions and the Labour Party. 'Choice' might provoke a toxic reaction from either or both. I noted in my diary that Blair didn't quite bang the table, but he might have done. 'Choice is choice,' he insisted. 'Why mince our words?' He added, 'It's going to be hell for a large part of the time we're doing this . . . [but] I don't see any point in being Prime Minister unless we take risks.'

This conversation about strategy took place shortly after the 2001 election. How would we approach not any specific reform, but our entire reform agenda? What were the principles on which we would base our reforms? In the run-up to the election, Blair had made a speech at Gravesend (in Kent), suggesting there should be three principles: namely, set standards and expectations; devolve power, budgets and responsibility to the frontline; and break down artificial barriers and demarcations between professional groups such as doctors, nurses and pharmacists.

Now at Chequers, the prime minister's out-of-London residence, which has an upstairs equivalent to the No. 10 Cabinet Room, we debated whether these three principles were a sufficient basis for a radical reform programme. Someone, probably knowing in advance that Blair would seize on it, threw choice into the mix. Shouldn't there be a fourth principle that, wherever possible, we would offer the patient, the parent, the citizen, choice?

It was the perfect issue to split the reluctant Blairites from the enthusiastic Blairites (the latter included, needless to say, the prime minister). The fact that unions and party would react against it weighed heavily with some, but only encouraged others. Blair was a master of running against his own base, as indeed Thatcher had been.

We worked out the argument for it, and it was compelling. The wealthy have the greatest choice, we argued, because they can opt for private healthcare or education, or they can easily move house to get their child into the school of their choice; whereas we wanted choice for everyone. When those with wealth already had choice, why should the poor have to put up with a take-it-or-leave-it single offer? In the end, choice is an exercise of power. Thus by extending choice we were empowering the powerless. We argued too that choice would be attractive to the middle class and help persuade them to remain committed to the public services, which in turn would mean they would be prepared to pay taxes to support them.

Once the principle and the case for it were established, certain policy prescriptions followed. For example, a diversity of provision would be required, so foundation hospitals would be given independence from the National Health Service and academies with similarities to charter schools in the US – independent state schools – would be established in education. Similarly, citizens needed information on which to base their choices, so transparency about performance would be vital; and advice for those who wanted choice but didn't have the confidence to exercise it, would be desirable.

The conversation at Chequers about principles flowed into strategy, which in turn determined policy. This is the key insight here, in contrast to what all too often happens, which is that a government simply generates a list of things to do.

In the plush, dark lobby of a London hotel, I met the top civil servant from the education department of an emerging Asian nation. Small, energetic and perhaps a little jetlagged, he had been encouraged to pick my brains on the way back from a UNESCO event in Paris. We hadn't met before, so while we relaxed in each other's company, I asked him about himself and about his country's recent election. Then I turned to his agenda for the meeting. 'How can I help you?' I asked. 'What are the challenges you face?'

'Oh,' he replied, 'it's tough. I've got sixty-nine initiatives to implement before Christmas!'

My heart sank. That word 'initiative'. As I've said before, I'd abolish it if I could. Success in achieving ambitious goals is not just hindered by lots of separate initiatives – they actively get in the way. I learned this in the Department for Education in Blair's first term. In the first couple of years, we were always looking for things to announce. Announcements and initiatives are first cousins! Some of them were very good, others less so, but there were simply too many of them.

On my regular school visits, I would set out the strategy for the staff and then listen to their comments. The first was almost always something like, 'Well, Michael, you might think there's a strategy; we think there's just one damn thing after another.'

That's the effect that initiatives have. They cause confusion. They undermine clarity about priorities. Sixty-nine initiatives before Christmas would be a lot of work and almost certainly make things worse. Yet there are management consultancies even now that advise governments to create a portfolio of initiatives . . .

This is a chapter about strategy – your broad approach to achieving your goals. There's nothing wrong with ideology as a starting point. In fact, it's a key ingredient of political debate. In elections, we are not just choosing between different leaders and different manifestos, we are choosing between different views of the world. Ideologies in other words. And if the government's ideology is clear enough (and is not devoid of foundation in reality), it can help get things done. Take Margaret Thatcher. After the first three or four years were spent, in her words, 'sorting out the supply side', she moved on to a series of privatizations of the state-owned enterprises before addressing the problems of health and education. During that time I happened to run into a Treasury official in a pub. He said, 'It's very simple for us because we know that whatever the problem is, the question she wants us to answer is "How do you make a market?"' Crucially, therefore, they were able to apply this perspective not just to the problems in the PM's focus, but also to those that lay ahead. Then, when the all-seeing eye fell on that problem, the thinking was already far advanced. A good example of how ideology can help.

This explains too why, at the start of his second term, Blair wanted to clarify and establish the four principles of public service reform which became the theme of a series of speeches. Blair had learned by then that the 'eye-catching initiatives' which he had demanded in his first term brought only superficial progress; they did not change how systems work. Not all of his ministers kept up. One was famously dismissive of the approach: 'Strategy is b*****ks!' he asserted and carried on announcing initiatives.

> **RULE 14**
> WORK FROM PRINCIPLES TO STRATEGY TO POLICY (and put a stake through the heart of initiatives)

In the modern world, ideological differences are not as stark as they were in the mid-twentieth century. 'What works' should be the mantra of the twenty-first century. The differences now tend to be differences of emphasis – some favour choice as a good in itself, others do not. Some would like to reduce tax rates over time, others have a modest preference for more public expenditure if they can make it work. Some have greater faith in markets left to themselves; some less so. These debates, such as that between Bhagwati and Sen mentioned in the Introduction, can be very vigorous and – at the extremes – broad as well as deep. Often, the widest, deepest political divisions are over cultural issues – gay marriage, the ordination of women, immigration and so on, as the Tea Party in the US exemplifies – rather than over core political issues.

Either way, there are a range of legitimate positions and many can be shown to bring benefits if reforms are well designed and there is a systematic approach to delivery. The problem is that such broad ideological positions don't necessarily tell you what to do in any given case and most certainly don't provide you with the detail.

Moreover, the evidence is important and it has clear messages which you ignore at your peril. But even with the evidence well assembled, there are judgements to make, for instance about the specific moment and context in which a reform is introduced. The other pitfall of much of the evidence is that it is subject-specific, relating for example to health, education, crime or welfare, but not necessarily connecting all of them.

The main aim in this chapter is to set out five broad approaches which are potentially applicable across a wide range of government responsibilities. In relation to each, there is a brief commentary drawing on the evidence. The central point of the chapter is that sound strategy is a precondition of a successful delivery. Strategy without delivery is vacuous; delivery without strategy is incoherent. In establishing the five approaches, I've drawn on my own previous work (see pp. 333–42 of *Instruction to Deliver*) and also on the excellent work of Gwyn Bevan from LSE and Deborah Wilson from Bristol.[1] They and others have focused on what they describe as 'the natural experiment' that occurred in the United Kingdom after the Blair administration introduced devolved legislatures and governments for Scotland, Wales and Northern Ireland. What this involved was the pursuit of divergent paths from largely similar starting points in health and education. The analysis that results has much more general applicability, as I hope to show (Fig. 11 below).

Five Paradigms of System Reform

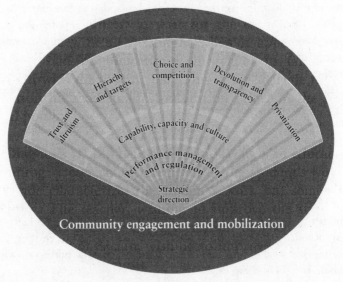

Figure 11

In addition to the five approaches there are three functions that the system needs to consider centrally. Taken together, these three constitute the concept of stewardship, which in essence means leaving a system better than you found it. Finally, there is the wider context of community engagement. This chapter deals with each in turn.

APPROACH 1. TRUST AND ALTRUISM

Trust and Altruism is the approach that everyone would like to work and which many governments have adopted and some continue to depend upon. It was for decades the way the UK's National Health Service was approached. It has also been the default approach to governing school systems across the world.

In this model, the basic idea of government is to fund the inputs (buildings, equipment, salaries and so on), staff the service with professionals who have been trained and have gained certain professional qualifications, and leave them to get on with it. Attachment to their professional ethics, it is believed, means they will do their best for those they serve, while the profession itself will ensure the professional learning and growth of its members. Seen from the point of view of the professions, the approach can be summed up in the phrase: 'Give us the money and get out of the way.'

It has many attractions for government too: not much action is required, there is no need to engage in a battle of ideas; it assumes the best of the public service workforce and leaves much of the decision-making to them. It assumes that accountability, data and performance management are not necessary. For these reasons, the approach suits public sector professionals too – pay without accountability has its attractions, needless to say. Moreover, when there is system underperformance, the strong presumption is that lack of resources is the cause of the problem and therefore the solution is to spend more. This means public debate focuses purely on inputs: the professions want more money and pay, and often the public supports them; governments have to balance competing demands and raise money through taxes, so there's a cap on their ability to respond. As a consequence, this approach results, surprisingly often given its basis in trust, not in harmony but in acrimony – usually over funding – between government and professions.

In his excellent account of professional motivation, Julian Le Grand distinguishes between 'knightly' motivation – altruism – and 'knavish' motivation – self-interest. Trust and Altruism assumes that all the public sector professionals are knights, not knaves.

Attractive all round though it may be, there is one significant problem with it. It doesn't work. As Le Grand points out, 'the assumption that knightly behaviour characterised those working within the welfare state proved ... vulnerable ... many politicians ... grew increasingly sceptical of the view ... that professionals were only concerned with the welfare of their clients'.[2] He was talking about Britain, but the insight applies generally. Bevan and Wilson, in their striking comparison of health and school performance in Wales and England, reach a firm conclusion:

> The consistent finding is that the [Trust and Altruism] model resulted in worse reported performance in Wales as compared with England on what were each government's key objectives of improving examination performance at age 16 and reducing long hospital waiting times.

While they accept that England's system of sharp accountability had some problems, they conclude that 'the benefits ... did indeed outweigh their dysfunctional consequences'. They continue:

> So we argue that our findings show that the [Trust and Altruism] model not only lacks the theoretical justification we identified earlier, but has been found wanting in our (and other) empirical studies.[3]

Reliance on Trust and Altruism also explains why so many school systems barely improved over the decades between 1950 and 2000. The cause of the failure is that the public service professions, while often full of very fine people, are not all knights; many – like all human beings incidentally – have some knavish elements and a few are very knavish indeed. Professions are powerful; their cultures are strong, which can be good (doctors responding to any emergency) or not (a quarter of India's teachers not turning up on any given day), depending on the time and place. The professions often hold governments captive too, through powerful unions, effective lobbying and in places – such as India and the US – direct involvement in elections themselves.

I've walked into an ordinary government school in a suburb of Accra, Ghana to see Trust and Altruism at its worst. The headteacher was warm and welcoming, but also resigned to his fate. The teachers took no notice of him and firing them was virtually impossible. He showed me into four classrooms; in three there was no teacher at all, though the sight of visitors brought two of them scurrying back; in the fourth classroom, the teacher was present, eating her lunch in the corner of the room; she did not look up once, even when spoken to by the headteacher, and studiously ignored the children.

This is not untypical, as everyone knows but prefers not to mention. The government of Ghana pays teachers well. In fact, their pay is such a big proportion of the education budget (over 95 per cent) that there is hardly any money left for anything else. There have been no new textbooks for years. While, of course, there are some heroic and dedicated teachers in Ghana's government schools, the overall effect is clear: the government is paying for knights and getting knaves.

There are places where the knightly assumptions work better. Finland is famed for having an outstanding school system, which consistently comes out well in international comparisons, though it has fallen away somewhat recently. It takes a fundamentally knightly view of its teachers, who are given extensive professional autonomy and deliver high quality across virtually all schools. At first the country was surprised by its success and unable to explain it. Now, a small group of Finnish educators, led by the indomitable Pasi Sahlberg, have made themselves famous by touring the world to explain how Finland does it.

The answer, in brief, is that teaching is a very tough profession to join in Finland. Education is highly valued and respected in the culture, so the country's brightest and best young people aspire to get into it. One British minister I know learned this first hand on a visit to Finland, where he was shown round by an impressive young woman from the Finnish foreign ministry. 'How did you get such an excellent job?' he asked her. 'I applied for teacher training and they turned me down,' came the reply.

With a talented intake every year and a strong, principled

professional culture, the teaching profession goes from strength to strength. In effect, it holds its own members to account through this strong culture. In addition, the society as a whole has a strong commitment to equity and expects these excellent teachers to do everything they can to enable children who fall behind to catch up. And they do. The system is high-performing, though the constant praise has led to a degree of complacency and a lack of further reform, according to Sahlberg, resulting in a fall in performance in recent years.

Aspiring to have a school system like Finland's has its attractions. However, in most parts of the world it would be rash to base a strategy on achieving it, partly because it is a very difficult thing to do and most systems already have professional cultures of a very different nature; and partly because Finland itself is highly unusual – small, homogeneous and with what sociologists call 'thick social capital'. It is a place where everyone's tax return is available online. Learn from Finland, absolutely yes; copy it, probably not. As

> **RULE 15**
> TRUST AND ALTRUISM IS POPULAR BUT DOESN'T WORK
> (other than in unusual circumstances)

they say at the end of some children's television programmes: Don't try this at home.

APPROACH 2. HIERARCHY AND TARGETS (OR COMMAND AND CONTROL)

This approach, Bevan and Wilson say, has 'a limited set of public targets that clearly signal priorities, with specified rewards for "successful" organisations and sanctions directed at those responsible for running "failing" organisations'.[4] It is much the same as the approach I have described in previous publications as 'Command and Control', defined as 'a top-down implementation of a change the government wants to bring about'.

As an approach, it has a bad name, mainly because it is unpopular with professionals who feel the pressure, but the evidence suggests

Performance Wedge

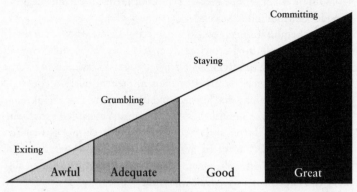

Committing

Staying

Grumbling

Exiting

| Awful | Adequate | Good | Great |

Figure 12

that, implemented well and sustained, it can be effective. Bevan and Wilson show how well it worked in England in reducing health waiting times and improving school performance, especially compared to Wales and Scotland, which preferred Trust and Altruism.

It is particularly effective in improving underperforming services or parts of services, which provides an opportunity to introduce another useful tool of policymaking, the Performance Wedge.

Jim Collins's book *Good to Great* is justly famous for its analysis of the leadership and strategies that take companies from good performance to great. It was one of the seminal texts I read while leading Blair's Delivery Unit. We found we had to add to his two-point scale two lower levels of performance, Awful and Adequate. Thus we arrived at the Performance Wedge. While there were great elements of services – such as a great hospital or school – none were universally great. By contrast, some were largely awful. For instance, fine collection in the UK was at 50 per cent when the Delivery Unit first took responsibility for it in 2001; by 2004 it was at 75 per cent. Big progress, but surely only from Awful to Adequate.

The adjectives above the wedge describe the attitude of citizens as performance improves. While it is poor, citizens will exit if they can; if it reaches adequate, they continue to grumble. It may be a huge political achievement to shift a service from awful to adequate, but the citizens are unimpressed; they think you should have done it years ago. Only when a service becomes good or great do citizens begin to consider dancing in the streets.

Hierarchy and Targets (or Command and Control) is particularly appropriate for shifting a service from Awful to Adequate. No point after all in trusting or relying on altruism where a service is awful; the time for that is surely past. Just make them sort it out! Of course, if you attempt Hierarchy and Targets and do it poorly, you might make things worse. For example, New York State struggled for years with its intervention in the poor-performing Roosevelt School District. You will need political courage because it will be controversial, but do it well and the citizens will benefit. (They may not applaud, because they always knew it was awful; why didn't you?)

Gwyn Bevan emailed me in April 2014 with his latest work on health performance to say:

> ... the interesting finding is that in response to the criticisms of the performance in Scotland as compared to England, the Scots strengthened their system of performance management and created a delivery unit within their department of health. The outcome has been that performance on waiting times in Scotland is now similar to England. Wales still lags behind.

In short, Scotland abandoned Trust and Altruism, adopted Hierarchy and Targets and reaped the rewards. In relation to health, Wales has yet to do so.

In my recent personal experience, the best evidence of this approach in practice has been the Punjab Education Roadmap, which began in 2011 and continues. Hierarchy and Targets has been applied across a province with over 20 million school-age children and 60,000 schools.

Enrolment, student attendance, teacher attendance and the provision of facilities and materials such as textbooks have all risen significantly as a result of setting targets and introducing effective hierarchical management. Even learning outcomes have improved a little. A system that was unmanaged and therefore Awful is now managed and is therefore becoming Adequate. A crucial ingredient of the Roadmap – monthly data on key indicators collected from every school – is representative of the Hierarchy and Targets approach generally: it depends on a steady supply of reasonably good data on which to base decisions. Incidentally, in polls of Pakistan's citizens in June 2014, around 65 per cent thought Punjab the country's best-run province.

The major challenge with this approach comes after it has been sustained for a while and is succeeding: that is, how to sustain the progress beyond Adequate to Good and then from Good to Great. It works to get to Adequate, but can it also get a system to Great? This is doubtful – in the words Joel Klein of New York City and I hit upon, 'You can mandate adequacy but you cannot mandate greatness; it has to be unleashed.'

Indeed the very idea of 'mandating greatness' seems absurd. You can make people meet the standards of adequacy; to bring about greatness you have to create the conditions in the system and foster it. Targets might still be desirable or necessary, but once a system moves beyond adequate, a different overall approach is required. This is where Daniel Pink's three elements – autonomy, mastery and purpose – come into their own.[5] They inform the next two approaches.

> **RULE 16**
> THE HIERARCHY
> AND TARGETS
> APPROACH WILL GET
> YOU FROM AWFUL
> TO ADEQUATE
> (if executed well)

APPROACH 3. CHOICE AND COMPETITION

As we have seen, Tony Blair was determined to put choice and competition at the heart of his second-term public service reforms. It has also featured strongly in school reforms in the US in places such as New Orleans and Boston and in the way healthcare is organized in many countries.

Julian Le Grand, whom we met earlier, is the best-known theorist of applying choice and competition to public services. He argues that the introduction of choice and competition empowers the citizen; extending his chess metaphor, they become queens instead of pawns. The effect is to incentivize public sector institutions and professions regardless of whether they are knights or knaves. In other words, the approach does not depend on assuming knightly behaviour as in Approach 1, or knavish behaviour as in Approach 2.

To make it work, the service user – patient or parent, for example – must be given real choice and the information on which to base the decisions; the money in the system must follow those choices; as a result the more attractive or successful providers will gain and the less successful will struggle.

So far, so good, but it is not straightforward. Public services are not pure markets in the way that mobile telephones or consumer durables are. In the pure markets, the consumer can easily move from one brand to another and indeed exit altogether. If some consumers opt out in such a market, that is not a problem. Also, the producer can vary the price in response to market signals. In a public service, there is public as well as private benefit. I benefit not just from ensuring my child is vaccinated, but from you and everyone else doing so too. I gain from my child being educated – and yours. Indeed, schooling is compulsory almost everywhere for this reason. Moreover, the government fixes the price – or more precisely, makes the service free at the point of use and pays the price. So, however much choice and competition are introduced, it is a quasi-market rather than a pure one.

This has practical consequences which political leaders sometimes find it hard to deal with. If the quasi-market results in some schools benefiting at the expense of others, how long can a failing school be allowed to wither away, offering poor education to fewer and fewer children? Surely not long. The government needs to intervene. If a quasi-market points to a hospital closure being required, will the politicians involved have the courage to see it through in the teeth of a likely vigorous, local, public campaign? Or in the case of a university under similar pressure? The evidence suggests this is politically very difficult. At this point the choice and competition policy may need a dose of hierarchy and targets to make it work.

Nevertheless, the policy can also be attractive to politicians both because some ideologically prefer markets and because, if the policy works, it frees the government from day-to-day intervention as the system becomes sustainable. As Bevan and Wilson put it,

'Quasi-markets have high transaction costs, but are popular with governments because pressure on poor performance comes from an invisible hand . . .'[6] Blair saw choice as a key ingredient in creating 'self-improving systems' – different words for the same basic point.

There is much academic debate about whether choice and competition work in the sense of driving up performance. The evidence so far is unclear, though cumulatively it is beginning to suggest that under the right conditions choice does work. Certainly low-cost private schools in the developing world are contributing to improved performance. And if choice is seen as something valuable in itself, the argument is stronger still.

The challenge when market thinking is applied to public services is to ensure not only that performance improves, but that equity is at least protected and perhaps even enhanced. Pure markets aim at efficiency rather than equity. Therefore, when market thinking is applied to public goals, the policy approach needs actively to promote equity. If, for instance, the money follows the student in a school system, then students from low-income families could receive more, as they do in England, but often not in the USA. In a healthcare system, advice could be targeted at those least able to seize the opportunity of choice. To quote a specific case, the vouchers in the Punjab school system – which can be redeemed at registered private schools – are only for poor families whose children are not in school. Here choice and equity are combined as a goal of policy. By contrast, the original voucher scheme in Chile in the 1990s was universal – everyone got the same voucher however wealthy or poor. The voucher for the rich became a subsidy of the private school fees they already paid; for the poor it enabled a rudimentary education in a public school. Equity gaps, already wide, widened further.

The other challenge for government with choice and competition is in ensuring that genuinely diverse options are available. Even if the customer has choice, and the money follows their decision, the choice is more apparent than real if all the options are broadly similar in style and substance. Moreover, in some locations, particularly rural ones, providing a range of options might not make sense, so diversity in practice is a largely urban phenomenon.

In relation to this challenge, much of the best thinking has been done among charter school advocates in the US, especially in its large, urban districts. In New Orleans now, the vast majority of children are in charter schools. A not-for-profit organization, New Schools for New Orleans, attracted charter providers to the city and helped them navigate the politics and regulation. This brought a diverse range of providers to the city. Meanwhile, the public authorities, through the Recovery School District, created a policy framework that offered parents choice and rewarded school providers who delivered outcomes.

Recently, the idea of the policy 'nudge' has become widely advocated, sometimes as an alternative to strategy and a systematic approach to delivery. In fact, it is entirely consistent with both, as David Halpern, Britain's leading nudge 'guru', affirms. It is best seen as a major contribution to thinking about how quasi-markets can work successfully in public systems. To summarize a somewhat academic or theoretical argument, the authors of *Nudge: Improving Decisions About Health, Wealth and Happiness* argue for what they call 'libertarian paternalism': 'libertarian' because they advocate choice in the public as well as private sectors; 'paternalism' because they believe that real human beings as opposed to 'econs' – the theoretical human beings beloved of economists – don't necessarily maximize either their own interests or those of their society. In these circumstances, they argue, it is legitimate for the public authorities to incentivize behaviours that are more socially desirable. They suggest, therefore, that in some circumstances, officials overseeing public provision might see themselves as choice architects – using a series of nudges to achieve better social outcomes. One way to do this is to turn the 'status quo bias' – the preference most of us have against change – to advantage. This is, in fact, exactly what Julian Le Grand, quoted at the start of this section, advocates: the creation of a choice and competition system so that the key players in it are incentivized to do the right thing whether they are altruistic or not.

Thus, while uniform systems seek to impose better outcomes, including equity, quasi-market systems seek to incentivize them. Drawing on language from the famous *1066 and All That* by Sellar and Yeatman (Cavaliers are wrong but romantic, while Roundheads are right but repulsive), Figure 13 illustrates the dilemma. Quasi-markets, left to themselves, will end up in the top left box, while traditional uniform systems will end up in the bottom right. No one wants the bottom left,

Equality and Diversity

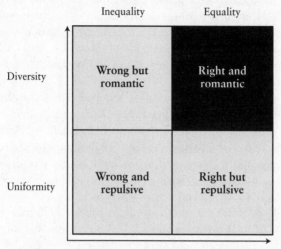

Figure 13

though some systems end up there by accident. The goal for most is the top right, and the strategy question is how to get there from wherever the starting point is.

Seen in this light, 'the science of choice' which the authors of *Nudge* describe and advocate is an increasingly important aspect of the science of delivery and crucial to getting this third approach to strategy right.

> **RULE 17**
> CHOICE IS BECOMING INCREASINGLY IMPORTANT IN PUBLIC SYSTEMS
> (it's a good in itself)

APPROACH 4. DEVOLUTION AND TRANSPARENCY

The fourth approach is particularly appropriate where choice doesn't work well: running prisons or immigration systems, for example. No one thinks prisoners or illegal immigrants should be offered choice. In services such as these, there is no obvious customer who can exercise choice because the customer is the government on behalf of citizens.

It involves devolving power and responsibility to managers close to the frontline and then, through transparent publication of data on outcomes, holding them to account. For this reason, what I describe as Devolution and Transparency, Bevan and Wilson call Transparent Public Ranking.

The classic pioneer of Devolution and Transparency in the public sector was the New York City Police Department under Commissioner Bill Bratton in the early 1990s. Policing is another service where individual choice doesn't apply, but Bratton wanted to create a similar pressure for improved performance on a police department that was notoriously inefficient in a city whose reputation at the time was at stake because its crime rate was so high.

His answer was to create Compstat, which was both a data system and a process. Weekly data on all major crime types was collected at precinct level and published regularly. Power and responsibility were devolved to precinct captains. The citizens of New York City (and its vigorous media) could see how crime varied across the city – almost in real time.

Meanwhile, Bratton organized regular sessions where precinct captains would be gathered together to watch one of their number being quizzed about performance. The precinct captain on show would find data about the precinct put on the screen in front of peers and then be asked to explain any successes or failures. The central team would prepare well for such meetings and could be quite aggressive, New York-style, in challenging an account. If, say, a captain claimed to be on top of litter, the central team might put up on the screen a photograph taken the previous day of litter in his precinct. The watching precinct captains would be invited to join in making suggestions as to how to improve this precinct's performance.

Note how, through the Compstat process, the data and devolution enable not just vigorous challenge but, crucially, learning about best practices or innovative ideas. In its first year or so of operation, the challenge element was at the forefront, and a significant proportion of precinct captains who couldn't stand the heat moved on or found themselves moved on. But over time it was the learning element that mattered most: the process enabled ideas to spread quickly across the city, which became a hotbed of trial, error and innovation. The pressure of Compstat provided the incentive to precinct captains to adopt ideas that worked. In other words, the process replicated one of the best features of markets, which is the incentive to innovate and adopt successful practices. Crime fell steadily in New York City from Bratton's time onwards. It may be true that some social trends helped, but it is no doubt true also that the increased effectiveness of the police department was a critical turning point. Through his changes, Bratton demolished the deeply held belief that crime was a remorseless tide that could not be reversed and convinced his officers – not least through smart new uniforms – that they could get a grip. Others took notice.

Anapolis is a small pretty town on the shores of Chesapeake Bay. The water laps and frets around the yachts in the harbour. Evening diners look out over the bay. A little way up the hill is the seat of Maryland's government. In strict accordance with America's belief in the separation of powers, the legislature and the governor's mansion are separated too, by tree-lined streets. Some of America's state capitals turned out to be a disappointment – Dover, Delaware hardly sets pulses racing – but Anapolis is special, with the unity of its classical architecture and views across the ancient bay.

Governor Martin O'Malley knows that not all of Maryland is as pretty as Anapolis. There are the sprawling Washington DC suburbs of Montgomery County on one side; and the mean streets and boarded-up houses – think *The Wire* – of Baltimore on the other. O'Malley had been mayor of Baltimore prior to his election as governor of the state. Learning from New York City, he had introduced Citistat, a successful attempt to drive Bratton-type reform through city government. *The Wire* had done him no favours, with its portrayal of a shady mayor playing both sides of the street, but O'Malley's own track record was impressive. Baltimore, a city with multiple challenges, made progress under his stewardship, and in 2006 his success there catapulted him into the governorship and the mansion in Anapolis. He had done his 10,000 hours of deliberate practice and was well prepared to be a successful governor. 'What's the difference between a goal and a dream?' he quips. 'A deadline.'

Once installed in Anapolis, he combined his Citistat experience with a small delivery unit modelled on our experience in Britain. He says the 'relentless discipline of delivery' is the key ingredient of 'a new wave of leadership'. Now, at the end of his second term, the results are plain. The key economic and public service indicators in Maryland suggest that it is in much better shape than it was. It is one of America's highest-performing and best-governed states. The recession has been tough everywhere, but Maryland has proved more resilient than most. O'Malley argues that you can embrace the new technologies to ensure openness, transparency and performance management. In fact, for the 'show me' generation, he believes there is no alternative. Citizens demand, in his words, 'timely, accurate information shared by all'. And he emphasizes 'all means all'.[7] For example, anyone can now see online what progress is being made on cleaning up Chesapeake Bay. Devolution and Transparency, it seems, worked well on its shores.

Ten time zones away in the Queen of Cities, Lahore, it worked well too. Ask the Secretary – Schools (from 2010 to 2013), Aslam Kamboh, what single factor drove up performance in Punjab in his three years in charge, and he will answer with a single word: 'rankings'. Each month, the data on key indicators – such as teacher presence or student attendance – was collected from every school. It was analysed in Lahore, enabling Secretary Kamboh to rank order his thirty-six Education District Officers. The top performers, on a ranking that takes into account progress and the varied starting points, are rewarded both financially and symbolically (a cup of tea with the chief minister being highly prized), while questions are asked of the bottom performers – and sometimes they are moved on. Kamboh's successor has maintained the tradition. It's still working.

The research evidence suggests that Transparent Public Ranking works, not because consumers make different choices on the basis of the data (often they don't) and not because committed professionals choose to learn from their peers (they are more likely to critique the data), but because, crucially, rankings put reputations at stake.

The precinct captain in New York City has a reputation at stake when he or she appears in front of peers; when data on performance is made public in Maryland, the managers concerned have a reputation at stake; and in Punjab, where face and reputation for individuals and families are so culturally powerful, the local officials know their reputation is at stake too.

J. H. Hibbard, the American healthcare researcher, has shown, as Bevan and Hamblin put it, that comparative data is more likely to be used if presented in a ranking system that makes it easy to identify the high and low performers. She argues that four characteristics are needed to ensure that Transparent Public Ranking will be effective:

- A ranking system
- Data published and widely disseminated
- Data easy for the public to understand
- Future reports which show changes in performance.

Another US-based healthcare study confirmed Hibbard's view: 'the impetus to use the data to improve has been limited almost entirely to hospitals that have been named as outliers with poor performance'.[8]

More recent data from the UK supports this case. In England, the star ratings of hospitals met Hibbard's criteria and drove improved performance. In Wales and Scotland, where Trust and Altruism ruled (at least until recently), there was little or no progress. In fact, here poor performers attracted extra cash. As the Auditor General for Wales put it in 2005, 'the current waiting time performance management regime effectively "rewarded failure" to deliver the waiting times targets'. In Scotland, two 'failing' boards were bailed out. In other words, these systems incentivized doing the wrong thing.

A further study, this time looking at Australia, Canada, England, New Zealand and Wales over the period 2000–2005 (exactly the time the PMDU began to have an effect in England, incidentally), found that:

> Of the five countries, England has achieved the most sustained improvement, linked to major funding boosts, ambitious waiting-time targets and a rigorous performance management system.[9]

To put it bluntly, 'name and shame' works, especially in moving Awful performance towards Adequate or Good. It's not clear that once performance reaches Good the incentive effect continues, but it will certainly put pressure on any unit in the system that falls behind.

For politicians, then, the evidence is clear. The issue is whether they have the political will to take on the interest groups, especially public sector unions, who will undoubtedly resist such transparency.

> **RULE 18**
> TRANSPARENT
> PUBLIC RANKING
> WORKS (don't flinch)

Contracting out services or commissioning them has been a major theme in public policy in the past couple of decades. Often the involvement of the business sector in the provision of government services provokes controversy: Are you for or against their involvement? Shouldn't public services be fully publicly provided?

This ideological debate should be over by now. The problems with purely public provision are twofold. First, the public sector doesn't have – and cannot possibly have – all the skills and capacity necessary to do everything that might be publicly provided – whether it's building an aircraft carrier, manufacturing a drug or publishing a textbook. Second, where public provision has been given a monopoly, it has sometimes become (as monopolies tend to) inefficient, occasionally grossly so. At its worst, public sector unions have such great sway over political decision-making that they not only represent their members, they also hugely influence the political authorities with whom they negotiate. No wonder in these circumstances that the public service is run in the interests of the workforce rather than the consumer.

I used to collect examples of what this looked like at its worst: Bill Bratton found when he arrived at the NYPD that the drug squad worked 9–5, Monday to Friday! There are Mental Health Services that close over Christmas and New Year, even though this is known to be the time when demand for them peaks; orthopaedic surgeons take Friday afternoon off to play golf; long lunch hours at courts suit judges, but not justice.

A seminal moment for me came when I was a councillor in the London Borough of Hackney in the late 1980s. The Direct Labour

Organisation (DLO), which did repairs for the large swathes of public housing in the borough, wanted a pay rise. Negotiations with council officials had stalled. The union representing the DLO decided to use its muscle inside the Labour Party to get its way. Since Labour had a huge majority in the council, if the Labour group of councillors supported the pay rise, the council officials would be overruled and the DLO would get its way. In spite of the fact that every Labour councillor knew that the service provided by the DLO was lamentable – they knew because their constituents never ceased to tell them so – in a meeting where the galleries were packed with aggressive DLO workers, the Labour group chose to support 'the workers' (i.e. the union) against 'the management' (i.e. the council officials). With two or three other Labour councillors out of fifty or so, I voted against the pay rise and was jostled and spat at on the way out for my pains.

This story has unfortunately been played out again and again in different forms – sometimes without the spitting – around the world, and it's the reason why public authorities began to contract out services in the first place. Our leader back then, Andrew Puddephatt, whom I came to admire hugely, finally called time on this kind of complicity, calling it 'theft from working people'. At last we were standing up for the consumers of the services rather than the providers.

Devolution and Transparency provides a good basis for contracting out, not for ideological reasons, but for pragmatic ones, because it makes clear which parts of a service are working well and which less so. In Britain the Cameron government is enabling private managers to take over poorly performing hospitals. In Massachusetts, the commissioner, Mitchell Chester, has intervened to take over the Lawrence School District where performance was shocking. In the latter case, while the takeover is by the state rather than by a private provider, the new leadership of the district, with significant success, has brought in a range of new providers to solve the district's serious problems.

In short, while the Choice and Competition model of reforms depends on the upward pressure of individual consumers making choices, the Devolution and Transparency model enables downward pressure – competition imposed from above – and also lateral pressure – peers learning vigorously from each other.

Given the numerous stories of failed contracting out, most infamously with large IT projects, it is worth pointing out that the evidence is not conclusive one way or another between public and private. This is not surprising, given that both sectors are capable of screwing up massively. Everything depends on how it's done. Are the contracts clear? Do the public authorities and private contractors

> **RULE 19**
> CONTRACTING OUT SERVICES BREAKS MONOPOLIES
> (but don't think it relieves you from management responsibilities)

build credible working relationships? And so on. What often worried me in the Blair years was that departments let contracts without having the necessary skills either to design them well or to manage them after they were let. Many civil servants seemed to believe that once a contract was let, they didn't need to worry about it any more. Out of sight, out of mind proved disastrous time and again.

There are some straightforward lessons that governments can apply to improve the effectiveness with which they contract out services and develop public–private partnerships. Alan Trager from Harvard has made himself an expert in this emerging field. He argues that governments need to set up the negotiation of a contract well. Drawing on the work of Lax and Sebenius (*3-D Negotiation*), he argues that the first consideration is the architecture of the negotiation, who should be involved and when and what is the scope of the conversation; second, he says, governments need to be much clearer about the overall design of the deal they want to do – what value, what substance, what outcomes, over what time period? Finally they need to think through the tactics they will apply at the negotiating table.

All too often governments skip the first two steps and go straight to the third. Moreover, they are frequently outgunned in the negotiation by a company that brings more experienced (and better paid) negotiators and lawyers to the table while the government muddles through. Trager also says any government negotiating team should 'bring a designated listener' so they are in a better position to reflect between sessions. Crucially, too, the government needs to be able to walk away before striking a deal and live with the temporary embarrassment.

Otherwise, its leverage in the negotiation is minimal. To illustrate, I recall with horror a time in government when I was finalizing a deal with a private contractor knowing that my political masters would not want to live without a deal and that this particular contractor was the only one left, the others having decided it was all too risky. We got a deal, but the impact over subsequent years fell well short of our aspirations.

Once a deal is done, contracts need to be managed and relationships built. They never take care of themselves. This requires senior officials with specialized skills to be involved. This is because many of the problems that contractors will work on are not 'simple and technical', but 'complex and adaptive' (to use the language of Ron Heifetz and Marty Linsky, also of Harvard). The practical implication of this is that however well set up the initial contract is, the world will change in unexpected ways and not every eventuality can be predicted at the outset. This is when the quality of the relationship becomes decisive. Dame Tessa Jowell, the politician who oversaw the London Olympics from concept to delivery, was a master of building these relationships. The 2012 Games were a huge triumph as everyone knows, but even here there were setbacks. The most visible was not long before the Games when the company G4S admitted it had not been able to recruit sufficient security people for all the venues. The military stepped in (and loved it), and all went well. When I asked Tessa to reflect on this experience, she said she wished now that they had embedded a senior civil servant inside G4S from the start so that communication would have been constant, and nasty surprises, such as the one the country got, would have been avoided. Relationships again. Marty Linsky, in the same conversation, put it more grandly, 'The work of transformational leadership is about human dynamics.' Incidentally, these points apply whether the contractor is a for-profit private or a social sector organization.

The other major consideration is whether there are any ideological issues to take into account; are there some aspects of a service which should be purely public; and any that should be totally private. In part, these are matters of political disposition. Julio Frenk was Minister of Health from 2000 to 2006 in the administration of Mexican President Vicente Fox. His crowning achievement was to bring all

Mexicans within a comprehensive health insurance programme, before which millions each year were bankrupted trying to fund healthcare for themselves or a family member.

He has thought carefully about where the private sector should and should not play a part in healthcare systems. He argues that the government on behalf of the public should set 'the rules of the game' and provide the funding; no role for the private in either of these spheres. Provision or delivery might be either public or private, or a combination of the two. Pharmaceuticals should be private, though of course within a regulatory framework set by government. As he himself says, there are political choices to be made, but what he outlines seems pragmatic, sensible and potentially generalizable.

One final point on contracting out: how much of a service do you need to contract out before the performance of the whole service changes for the better? After all, part of the point of contracting out is not just to improve performance where the service is contracted out, but to incentivize improvement across the board.

If there is convincing research on this question, I have yet to see it, but experience suggests the answer is in the range of 10–15 per cent – once private prisons provide 10–15 per cent of the total prison service, the competitive threat will be sufficient to ensure that the other 85–90 per cent improve. Once 10 per cent of the knee and hip operations are privately provided, orthopaedic surgeons across the country will begin to wonder about taking Friday afternoon off. Once ten or twelve local authorities out of 150 with poor education services are on the receiving end of intervention, the rest will begin to improve.

APPROACH 5. PRIVATIZATION (AND VOUCHERS)

As a young Labour Party activist in the 1980s, I must admit I was no fan of Nigel Lawson. The slightly arrogant gaze, the over-ebullient ties, the shock wave of black hair swept back and the uncompromising case he made for Thatcherism all combined to put me off. Even then, though, I could see he was an ideologically influential figure as well as a powerful Chancellor. Now, all these years later and having read his impressive autobiography, I am compelled to believe, in spite of my reaction back then, that he had a powerful case at the time which on the whole history has endorsed: the case for privatization.

The previous four approaches are different ways to reform a public service while keeping it public. Privatization is a different solution altogether – it simply says: Why waste time on reform? Let's sell it off and let the market deal with it. As one of Sinclair Lewis's characters observes in *Main Street*, 'And you want to reform people like that when dynamite is so cheap?' Of course, privatization is not appropriate for every service – no government has (yet) chosen to sell off an entire school system or even large parts of it, for very good reasons, but in Britain in the late 1970s, huge swathes of the economy were under public ownership – gas, water, electricity, the post office, telephones, much of North Sea oil, the railways . . . on and on. In 1982, the nationalized industries accounted for over 10 per cent of total national output and employed approaching 2 million people. Moreover, everyone in Britain knew that the services were often poor. In 1980, I moved into my own flat for the first time and called (from a phone box) to order a telephone. The only question I was asked was 'What colour do you want?' To be truthful, I hadn't thought about this before I rang, and when I did think about it I didn't really care. Black would be fine. What I did care about, though, was how long it would take before someone could come round and install the phone. That would take a while, I was told. More worryingly still, the person I spoke to told me they were running out of numbers. Running out of numbers? This was not something I had worried about before either. I began to imagine a lucrative career smuggling illegal Colombian sixes into the country . . .

Thanks to Nigel Lawson and his colleagues (and some serious technological change), this seems like ancient history now – but in parts of the modern world, the privatization revolution has still not occurred and much of the economy remains in public ownership – state-owned enterprises in the modern jargon. Often they are heavily subsidized. Some countries have massively improved the performance of these companies by setting up an efficiently run state holding company which applies modern management disciplines. Khazanah, the excellent state holding company in Malaysia, is a very good example; sometimes once a company has been improved it can be sold off, other times it will be kept in public ownership, but either way it will be properly managed, and generating revenue for the taxpayer.

In some other countries, there remains a huge, moribund state sector riddled with inefficiency and sometimes mired in corruption. The Sharif government in Pakistan, elected in May 2013, inherited just such a sector. In a country which has big debts, difficulty collecting tax and an expensive military, public money is extremely scarce and it makes no sense to be pouring it into subsidies for an inefficient and corrupt state-owned energy sector or for Pakistan International Airlines.

Effective privatization is, therefore, very much an issue of the present globally, which takes us back to Nigel Lawson.

In a series of ministerial positions in the 1980s, Lawson was the ideological core of the privatization agenda. When he thought there was any risk of his colleagues backsliding or becoming faint of heart, he would fire off a memo to them. As a successful former journalist, he wrote with clarity and punch.

Most of Britain could see what he saw: the nationalized industries had not delivered what they had promised. They had been intended to improve industrial relations but by the 1970s and 80s were often strike-ridden. They were meant to contribute to full employment, but in practice had resulted in state-subsidized overstaffing. They were supposed to improve productivity, but on that measure Britain was falling behind other countries. With their failure to perform, the case for them had unravelled. The boards that oversaw them, and their chairmen, did not leap from this analysis to privatization. Instead, they proposed another round of changes in governance and management.

Lawson took on this (as he saw it) woolly thinking in no uncertain terms. 'We have created industrial baronies,' he exclaimed, 'not truly accountable to anyone – Parliament, Government, shareholders or the marketplace.'[10] His prescription, set out most clearly in a note to his colleague Nicholas Ridley on the subject of the water industry, was full-scale privatization, even for so-called natural monopolies, of which water was a case in point. This is a summary of his argument:

1. Businesses are more efficient in the private sector than the public.
2. Water and sewage is a business like any other.
3. A quarter of the [water] industry is already in the private sector.
4. Of course it will need regulation to protect the consumer and the environment.
5. Even though a natural monopoly, once privatized the industry will have to compete for capital in the private sector and face a published daily share price – a comment on performance and a spur to management.

Egged on by Lawson, the Conservative governments of 1979–97 saw through a huge programme of privatization. They learned lessons as they went. There were three basic issues that needed to be resolved in the process – first, what price should it be sold for? Too high and no one will come forward, too low and the taxpayer has been ripped off; second, how should the industry be broken up – by region as with water, by function (track and train operators separated in the case of rail), or should it not be broken up at all (as with telecoms initially)? And third, what form of regulator was required and what regulatory framework should it set?

They did not get all of it right by any means, but the overall effect, accepted broadly now, was of much improved service. Tellingly, not a single one of the industries privatized in that era has been brought back into public ownership, nor has any government seriously considered doing so.

By luck more than judgement, the British became world leaders in privatization just before the Berlin Wall came down and Communism across central and eastern Europe, followed by the former Soviet Union, imploded. Privatization marched boldly across the former Communist bloc, learning more lessons as it went. In Russia it became obvious that if you privatize in a hurry before you have some basic functions of a market economy – accountancy standards or robust banking – you risk replacing monopoly with kleptocracy, which is what happened there. Around 1,500 people ended up owning half of Russia.

This fear that the well-connected few will benefit from a fire sale of public assets is not without foundation in some parts of the world. The government in Pakistan is right to consider privatizing some of its state-owned assets as a way to improve performance and cut costs, but it is not surprising, given the country's history, that some are fearful. In September 2013 a newsletter from *Rise for Pakistan*, an e-journal of passionate Pakistani youth, argued:

> Say No To Privatisation . . . Privatisation is promoted and supported with the claims of reducing economic burden on the government and improving the efficiency of the institutions. But past history of privatisation process not only in Pakistan but all over the developing world, shows that rather than accomplishing these goals, it ends up lining the pockets of top bureaucrats, politicians and other top officials involved in this process.

It is impossible to deny the risk to which it draws attention. But this is not an argument against privatization in principle, merely an argument for undertaking it in an open, transparent and measured way. Where corruption is rife and the state or the other basic institutions of a market economy are weak, this is easier said than done. However, in these circumstances, clinging on to the state-owned assets is likely to result only in a drain of cash and continuing execrable performance.

The key is to get the details of the regulatory framework right and, along with it, ensure transparent governance of the businesses that emerge. Government can learn from regulatory regimes that failed as well as from those that succeeded. And the regulatory regime needs to move on to keep up with changes in the economy and technology. As Joss Garman argues in relation to Europe's energy requirements, there may be long-term economic benefits in regulations that are more stringent in requiring 'cleaner, more efficient and home-grown' energy supply. This is because both geo-politics and technology are continually moving on.[11]

As Poland, the Czech Republic and the Baltic states, as well as Malaysia, show, well-designed privatization is a serious policy option to consider as states and societies modernize themselves for the twenty-first century. Critically, it reduces the size of the state, helps raise revenue and enables the state to focus on the things that matter most to citizens – increasing security, reducing crime, improving health and education and providing a climate for investment and economic growth.

Vouchers have always been the subject of controversy. The basic idea is that where a state wants to make a service available,

RULE 20
WELL-DESIGNED
PRIVATIZATION CAN
IMPROVE
EFFICIENCY
(it can also lead to smaller, more effective government)

instead of funding it directly, it gives each consumer/citizen their share of the money and enables them to buy the service themselves. It is a simple idea predicated on the view that markets are more likely to provide quality than monopoly public services. In this sense, vouchers are merely the most radical version of Choice and Competition, described above, but because they are the most extreme version, I have included them here.

Ever since Milton Friedman advocated vouchers for school education, as long ago as 1962, they have been debated, and indeed the experiments have largely centred on their applicability in school systems, where the parent receives the voucher and spends it on behalf of the child. Before plunging into the debate briefly, it should be pointed out that, at least in theory, vouchers could work for numerous other services including aspects of social care and healthcare or for further and higher education.

While the basic principle, in part due to its simplicity, has real appeal, in practice there are a number of problems to overcome. One is that if you introduce a universal voucher scheme you will be giving vouchers, paid for by the public purse, to some parents who have already opted out of the state school system and into the private one. This is a deadweight cost – a state subsidy to parents who evidently don't need it.

A second problem is that the administration of vouchers is quite challenging in practice. In the voucher scheme for poor families in Punjab whose children are out of school, there are three substantial administrative tasks – finding the deserving families, which in a country with poor records and no census since 1998 is by no means straightforward; registering the private schools eligible to receive the vouchers and ensuring they conform to certain minimum standards; and finally making sure that the voucher is as corruption-proof as it can be and that the intended children actually become the beneficiaries. None of this is simple, but we are persevering successfully because of the potential benefits in access, quality and cost efficiency. As of the summer of 2014, over 200,000 children from poor families are getting an education they would otherwise not have had.

In the end, as Gabriel Sahlgren points out in his rigorous analysis, the issue is not an ideological one – there is too much polemic on both sides of this subject – it is a matter of getting the design right. 'The conclusion,' he says, 'is that school choice and competition have the potential significantly to increase school quality, but that design matters.' He quotes Terry Moe, long-standing US advocate of school choice: 'choice always operates within a structure . . . which in turn shapes the kinds of outcomes that choice will ultimately generate . . . Different structures, different outcomes.'[12]

So in Punjab, which has the fastest-growing voucher scheme in the world, we have focused it on poor families who are out of school. We have helped strengthen the administrative capacity of the Punjab Education Foundation, which oversees the scheme. We have kept the quality assurance process simple and objective – any private school that accepts voucher children must allow all the children to be tested annually (by an independent organization) and show that

> **RULE 21**
> A WELL-DESIGNED VOUCHER SCHEME EMPOWERS THE BENEFICIARIES (and can promote equity)

the vast majority of its pupils are making progress. And periodically we audit the process to identify and tackle any abuses. So far the evidence is positive, not just for the children who get vouchers, but for the system, because the competition provides a wake-up call to the government sector.

In the long run, if experiments such as that in Punjab prove successful, it is possible to imagine governments in the developing world adopting vouchers as a universal strategy. After all, the evidence from the developing world suggests that millions of parents on low incomes

Summary of the Five Paradigms

	Trust and Altruism	Hierarchy and Targets	Choice and Competition	Devolution and Transparency	Privatization
Relevant sectors	Public services such as health and education	Public services such as health and education	Public services where the citizen/ consumer can make real choices	All major public services including police, prisons, railways	Large state-owned utilities/enterprises such as telecoms or energy
Where on performance scale	Most relevant to Good to Great or above	Most relevant to Awful to Adequate	Most relevant to Good to Great and beyond	Most relevant to Adequate to Good and above	Adequate to Good. If service is Awful, may need improvement before privatization
Evidence of effectiveness	Thin	Solid	Growing	Strong	Strong
Combines well with	None	Devolution and Transparency	Devolution and Transparency	Hierarchy and Targets	Choice and Competition
Main challenge of implementation	• Government gives up leverage • Performance debate turns into one about money	• Political will and focus • Designing good targets	• Creating real alternatives • Ensuring choice is real for the poor • Market information	• Political will to make performance transparent • Need for good leadership at frontline	• Design • Reliance on the institutions of a market economy (e.g. accountancy)
Telling examples	Finland schools (good) Ghana schools (bad)	• 2001–10 UK Accident & Emergency and surgery wait times • Punjab school reform	• Punjab schools • NHS in England • Portfolio School Districts in US	• NYPD • UK rail performance • Citistat Baltimore • Maryland	• Khazanah in Malaysia • UK 1980–97 • Poland 1995– 2005

Table 7

have chosen low-cost private schools because the government schools are so poor; furthermore, the low-cost private sector achieves better outcomes at much lower cost. In these circumstances, there has to be a temptation for a government to switch much, perhaps eventually all, of its funding from the moribund and wasteful to the effective and economical. This would be consistent with the Julio Frenk view of the world: government sets the rules and pays, public and private compete to provide.

In the meantime, the electronic payments systems that are proving so helpful to economies in the developing world – more than one third of payments in Kenya are now made on mobile phones – could help resolve at least some of the administrative challenges. Indeed, there are already experiments with conditional cash transfers as a means of combating poverty.

STEWARDSHIP: THE ROLE OF THE CENTRE OF A SERVICE

Whichever of the five approaches – or combination of them – is chosen, it is easy to miss a startlingly obvious point: someone at the centre of the system has to oversee it in its entirety and secure its long-term interests. This is stewardship, a fundamental responsibility of government. As the fan diagram above (p. 64) makes clear, there are three aspects of stewardship. Sometimes governments delegate part or all of these functions to a regulator – usually an agency of government – but even then the (ultimate) responsibility lies firmly with government, as we discovered in the financial crisis. The authors of *The Gardens of Democracy* use a gardening metaphor: 'Tending and regulating . . . signify the same work but tending frames the work as presumptively necessary and beneficial rather than as something to be suffered.'[13] This tending is an essential function of government, whether your preference is for small or large government.

First, strategy: of course, you can choose not to have a strategy at all and simply muddle along. This may even be popular, especially with the public sector workforce – but it remains a choice nevertheless, and what it amounts to is Trust and Altruism by default . . . or to put it more crisply, drift. Generally speaking, though, a well-run sector needs government or the regulator to survey further possible technological change, shifts in global patterns of provision, likely demand and so on. As Francis Fukuyama argues, legitimacy comes in part from delivering results, but in part also from being able to anticipate and respond to changing citizen demands.[14]

Strategy remains a responsibility even after privatization, where the nature of regulation, for instance, or the extent of any subsidy – for a transport system, for example – are clearly government functions. Singapore has a government that excels at this aspect of stewardship.

As the fan diagram also makes clear, the second is to put in place the means of monitoring performance across a system. In the case of a privatized industry, such as energy in many countries, this role generally falls to a regulator; in a state-run system such as schooling in Punjab or Louisiana, the role falls to government. Sometimes some governments choose not to measure outcomes in any effective way, perhaps in response to professions fearful of the impact of comparative data on crime, health outcomes or school performance. But where government abdicates this responsibility, the effect is to shift the debate to a focus on inputs. Alternatively, the media steps in where governments fear to tread – this often results in comparative data of less value and less quality, but no less impact. Better, then, for government to take responsibility. This is why when Dalton McGuinty, then premier of Ontario, announced that the government would publish school test scores rather than leaving the task to the *Toronto Globe and Mail*, he gained the unlikely distinction of a standing ovation from teachers.

Given the rise of 'Big Data' – the capacity to collect and analyse massive quantities of data in close to real time – which is currently transforming much of business, it is unthinkable that government-funded or regulated services could stand against the tide, even if there was a good case for doing so (which there isn't). The issues are therefore what data to collect, which indicators to value, and how to present the data in a way which has integrity and vividness.

Moreover, it is not just a question of performance data, but also of setting regulation and checking for compliance. If a water company is not meeting environmental standards, the public needs to know. If pricing policy is being abused to enable unwarranted profits, the public wants something done.

The third and final essential task of the centre of government is to ensure that the necessary human capital is in place, properly regulated, with the required skills and motivation. It takes seven years or more to train a doctor, and almost as long to train an engineer or an architect, so the supply of such scarce skills needs planning ahead.

And because trust in professionals is such a key aspect of their capacity to play their part, even in a largely private and self-regulating profession such as engineering, there is a role for government in creating the circumstances that allow such self-regulation and in ensuring dialogue with the profession's leaders about matters such as access to and content of engineering degrees and training. Where the profession is also part of a public service, such as teaching, the government responsibility is all the greater.

In a market, firms may be able to recruit and train the staff they need, but even the larger ones cannot ensure the national supply of the necessary qualified people. Government has a clear responsibility here, and in a public service much more so. Having experienced in 1999 being in the Department for Education during a period of acute teacher shortage – with headteachers expressing constant anxiety and the media hyping up every school which claimed it had closed due to staff shortages – I know what failure in this respect feels like. We had increased school budgets, which schools evidently welcomed, but we failed to anticipate the obvious truth that the schools would spend the extra cash on recruiting more teachers.

> **RULE 22**
> GOVERNMENT SHOULD TAKE ITS STEWARDSHIP RESPONSIBILITY SERIOUSLY; THAT INCLUDES STRATEGY, REGULATION AND THE SUPPLY OF SKILLED PROFESSIONALS

The result was that schools in more comfortable and less expensive locations recruited the staff they wanted, and those in challenging and expensive locations suffered badly – which is why the rougher parts of London screamed loudest.

The positive outcome of the crisis was the most thorough-going reform of teacher preparation, pay and incentives of the past generation, which had long-lasting beneficial consequences. But it has not erased the memory of the crisis, which I wouldn't wish on anyone responsible for any major public service. The moral is that ensuring a supply of the necessary professionals is an essential function of government. Even in the good times, never forget it!

Supply, though, is not the only issue. There is also the ongoing question of the relationship between governments and the professions who work in the public services. Often around the world this is tetchy, or downright dysfunctional. In the three years I have been working in the Punjab, there have been strikes by both teachers and doctors, as well as a range of other public servants. Acrimony between teachers and government is common across Africa, as well as Britain, Canada, Australia and parts of the US. Doctors, nurses and other healthcare professionals too often find themselves at odds with government, as do police officers. Sometimes the issues at stake are pay, conditions, pensions or workload; sometimes they are about policy itself. For reasons that become apparent at various points in this book, some tension is inevitable. Public servants will always want improved pay or conditions, while governments, unless they are irresponsible, will always face financial constraints. Public servants will always want a say on policy because it will be their job to implement it, and they are knowledgeable, while governments often have an electoral mandate and will want to deliver their promises. Public service professionals will want to advance slowly and incrementally (and stay in control), while (some) governments will be in a hurry.

Julio Frenk describes a process by which a strategy decays through a consultation process. The vision is outlined; consultation with professionals and others blurs it; a proposal is made; its radical cutting edges are bevelled and smoothed and rounded through further consultation; the legislation is introduced and legislators are lobbied; the legislation becomes still less radical, still more incremental; and up to this point, implementation has not even begun. We'll see (in the chapter on irreversibility) how this process of decay can be fatal. At this point it is sufficient to note how easy it is in this process for the relationship between government and professionals to decay too.

Meanwhile, as the debate about a set of proposals evolves, the public watching are wondering what on earth is happening to their public services and what value they are likely to get for the money they deliver up through their taxes. Often they are thinking 'a plague on both your houses'. At the same time, perhaps, those who can afford it are opting out into the private sector. An incredible 70 per cent of the children in Delhi, Lahore and Accra have already done so – so this is not just the wealthy, it's the poor too. Of course, it's not always like this, but the scenario I've described is not uncommon, and it illustrates why it is an important function of government to think through how to build this relationship with the public service professionals.

There is a tendency to believe that the way for government to buy peace in this relationship is to be soft or passive. However, the evidence suggests, as we have seen, that the Trust and Altruism implied

The Relationship between Government and Professions

Phase of development	Awful to Adequate	Adequate to Good	Good to Great
Chief focus of system	• Tackling underperformance	• Transparency • Spreading best practice	• World-class performance • Continuous learning and innovation
Role of government	• Prescribing • Justifying	• Regulating • Building capacity	• Enabling • Incentivizing
Role of professions	• Implementing • Accepting evidence • Adopting minimum standards	• Accommodating • Evidence-based • Adopting best practice	• Leading • Evidence-driven • Achieving high reliability and innovation
Nature of relationship between government and professions	• Top-down • Antagonistic	• Negotiated • Pragmatic	• Principled • Strategic partnership
Time horizon	• Immediate	• Short and medium term	• Continuous
Chief outcome	• Improvement in outcomes • Reduced public anxiety	• Growing public satisfaction	• Consistent quality • Public engagement and coproduction
What the public think	• 'You should have done that years ago.'	• 'Maybe... we'll believe it when we see it.'	• 'That's what we wanted all along.'

Table 8

will not work; nor in all likelihood will it buy peace. Much better is confident, assertive leadership, both in government and among the professionals. The strategic implications are set out in Table 8, which is a summary of how these crucial relationships might evolve as the quality of a service moves up the Performance Wedge.

Bringing about this shift in performance requires, among other things, attention from both government and the professions themselves to the need for a constant refinement and development of professional skills; easy for government to neglect, but fundamental to delivery of constantly improved outcomes and an essential aspect of stewardship.

These, then, are the five approaches to reforming or transforming large public systems and the three essential aspects of stewardship. The five vary in their effectiveness; all can work in certain circumstances, though some are less likely to work than others. Choosing between them will in part be a question of ideology and in part a question of the nature of the challenge or the goals that have been chosen. For Awful to Adequate tasks, Command and Control plus 'naming and shaming' are most likely to succeed. For Good to Great tasks – because greatness cannot be mandated – Devolution and Transparency or Choice and Competition are better placed to succeed – and indeed where there is a strong professional ethic, as with teachers in Finland, there are the circumstances when Trust and Altruism might turn out to work after all.

And that leaves just one further point to make. In any given large service there is likely to be significant variation in performance, so the strategy as a whole might weave together elements from among the five approaches – Command and Control for the poor performers, Transparency for all and increased autonomy and room to expand for the top performers.

Overall, then, getting the reform model right is a sophisticated challenge for any government or specific government service, but not an unthinkable one. The key is to make the time for informed discussion of the principles on which you want to base policy. In the whirl of activity and crises that is government everywhere, time for discussion of principles and strategy is remarkably difficult to find. It is worth it, though, because the alternative is coming up with one of those 'portfolios of initiatives' beloved of consultants and that, in spite of the good intentions, is without doubt the road to hell.

COMMUNITY ENGAGEMENT

On 14 August 1908, Mohandas K. Gandhi, not yet Mahatma, wrote to General Jan Smuts, Transvaal Colonial Secretary, to tell him that the Indian community in the province planned to burn their registration certificates. They would accept an education hurdle for the entry of Indian immigrants into Transvaal, but not a racial one.

Two days later, the burning began, as the *Transvaal Leader* described:

> Paraffin was poured in and the certificates set on fire, amid a scene of the wildest enthusiasm. The crowd hurrahed and shouted themselves hoarse; hats were thrown in the air and whistles blown.[15]

How had Gandhi unlocked this extraordinary level of community engagement in a course of action which would soon result in not just Gandhi himself being locked up, but also 2,500 other members of the South African Indian community?

First, there was moral strength in the case. As Gandhi put it:

> Unenfranchised though we are ... it is open to us to clothe ourselves with an undying franchise, and this consists in recognising our humanity ... I say that no matter what legislation is passed over our heads, if that legislation is in conflict with our ideas of right and wrong, if it is in conflict with our conscience, if it is in conflict with our religion, then we can say that we will not submit to the legislation.[16]

The identity and dignity of the Indian community were at stake and, powerless though they appeared to be, no one, not even General Smuts, would be allowed to take those away from them.

Second, the way they made their case had great moral power. Some argued for simply lobbying, sending letters, arranging meetings; others argued for violent confrontation. Gandhi rejected both, and instead advocated what became known as Satyagraha.

The movement in the Transvaal, with which I have identified myself, is an eloquent and standing protest in action against such methods. The test of passive resistance is self-suffering and not infliction of suffering on others.[17]

General Smuts was at a loss:

In more primitive times one would have met [this campaign] by simply issuing a declaration of war. But in these times it is impossible to do that and therefore the situation became a very difficult one for us to handle.[18]

Those early Satyagraha campaigns in South Africa struck both their participants and the governments against whom they were aimed as an innovation in public protest. No wonder Smuts was unsure how to proceed – how do you face down a committed community whose protests harm only themselves, not anyone else?

Now imagine if that level of community engagement could be unlocked in favour of a public programme. Imagine that level of belief in support of a major government reform. That is why the fan diagram is set against the background of an ellipse entitled Community Engagement. Hard to do, of course, but suspend disbelief for a moment.

The education of children, the health of a nation, the safety of urban communities: these are all causes in which people believe and about which they have strong views. There will sometimes be protests – against a hospital closure perhaps – but imagine if the energy of the community was unlocked and channelled into delivering the outcomes that people want. In the end, however much government invests in doctors, nurses and medical technology, only families and communities can make sure all children eat healthily and exercise regularly; only individuals can decide to stop smoking; only parents can see to it that homework is done, perhaps even enjoyed; and only citizens can ensure their streets are safe.

One problem with the post-war era and its welfare state was that people began to expect the state to provide; they became passive recipients of a service; they became dependent. If, instead, they were active participants – exercising choice, taking responsibility and demanding quality – the services would deliver much higher performance at no extra cost. The key here is motivation. Dangerous territory for a political leader – make the case in the previous paragraphs, and you risk being accused of softening up the service for cuts and abdicating responsibility. This is what happened to David Cameron when he proposed 'the Big Society' – a good idea shot down before it reached its prime.

Similar extended periods of failure of government dampen people's expectations. Because they expect little, they cease to make demands. Those on the inside of the ineffective government then blame the citizens for having low expectations. Sania Nishtar, who was briefly minister of health and education in Pakistan, wondered why there was no 'upward pressure' on government to deliver. She even stopped her ministerial car randomly to ask women walking by why they did not demand more. The answer was that they had given up. They expected little of government and it then lived up to their low expectations.

It is vital, therefore, that those responsible for government and public service – if they are to focus on delivering the best possible outcomes for the precious taxpayers' money invested in public services – find ways to unlock and harness public engagement.

There is an extensive literature on this subject, well tackled in the think-tank world. Here are some of its topics:

- **Transparency**
  Provide information – about services, outcomes and threats (Australians now routinely guard themselves against the hot sun in a way they didn't a generation ago).
- **Open debate**
  Encourage dialogue between professionals and public, both at the point of delivery – the GP's surgery for example – and publicly.
- **Empowered communities**
  Enable community groups to take on services (and budgets) that in the past have been 'provided' by government (free schools in England, charter schools in the US).
- **Social enterprise**
  Make it easier for people to establish social enterprises and for them to compete when services are being contracted out.

- **Social alchemy**
  Celebrate social alchemists – those who assemble the disparate elements that change the game at local level (such as the Harlem Children's Zone).
- **Competition**
  Shift the burden of proof so that services are contracted out unless there is a good reason for them not to be.
- **Learn from business**
  Ask yourself why some major companies – Apple or Starbucks – generate such passionate commitment.

Some or all of these options will make a difference. As you consider the five paradigms and the three stewardship responsibilities, never forget the potential of public or community engagement to transform outcomes.

POLICYMAKING

Somewhere between strategy and implementation you find policy. Much of government goes straight to policy, forgetting strategy. And then, as we've seen, underestimates implementation. Indeed, many civil servants claim their real expertise lies right here, with policy. But policy without strategy is rarely transformative; and policy without implementation is worthless.

It is true that there are some things where implementation will take care of itself. For example, assuming there is general support for it, a ban on smoking in public places will take care of itself because citizens will enforce it. But the 'big' changes that transform outcomes for citizens are mostly much more challenging than this to implement, which is why we need a science of delivery. At this point, though, it is worth emphasizing that policy matters, matters a lot, as long as it's in its rightful conceptual place between strategy and implementation and takes account of both.

Reams have been written on the subject and don't need to be repeated. For our purposes, we just have to know what questions you would need to ask yourself if you were tasked with preparing the policy on anything.

A good first question would be: How does it relate to the strategy (if there is one)? After that, I have not found anything better than the document circulated in the Department for Education in England by its permanent secretary Chris Wormald, who also heads the cross-government policymaking profession.

The Five Policy Tests

1. **WHAT'S THE POINT?**
   PURPOSE – Are you absolutely clear what the Government wants to achieve?
2. **WHAT'S IT GOT TO DO WITH *US*?**
   ROLE – Are you absolutely clear what Government's role is?
3. **WHO MADE YOU THE EXPERT?**
   EVIDENCE – Are you confident that you are providing world-leading policy advice based on the very latest expert thinking?
4. **IS YOUR ADVICE PREDICTABLE?**
   CREATIVITY – Are you confident that you have explored the most radical and creative ideas available in this policy space . . . including doing nothing?
5. **BUT WILL IT ACTUALLY WORK?**
   DELIVERY – Are you confident that your preferred approach can be delivered?

And then, just to be really practical, Wormald asks four more questions which reveal his knowledge of Whitehall.

Satisfied you pass those tests? Then ask yourself this . . .

1. **WOULD I BE COMFORTABLE EXPOSING MY POLICY THINKING TO THE HIGHEST LEVEL OF CHALLENGE IN THE DEPARTMENT?**
2. **IS MY POLICY ADVICE ARGUED LOGICALLY AND CRISPLY, AND FREE OF JARGON?**
3. **IS IT FREE FROM ERRORS?**
4. **WILL MY ANALYSIS AND THINKING BE AVAILABLE FOR OTHERS TO USE AND LEARN FROM?**

Successful governments, then, think strategically, adopt proven methods of reform, take their stewardship responsibilities seriously and ensure they engage with stakeholders and communities. They also ensure that the policy advice they receive is of high quality.

So, looking back, that meeting at Chequers in June 2001 was profoundly important. It was the moment when the prime minister and his team understood not just their approach to public services, but also how to turn strategy into delivery. Now all we had to do was turn the strategic approach into policies and plans, service by service. The struggle governments face in doing that is the subject of the next chapter.

4

Planning

On 15 May 1944, just three weeks before the big day, General Bernard Montgomery – Monty to his British admirers – summed up what his boss, the Supreme Allied Commander, had achieved: 'Plans and preparations are now complete in every detail. All difficulties have been foreseen and provided against. Nothing has been left to chance. Every man knew exactly what he had to do.'[1]

By completing these preparations, Dwight D. Eisenhower, known as Ike to his friends, had made history long before he was elected president of the United States in 1952. A stellar military career resulted in his appointment by Roosevelt in December 1943 as Supreme Allied Commander in Europe. In this role, he was personally responsible for planning and implementing one of the most challenging military campaigns of all time – the Allied invasion of Normandy known as Operation Overlord, which was the first step towards the liberation of France, and eventually all of western Europe, from Nazi oppression.

D-Day, 6 June 1944, involved 12,000 planes to attack the enemy, 7,000 vessels to transport soldiers across the Channel from England and almost 160,000 troops. Within a couple of months, more than 3 million Allied troops from several countries were involved in the liberation. The night before D-Day, Eisenhower wrote a note to himself which reflected the loneliness of the leader at an historic moment such as that: 'If any blame or fault attaches to the attempt it is mine alone.'[2]

As an exercise in planning, Operation Overlord is logistically mind-boggling. Think not just of the planes, vessels and troops, but also of the military equipment, not to mention the food and basic supplies. Ike had overseen the planning in advance and took command as the plan became reality. To add to the complexity, the task was made that much more difficult by the giant-size egos Eisenhower had to deal with as the plans were made. He had to argue with Roosevelt about the role the French would play; with Churchill about the bombing strategy; and about everything with his subordinate George S. Patton, whose combination of genius and prickliness was legendary. In each case, Ike prevailed. Reflecting on the whole process long after these momentous events, he remarked famously, 'In preparing for battle, I have always found that plans are useless but planning is indispensable.'[3]

Eisenhower's wisdom had somehow not seeped into the Whitehall culture by the time the Delivery Unit was established in 2001. One of the first things I read after I had been appointed was a paper by two external advisers to the Treasury who had been asked to review how departments were making progress with the targets they had agreed to in the year 2000 as part of Gordon Brown's spending review. A number of things surprised the advisers, but none more so than the fact that, in most departments, as they put it, 'there was no plan'. It seemed to defy common sense that goals had been set and multimillion-pound budgets allocated, but there were no plans. This was a seminal insight for me, not least because I was about to ask departments for plans to deliver the priorities established by Blair and approved by the cabinet in the few short weeks after the 2001 election.

In my four years in the education department, I had learned to expect better. Well, a little better. There I had discovered that when asked for a plan, civil servants would jump to it ... and they would come back a few weeks later with something more like an essay, often very well written and, if you were lucky, decorated (as one of my No. 10 colleagues later put it) with the occasional number. It just required the glossy cover to round it off.

This, then, it seemed, was the choice: on the one hand, no plan at all; on the other, an essay. In these circumstances, successful delivery seemed improbable. In Ike's terms, we would get neither the plan nor the planning. The civil service appeared not to have grasped the underlying truth that Ike understood: that until you grapple with the messy, day-to-day realities of getting something done, you simply can't understand what it takes. When I read in business strategy books that leaders deal with 'the big picture' and 'overarching strategy' while delegating all the detail, I groan. Serious leaders never do that, because they understand Ike's point. Their challenges are not to avoid the messy, ground-level reality, but to be selective in deciding when, where and how to intervene and in which details; and of course to build an effective team (at which Ike, incidentally, excelled).

So we told Whitehall back then exactly what we did and did not want. No essays. No glossy covers. Instead, we asked for real practical plans, with folds and creases, scribbled notes in the margins and coffee stains. Above all, we wanted to know what was going to be done, when it was going to be done and who was responsible.

It was not just Whitehall that had this challenge. In Punjab, Pakistan, there had been an Education Sector Plan for years prior to the start of the Education Roadmap in 2011. The World Bank and the Department for International Development (DFID), along with Punjab officials, had put years of hard work into that Education Sector Plan . . . but it was a descriptive essay, not a real plan. In this case, there was a plan but no planning. Nor was anyone responsible for checking that the elements of the plan got implemented. Small wonder that the province was not making progress towards the Millennium Development Goal and that the chief minister had no idea that his province was not making progress. In 2014 we discovered an almost identical failure in Punjab's health sector.

This is a chapter about putting that right. About ensuring that Ike's kind of planning gets done and that political and official leaders have a plan that they can use, and constantly update, to drive delivery of the goals they have set. We'll come to the qualities of a good plan in the final section of this chapter but, taking Ike's advice, there are four sections on aspects of planning that come first.

UNDERSTAND THE PROBLEM

In September 1776, all was not going well for George Washington and the Continental Army. They had been trying for some weeks to defend New York from conquest by the British, who had sent the greatest armada that up to that point had ever crossed the Atlantic to accomplish the task. In August, the British had driven a dishevelled Continental Army from Long Island. Indeed, had it not been for the good fortune of a dense fog on the morning of 20 August, it is doubtful whether the Americans would have escaped across the river to Manhattan to fight another day.

The situation did not improve for them there. When the British followed them onto Manhattan, on 15 September, the Continental Army did not stand and fight. It fled. 'The demons of fear and disorder seemed to take full possession of all . . .' commented one soldier present that day. Only the heroics of a then-unknown American officer, Thomas Knowlton, at Harlem Heights salvaged any pride at all. And even after that, Washington knew he and his men were in the direst of straits.

At the Continental Congress in Philadelphia, William Hooper of South Carolina saw the early glimmer of hope in the situation:

> It becomes our duty to see things as they really are, divested of all disguise and when the happiness of the present age and millions yet unborn depends upon a reformation of them, we ought to spare no pains to effect so desirable a purpose.[4]

Marty Linsky of Harvard Business School makes a similar point in modern language. He urges leaders to be 'relentlessly optimistic about the possibility of changing the world and brutally realistic about the difficulty of getting it done'.

The start of good planning, then, is – in John Kotter's words – to 'confront the brutal facts'.[5] That is precisely what George Washington and his team proceeded to do in 1776. For five days from 20 September, while New York City burned, they assessed the state of the Continental Army, which historian Joseph Ellis summarizes as 'deplorable'.[6] Having not flinched from seeing things as they actually were (rather than as they wished they would be), they came up with a plan. If instant success was not possible, they reasoned, they had better prepare for a long war in which they would wear out the British rather than defeat them. That required an army of 60,000 with men conscripted 'for the duration' rather than seasonal volunteers from the thirteen state militia. Two weeks later, the Continental Congress approved the plan and the stage was set for the long grind to the ultimate triumph of American independence ... though the first step was inevitably a further chaotic retreat.

More recently, a similar exercise in recognizing reality took place in Lahore in October 2010. I visited Pakistan regularly from 2009 on in my role as the DFID's Special Representative on Education in Pakistan. As a result, I came to understand its (deeply dysfunctional) school system and what needed to be done about it. The problem wasn't knowing what to do, it was finding someone with the courage to do it. Everyone had been telling me that the one politician with the courage and executive mindset, as well as the position, to act was the chief minister of Punjab, Shahbaz Sharif. That month, Fenton Whelan and I managed to get to see him and a handful of his officials without the stultifying presence of the massed ranks of the aid industry. We showed him the data that demonstrated Punjab was not on track to hit the Millennium Development Goal of universal primary enrolment by 2015. Clearly this was news to him – neither his officials nor (even less forgivably) the aid agencies had told him the inconvenient truth. What really shocked him were the two pictures below.

They laid bare the scale of the problem in a way that no amount of data could. In spelling out a problem, it is as important to affect

Improving Basic Management Would Make a Huge Difference

Children without facilities   Facilities without children

Figure 14

the emotions as it is to engage the intelligence. Shahbaz turned to his officials: 'Is this true?' There was a silence that seemed to last for an age. His officials looked at their shoes. Eventually I chipped in: 'It is true. The only question is, what are we going to do about it?' On the way out of the meeting, one of Shahbaz's officials commented tersely, 'You should never tell people what they don't want to hear.' Inadvertently, he had explained in a sentence why Punjab was so severely off track – no one up until then had been prepared to confront the brutal facts. Now that the chief minister had done so, we were ready to start planning.

> **RULE 23**
> UNDERSTAND IN YOUR HEAD (and feel in your heart) THE GAP BETWEEN YOUR ASPIRATION AND THE UNVARNISHED REALITY

The Punjab Education Roadmap was born in that moment. (At the meeting in which the Punjab Health Roadmap was born in April 2014, the chief minister was similarly affected. He turned to his staff after looking at the data and asked: 'How can you sleep at night?')

An essential element of that meeting in Lahore? The appeal to emotion, to the heart as well as to the head. Similarly, in William Hooper's advice he makes an emotional case – the future happiness of the world is at stake! Dispassionate, cool analysis *and* emotion. Not one or the other, both.

WORK OUT HOW YOU WILL DRIVE CHANGE

The next step is to decide what to do. At this point, it is important to remember the content of chapter 3. What is your overall approach to changing reality and advancing towards your goal? Which of the five paradigms, or what combination of them, will you rely on? How will you ensure that at the centre of your system you can play the three essential stewardship roles? How will you approach any policy changes you need? At the planning stage these almost philosophical approaches need to be turned into a timetabled sequence of actions. Remember, the keys to a plan are deciding what actions need to be taken, when they need to be taken and who is responsible for each of them.

The big danger at this point is over-complexity. It is essential to avoid it. This is what we did successfully in Punjab, after that seminal meeting with Shahbaz Sharif. First we looked for school systems of a similar nature which had succeeded in making progress and examined what they had done. As it happened, this work was already in progress for a report we were preparing for publication. The stories of Minas Gerais in Brazil, Western Cape in South Africa and Madhya Pradesh in India were powerful and clear – in each case the school system had improved because it had ceased to rely on Trust and Altruism and had applied a version of Hierarchy and Targets. Given they were on an Awful to Adequate journey, this was the right approach and it was working. Thus we knew what the drivers of change were.

Learning from these stories, we were able to develop a Roadmap or plan for Punjab with five elements.

1. *Data and Targets*
   Targets would be set for the province as a whole and for each district.
2. *District Administration*
   All appointments would be made on merit, instead of on political connection, and the new district leaders would be trained to deliver the Roadmap.
3. *Teacher Quality*
   We would prepare lesson plans for every one of 200,000 primary teachers in the province in English, Maths and Science and train them to use them.
4. *Punjab Education Foundation*
   We would use the PEF, an autonomous organization with government and donor funding, to bring in an element of choice and competition, by funding low-cost private schools and expanding a voucher system for poor families.
5. *Supporting Functions*
   We would improve facilities at schools, and include a number of practical developments which the Secretary – Schools wanted as part of the Roadmap.

It was a very simple plan. It was also incomplete – nothing in it at that early stage about school principles; nothing about strengthening the enrolment drives the system undertook (ineffectually) every year. That doesn't matter; these other aspects came later, as we regularly updated the plan. The point is, it was a good enough plan to get things started once we

> **RULE 24**
> UNDERSTAND THE POTENTIAL DRIVERS OF CHANGE
> (and base your plan on them)

had broken the actions in each of the five areas into specific practical steps with a deadline and a person responsible. Table 9 shows a typical page of the Roadmap plan from 2012.

The difficulty wasn't arriving at the plan, it was pulling the people at the centre of the Punjab education system together around the plan. In December 2010 and January 2011, in spite of the evident commitment of the chief minister to the emerging Roadmap, the other interested parties – the Punjab officials, Pakistani government people,

Extract from Roadmap Delivery Plan

G	
G	On target
AG	
AR	
R	Off target

Actions	Action by	Timeline	
40 Plan and conduct first teaching quality DTE training pilot	Sir Michael's delivery team, DSD	1 Sep 2012	G
41 Co-develop and carry out further testing and deeper statistical analysis to understand the extent of changes in learning over the last year	PEC, PEAS, DSD	30 Jun 2012	AR
42 Develop and implement a plan to address issues with the PEC examinations as quickly as possible with third-party support as required	PEC	30 Nov 2012	AR
43 Allocate additional funds for toilets and drinking water in schools which still lack them and disburse to school councils	Sec Schools	August 2012	AG
44 Grant project allowance for education sector institution staff (i.e. PMIU, DSD) in order to maintain capacity	Chairman P&D Secretary Finance	August 2012	AG

Table 9

the World Bank, even key people in the DFID, which was supporting my work there – were at odds either with the idea of the Roadmap or with aspects of it, or with each other. To be honest, for much of that time, myself and my team in Lahore felt pretty much alone.

This state of conflict around a plan in the early stages of a change is not unusual. At a much grander level it was part of Eisenhower's planning for D-Day, as we've seen. There are two ways to resolve these conflicts – one which works and one which is almost certain to be fatal. Often civil servants, sadly, choose the latter.

The first way is to keep going back to the evidence, to the chosen model of reform and keep making the case for why the emerging plan should work – and refine, refine, refine. If, as in the case of Punjab, the leader himself is on your side, this will help, but don't rely purely on the time-honoured 'the PM (or CM) insists . . .', especially if you're not quite sure what he or she thinks. Listen and see how, on the basis of vigorous dialogue, you can refine or improve your plan. Be ready to learn always, but don't compromise. You might make adjustments to the timetable perhaps, but even here the weight of argument will always be for delay, so someone needs to make the case for urgency – every day of not acting on the plan is another day of the system failing citizens, in this case the families and children of Punjab. This won't be fun, but resting your case on the fundamentals, and perhaps the leader's support, has its rewards.

The second approach, so often chosen, is to make one concession after another in order to get 'buy-in' or 'shared ownership' from each of the warring stakeholders. Civil servants often advocate this way forward, always supported with plausible arguments about the importance of 'winning hearts and minds' or the influence of certain stakeholders ('We really need to ensure the World Bank is onside'); but the main reason they take this line is that it avoids conflict (which they abhor) and ensures, as far as possible, a quiet life. The problem – known in negotiation theory as 'the theory of side payments' – is that if you make all the concessions required, there is a good chance you will emasculate your plan before implementation has even begun. It's like designing a plane, putting it on the runway, weighing it down with boulders, weakening its engines, clipping its wings perhaps, and then wondering why it doesn't take off. The argument for doing less or doing nothing often looks plausible (and is of course sometimes right); whereas the case for being bold needs constantly to be made.

Avoiding emasculation before implementation was exactly my challenge at the beginning of the Punjab Roadmap. As I wrote in my diary at the time of one very senior federal official – 'she doesn't have a strong view, but wants her friends in . . . government to be happy . . .' Meanwhile, a top consultant to the DFID was advising me to 'assemble the international community'. The next comment in my notes simply reads: 'inclusive vs getting things done', which says it all. 'Inclusive' sounds warm and appealing, and if it is possible, so much the better – but it can also be an excuse for procrastination and dilution.

The reality in some governments can be even worse than this. Some of the stakeholders aren't just sceptical, they actually want to block what you are doing, though they might not say so overtly. Stein Ringen quotes the political scientist Charles Lindblom on this theme: 'Many people constantly try to change the social world. An explanation of their failure more plausible than that of inertia is to be found in the great number of other people who are vigorously trying to frustrate social change.'[7]

Since this is often the case, it is as well to be aware of the reality. This is why success in government requires not only good planning but also political will. The combination is crucial because, with both in place, as soon as implementation begins, progress is possible and people who once opposed it will start to come round.

In Punjab, we were able to build sufficient support in the end – though it was touch and go for a few weeks – to get started in January 2011. My team began to build the three stewardship functions crucial to the centre of the system (see chapter 3) as the early phase of implementation began. With the strategy broadly established, the key was to set up the data collection system. The World Bank had made a significant contribution by creating inside the Punjab government the Performance Monitoring and Implementation Unit. The idea was great – monthly data from all districts on key indicators of educational progress – but the execution until then had been poor: only a few districts were collecting and submitting data and even then with a long time-lag. (The developing world is littered with half-finished institutions such as the PMIU at that time: 'It would have been marvellous,' the aid agencies assure themselves, 'but they didn't implement it properly.') One key Punjab official, with the help of my team, turned the PMIU into a purring, smooth-running data-collection machine.

The Punjab example illustrates several crucial steps towards a credible plan.

- Keep it simple; it doesn't need to be perfect, just good enough to get started.
- Expect conflict.
- Adhere to the principles and evidence; don't make so many concessions to get 'buy-in' that you end up with an inedible soup.
- Don't forget the three stewardship functions – even if you plan to devolve.
- Try to have the leader on board.
- Get started.

> **RULE 25**
> PREPARE A PLAN TO IMPLEMENT YOUR STRATEGY THAT IS GOOD ENOUGH TO GET STARTED
> (and don't make concessions for a quiet life)

LABS

Idris Jala brought to government policymaking in Malaysia a new approach which he had tried and tested in previous roles with Shell and Malaysia Airlines. He calls this a 'laboratory' or just 'lab'. He explained his thinking in an interview he gave to a researcher from Princeton.

> When I first went there [into government] it was me and my assistant and then we built a small team. But because we wanted to hit the ground running, the first thing we did was to run laboratories, so within a month of my arrival we started running six laboratories.[8]

There was one lab for each of the six National Key Results Areas. Each lab involved between forty and fifty people, a mix drawn from within government and the relevant field, public and private, who could bring different perspectives to bear on achieving the NKRA – reducing crime or improving urban public transport, for example. Idris locked them in a hotel for six weeks, provided a trained facilitator, lots of data and the occasional prime ministerial visit and set them the task of finding ways to meet the prime minister's ambitious goals. To participants, he likes to quote the line from the Eagles in 'Hotel California': 'You can check out, but you can never leave.' Note how different this is from standard policymaking – in a lab, people concentrate full-time for six weeks and have to emerge with solutions and a plan of action. Quite different from the desultory, once-a-month project meetings where there is plenty of talk but little action, and between meetings still less.

Idris explains the key to success:

> ... the labs began [with] very, very tall targets, almost what you call impossible targets, targets that will cause you to have fear of failure ... If we came with an incremental target ... there is no need to transform ... [stretch targets] require a radical approach and outside-the-box thinking ...[9]

Then he adds:

> I always believed this, people actually know the solutions but the reason why they don't execute it is because there are a lot of roadblocks along the way ... The ideas were already there ... but to move it from idea to results there are hurdles such as technical hurdles, political hurdles, administrative process hurdles ... We were really focusing on ensuring that the hurdles that prevented us from doing this before are now removed in the labs.[10]

What makes the lab different? Idris Jala's team answer:
- Bringing together key relevant people from the public, private and NGO sectors.
- '3 feet' implementation programmes.
- Budget request as part of the output.
- Key performance indicators assigned to relevant stakeholders.
- Syndication sessions with top leadership.

In short, it is an intensification and acceleration of much of what is in this chapter.

That phrase '3 feet' needs elucidation. Idris Jala points out that people are always talking about a '30,000 feet' perspective, as if somehow that is enough when it comes to planning. There are numerous euphemisms – '30,000 feet', 'strategic', 'high-level', 'high-level overview', etc. – but they all mean the same thing: vague. To avoid the '30,000 feet' perspective Idris insists on '3 feet' implementation – that is, close-to-the-ground reality. Six weeks locked in a hotel is, he says, usually long enough for people to get over their interpersonal tensions and really plan in practical detail. He admits that the output of a lab will not be perfect, but it will be enough to get started.

Labs had worked in Idris's business career. Now they worked in a government setting. The key lesson in each case, he argues, is to be very clear about the performance indicators you want to shift. In business it is likely to be profit; in government there needs to be a hard (and ambitious) indicator too, such as falling crime rates or improved health outcomes, which takes you into the debate elsewhere in this chapter about trajectories.

LEGISLATION

As you plan, you may discover you have to change the law, in which case you will need to legislate. The approach varies according to the constitution. In consensual countries such as Germany or Norway, there is a laborious process of consultation and a set of procedures to follow. In congressional systems such as the USA or large parts of Latin America (and now Kenya), the executive has to lobby the members of Congress in small groups or even one by one, as Julio Frank remembers doing assiduously to push his health reform through in Mexico. Talk to Melody Barnes, Obama's director of the Domestic Policy Council in the first term, and again and again you hear her talk about day after day spent 'on the Hill' lobbying members of Congress.

In parliamentary systems, the government usually has a majority in Parliament and therefore securing the passage of legislation is easier. Even here, though, attention to factions and individuals, especially in the governing party or parties, is vital. Tessa Jowell, Britain's minister for the Olympics, remembers assiduously courting individual ministers and key figures in all major parties to win support for London's bid.

The tactics of passing legislation, which clearly varies country to country, are dealt with extensively in the literature and this is not the place to delve into it. It is sufficient here to make two vital points. One is that legislation is not only vital from a legitimacy and constitutional point of view, it is also an opportunity to test the narrative, the strategy and potentially the organizational approach in the court of public opinion. By generating public debate, it can also help to define dividing lines between supporters and opponents and to create momentum. Get it wrong and the opposite applies.

The second is that compromise may be necessary to build a coalition in the legislature capable of passing the law. After all, a majority is required. A sense of realism in government is essential about this – but equally it is vital to guard against making so many compromises that the original intent becomes impossible. And of course the opposition know this and will choose their tactics accordingly. If they can't win head-on, emasculating the bill with a string of minor amendments is an attractive option.

Be on your guard.

THE DELIVERY CHAIN

Have you ever read one of those medieval history books full of lines like this: 'Edward gathered an army and hastened north . . .'? Hang on a minute! How did he do that? There he is at Westminster or Winchester and someone, perhaps a messenger, comes in with a piece of news that prompts the thought 'I need to head north with an army.' What do you actually do next (in a world where nothing moves faster than a horse)?

The answer is, you depend on a delivery chain. You gather what barons and men you have with you at court, but in all probability that will not be enough, so you send messengers to the leading barons wherever they are and tell them to meet you in Derby or York. They receive the message and – unless they see an opportunity in this moment of crisis to overthrow you – they send a message to their knights and retainers, who in turn scrape together the no-doubt reluctant peasants, and eventually, if you are lucky, everyone is heading north.

There are many opportunities for this to go wrong. Put another way, there could be weaknesses in the delivery chain. Perhaps the messenger got lost, was stopped by bad weather, or was killed by an enemy agent. Perhaps he is like Baldrick in the BBC comedy series *Blackadder* and garbles everything you tell him. Perhaps the baron receiving the message doesn't fancy hastening north and comes up with an excuse, or perhaps he simply wasn't where he was thought to be – maybe he's visiting his estates in Normandy . . . and so it goes.

The truth is that to gather an army and hasten north to fight the Scots was a staggering logistical challenge. It is all very well for Shakespeare to put inspiring speeches in the mouth of Henry V – and the historical record suggests the man himself was inspiring – but what made him successful was his mastery of the delivery chain and the associated logistics. He hastened south to fight the French (if crossing the Channel in a tub of oak counts as 'hastening'). His army arrived equipped for the task. Every time I read one of the many books about inspirational leadership, I think about how Henry V made sure that all his archers had functioning long bows and quivers full of arrows.

That was then. Now is no different; however noble the objective, however brilliant the motivational speech and however detailed the plan, without an effective delivery chain, nothing gets delivered. Jonathan Powell, Tony Blair's chief of staff, put it this way: 'A new Prime Minister pulls on the levers of power and nothing happens.'[11] The moral is that the plan you develop has to include an understanding of the delivery chain and how it needs to be strengthened. It is important to be clear that this is not a centralizing idea at all. It is simply a statement of fact – if you are a prime minister or minister or top local government official, or in charge of delivering any major objective in any large organization, even if your goal is to decentralize, you have to understand the delivery chain, otherwise you'll end up feeling the way Tony Blair did when he was new. In the Prime Minister's Delivery Unit, we were quite blunt about this: If you can't draw the delivery chain, you can't deliver.

My first experience of thinking this through for a large system was for the National Literacy Strategy in England in the late 1990s. Here is the way I thought about it. David Blunkett had to improve standards of reading and writing among eleven-year-olds. Implicit in this commitment was that in one way or another he intended to influence what happened inside the head of an eleven-year-old in, say, Widnes. The delivery chain is what makes that connection explicit; so how can we connect the child in Widnes to the minister in Westminster? What happens inside that eleven-year-old's head is influenced chiefly by her teacher – the first link in the chain; the teacher is influenced by the school's literacy co-ordinator, who, in turn, is influenced by the headteacher – the second and third links in the chain. The headteacher is influenced by the school governors and the local authority, who are influenced by the regional director of the National Literacy Strategy, who answers to the national director of the strategy. He in turn answers to the head of the Standards and Effectiveness Unit in the DfES, who answers to the secretary of state. And thus we have established the delivery chain.

Figure 15 is an example of a delivery chain from Punjab, Pakistan.

There are two crucial aspects of creating or reviewing a delivery chain. The first is to check whether *the actors* at each point in the chain have the will and capacity to do what is being asked of them. Remember that, as you go out along the delivery chain, the number of actors increases. In the National Literacy Strategy, the numbers were as set out in Table 10.

When you examine the will and capacity at each level, you should expect variation. It might be excellent, as it was in Blackburn, Wigan and Tower Hamlets, or problematic, as it was in Bristol, Walsall and Norfolk. Clearly you need to monitor this as the strategy unfolds, and where the problems lie will change over time. At the beginning, though, you just want to check that as far as possible across the system people are ready to go.

The second, equally crucial, aspect is not the actors, but *the links* between them. You might have someone marvellous in charge of literacy in one of the local authorities, but if that authority is in conflict with the headteachers, success is unlikely. Similarly, one of the regional directors may have a poor relationship with one of the local

Delivery Chain – Punjab, Pakistan

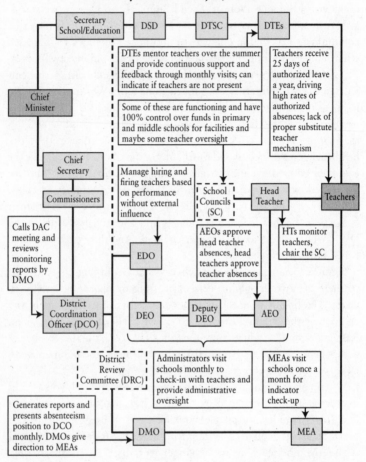

- For successful implementation it is essential that every level of the system is functioning at high capacity and has strong relationships

- A delivery chain maps out all the crucial stakeholders, dependencies and relationships, from the leader of the system to the front lines

- The weaknesses at every level and in the relationships are identified and remedied

Figure 15

1	Person responsible for delivering the result (me)
1	Director of the National Literacy Strategy
15	Regional directors
150	Local authorities, each with someone playing my role at local level
400	Literacy consultants
19,000	Headteachers, each with a literacy co-ordinator (so another 19,000)
190,000	Teachers teaching literacy hours
3.5 million	Children, lapping it all up

Table 10

authorities he or she is responsible for. In short, the links in the chain are as important as the actors themselves. In my experience, consultants with organization charts remember the actors, put them in boxes, and forget the relationships. Yet it is the relationships that matter most. As Lawrence Freedman put it, 'A chain is as strong as its weakest link, the more links in the chain, the higher the odds that something might go wrong.'[12]

When we started on the thankless task of improving railway performance in the Blair administration, the link in the delivery chain between the Department for Transport (DfT) and the train-operating companies was not so much flawed as (almost) irretrievably broken. The officials in the DfT believed that, the railways having been privatized, the punctuality of trains was nothing to do with them; the train operators despised the officials anyway and wanted to be left alone. Meanwhile, the passengers were, understandably given the execrable performance of the trains, screaming, 'What's the government going to do about it?' and the prime minister was saying to me, 'Michael, what are you going to do about it?' And I answered that we would fix the delivery chain,

> **RULE 26**
> STRENGTHEN THE DELIVERY CHAIN
> (don't think you can get away without doing so)

which is what we (painstakingly) did. And eventually performance began to improve steadily.

DATA AND TRAJECTORIES

Sir Bradley Wiggins became a true British hero in 2012 when he became the first Briton to win the Tour de France. Shortly afterwards, he added to his already substantial tally of gold medals by winning the time trial at the London Olympics. Sheer talent at the peak of form. Well, yes, but that's not quite all there is to it.

Wiggins and Team Sky, led by the relentless Sir David Brailsford, had been planning a British win at the 2012 Tour de France for well over a year. In the language of delivery, they had a target. They also had a plan: Wiggins was entered in five races in the year before the Tour, including setting out to win the Paris–Nice race in the months immediately prior to it. As Wiggins himself put it in his own inimitable style, 'to win Paris–Nice you still have to be bloody good . . . I was in bloody good form, at 95, 96, 97 per cent, but that last few per cent [required to win the Tour] is going to come from fine-tuning.' In other words, they had a trajectory too; 100 per cent performance in July meant 95 or 96 per cent performance a few weeks earlier.

And his coach had a mass of data on his weight, his blood pressure, his speeds and above all his power – the amount of force he was exerting on the pedals minute by minute. Their approach involved poring over the data day after day and addressing Wiggins's weaknesses as well as his strengths. One of his weaknesses was hill climbing. It wasn't that he was bad at it; rather that he was quite good but needed to be brilliant. The plan involved focusing on this between March and June of 2012, during which time Wiggins would cycle up 10,000 metres each week – 'a little bit more', as he puts it, 'than the equivalent of going from sea level to the top of Everest . . . daily grind. It's bloody hard work.'

So yes, Wiggins is an exceptional talent and was at the peak of his form that July when he won the Tour de France, but that was only the visible part of the performance, when the television cameras clicked on. To enable that, he and his team had a goal, a plan, a trajectory and a mass of data, which enabled them to see whether he was on track or not, and to tweak the plan when they needed to. Could he have won without all this? Not according to him: 'The critical thing is that I couldn't have done any of this without all the background training going back to November . . .'[13]

We want our triumphs, whether political or sporting, to be romantic – triumphs of brilliant ideas or moments, triumphs against the odds. Victories snatched from the jaws of defeat. Occasionally they might be like this but, whisper it if necessary, mostly they won't. They'll be victories ground out, perhaps incrementally, step by step through attention to detail. As Matthew d'Ancona, one of Britain's best political commentators, put it when I was in No. 10, 'There is no drama in delivery . . . only a long, grinding haul punctuated by public frustration with the pace of change.'[14]

The trajectory is the key to establishing this mindset. You know where the data is now on your chosen metric; and you know where you'd like it to be because you've set your aspiration. Go away and draw the line that connects the two points: that, at its simplest, is what a trajectory is.

How hard can that be? It turns out, quite hard. First of all, there are psychological barriers. If you are a civil servant, and your minister or

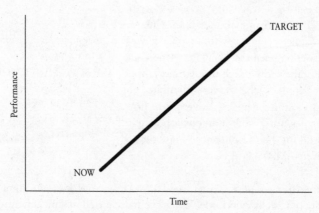

Figure 16

someone who works for a prime minister asks you for a trajectory, your first reaction is not 'How will I do that?', it is 'What will they think (or do) if I get it wrong?' So, when asking for a trajectory, it is necessary to anticipate this reaction and state the obvious: 'Of course you'll be wrong!' After all, how many people who predict what will happen four years into the future turn out to be right (except perhaps by sheer chance)?

You then have to anticipate the next reaction, which is obvious too. If you know the trajectory is going to be wrong, what's the point in tracing it? And here we get to the fundamental point about trajectories. The reason for drawing a trajectory is that it forces you to think about the connection between the actions you are going to take and their impact on the outcomes.

This is truly profound. It means that, as the plan unfolds, those responsible can check whether the actions set out in it have the effect that was intended; and if they don't, they can learn from what actually happens and tweak the plan. Sometimes, even if everything is on track, it is worth double-checking. When we were monitoring health wait times in England, once the plan was in place they fell steadily from one month to the next. But just to be sure, we checked the sub-trajectories for each type of operation. All were heading in the right direction except orthopaedics, where we were then able to intensify the strategy.

In short, a trajectory is a wonderful thing, and no one should plan a major government reform without one. It was an essential element of winning the Tour de France. How much more important is it to apply such proven techniques to massive (and expensive) government programmes on which millions of people depend for their fulfilment or maybe even their lives?

> **RULE 27**
> NEVER GO ANYWHERE WITHOUT A TRAJECTORY
> (you'll learn better, faster and deeper)

It is one thing to decide you should have a trajectory. It is quite another to draw a really good one. When we first started asking for trajectories during the PMDU days, we used to quip that the officials concerned went racing back to their departments and got out their most sophisticated piece of analytical equipment – a ruler – with which they drew a trajectory very much like the one in Figure 16 above. There are two serious limitations to this approach. One is that it enables the relevant officials to avoid doing the tough, analytical thinking required to connect their actions to the outcomes; in other words, to avoid the whole point of developing a trajectory in the first place.

Constructing a Trajectory: The Key Questions	
1. What is the performance indicator?	What data set are you going to rely on for your trajectory? What are its strengths and weaknesses?
2. What is the target?	What target have you set? And what is the deadline?
3. How will you collect the data?	Is your data-collection system reliable? Does it give you the level of detail you need? Is it timely?
4. What is the historic data run?	What happened in the past with this indicator? Are there interesting blips or outliers?
5. How will you estimate the future?	Remembering of course that the human world rarely travels in straight lines…
6. Can the data be broken down by locality?	Will you be able to see which regions/localities/hospitals/police forces, etc. are doing well and which aren't? Could you look at quartiles and track them separately?
7. Can the data be broken down by category?	Can you separate out different crime types? Or types of operation? Or students by race and ethnicity? All these will help you understand.
8. Can the data be broken down by policy?	Will you be able to see the impact of each of the different strands of your policy? Which are the big drivers of change? And which aren't?

Table 11

The other is simpler but just as problematic: the truth, obvious for anyone who stops to think about it, is that the human world rarely travels in straight lines. A hundred years ago we discovered, thanks to Einstein, that even the straight lines of Newtonian physics weren't quite as straight as we thought; and social science is far less predictable.

In the Delivery Unit, and tried and tested elsewhere on many occasions, we developed a set of questions to ask yourself when preparing a trajectory. These are set out in Table 11. As in everything else in the science of delivery, attention to detail pays dividends.

Once these questions have been addressed, it is possible to get to the next level. While trajectories are rarely straight lines, there are sometimes patterns. One common shape for a trajectory is shown in Figure 17.

This shape of trajectory is common because there are some things which improve rapidly once you focus on them, and then get harder. Literacy in primary schools is like this – you get a jump from the focus and accountability. Social science calls this the Hawthorne Effect, after an experiment in which performance on a production line improved, not because of the amount of light – which was the research question – but because the workers on the line knew they were being researched. These are the kinds of reforms where people talk about 'picking the

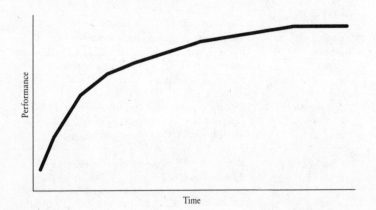

Figure 17

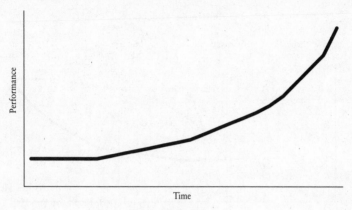

Figure 18

low-hanging fruit' or 'the quick wins'. (Too often that is all they do, and progress is not made irreversible.) After that all progress depends on grinding out improvements in the quality of work, which is hard.

Figure 18 exemplifies another common shape for a trajectory. This type is appropriate where there is a lot of hard work to do in the preparation phase or a lot of investment required up front before improvement can occur. It has to be said, though, that in the Delivery Unit and after, I have always looked at trajectories of this shape with *intense suspicion*. Too often you would see a trajectory like this and realize that the first significant improvement was three or four years in the future and you knew the official (and maybe the minister) was thinking, 'by that time, I'll be in another job'. However, they might really have had a point, in which case you needed to know what milestones – actions taken – would be met in the three or four years before improvement would occur.

Once the broad shape is clear, the key actions and the trajectory should line up as illustrated in Figure 19.

Now you need to pay attention to some minor details which, if you forget them, might lead to confusion. A good example is seasonal variation. In Punjab, February is exam season. Student attendance drops. April is the wheat harvest. Again, it drops. In Britain, in winter

Illustrative Trajectory

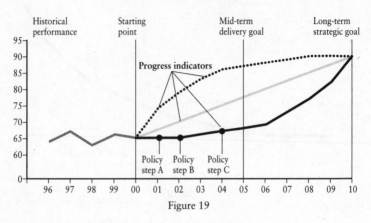

Figure 19

people are more likely to get ill, so waiting times for operations will be under greater pressure. When it gets dark earlier in the evening, certain types of crime become more likely. If you want to get even further into the detail, young people are more likely to get drunk on a Friday night and (at least in the UK) hit each other over the head with beer glasses. This, in turn, means that Accident & Emergency departments are more likely to feel under pressure at that time of the week – so numbers and perhaps wait times there will go up. Then there is the famous problem on the railways of 'leaves on the line', a cause of delay and hilarity in the UK (and just delay in New York City). Seasonal patterns can be anticipated (though they should not be excused – if Friday night is a busy time for A&E, increase the staffing) and built into trajectories.

Once done, the trajectory becomes a crucial monitoring tool. Those responsible at every level, including the delivery unit, can monitor progress against trajectory and learn from the deviations. All this requires collecting the data in the first place, and in swathes of the public services this can be a stumbling block. However, at the PMDU we had Tony O'Connor, one of the founding fathers of the science of delivery.

Tony set up a small team of four people to be the number-crunchers at the heart of the Delivery Unit's work. Over the years that followed, Tony taught us all three important lessons about how to ensure data has influence – you have to collect it, then you have to ask the right questions, and finally you have to present the data in a compelling way. Each of the three is essential. If you don't have the data, you're stuck of course; if you ask the wrong questions, or interesting but irrelevant ones, at best you are an academic; and if you don't present the data well, the chances are that the minister or prime minister will miss the point altogether, sometimes because numbers are not quite their speciality, but often simply because they are very busy and they don't have the time or patience to make sense of a complex table.

Tony's *pièce de résistance* was a moving PowerPoint graph of the huge increase in teenagers involved in street crime in 2001–2. As the line shot across the screen, there was a sharp intake of breath from the PM and the ministers in the Cabinet Room. From then on, I knew we'd have collective commitment to solving the problem. Some years later, I had a similar sense of triumph when the chief minister in Punjab looked at a beautiful map of enrolment by district across his province and said, 'I'm going to sleep with this map under my pillow.'

> **RULE 28**
> COLLECT DATA, ASK THE RIGHT QUESTIONS AND PRESENT THE ANSWERS BEAUTIFULLY
> (and don't forget integrity)

Tony made another equally important contribution. His job was to make sure that any slide we produced for the prime minister had integrity. It was tempting for someone in a position like mine to tell the prime minister a compelling and plausible story – but what if it wasn't true? 'You are the conscience of the Delivery Unit,' I used to tell Tony and his colleagues, and they took the role to heart.

Data is hard to collect on a systematic basis, at least in the initial stages; and as any number of people will point out, however well you collect it, there will be flaws in it and it won't tell you all you need to know. Added to that, some will oppose data collection because they fear what it will show. Incredibly, the very same people who make one or more of these arguments against collecting regular data, in the next breath purport to advocate 'evidence-based policy'.

If you want evidence-based or evidence-informed policy, there is no alternative but to collect good data. When designing the data collection system, Table 11 above is crucial. It is important to think about how much detail is needed. Clearly it is cheaper and easier to rely on a sample, say an opinion poll, but if this gives you only system-level data, it may not be enough. For example, it is helpful to know whether crime is going down or up at the level of the country, but much more helpful operationally to know in addition which places are seeing the biggest falls and rises, as well as what is happening to different crime types. Another vital aspect of the design of data systems is the timeliness of collection and analysis. Too often in government you find that data is collected, but by the time it is gathered at the centre of the system, many months have passed. By the time it has been analysed as well, many more have passed; and by the time it's available to the system leader responsible or the public it is barely relevant any longer because the world has changed so much in the meantime. Data on long time-lags is of no use at all to those managing the system because any decisions it might have informed are long since gone.

This is not an argument against large-scale academic evaluations which take place after the event. If done well, such research can, and should, be of huge value to future policy. While I was in the Department for Education between 1997 and 2001, two major studies were commissioned which have proved to be of global significance. One was the evaluation of the National Literacy and Numeracy Strategies undertaken by Michael Fullan and his colleagues, which proved to provide a platform for the ten-year reform of Ontario's school system between 2003 and 2013, in which Fullan himself played a leading part.

Similarly, the study we commissioned from professors Kathy Sylva and Pam Sammons (now of Oxford University) has enabled the tracking of successive cohorts of children for over a decade, and provides insights into such important questions as 'Does the type of preschool education children experience between ages three and five have measurable effects on how well they do at the end of primary school at age 11?' (The answer is yes.)

Insights such as these are vital to building the evidence for future policy, potentially across the globe, but they are of limited value in real time at the point of decision. Of course you can consult the researchers as you go and it is desirable to do so, but they are often cautious about reaching conclusions too soon – before they've done the research in fact! As a result, sometimes researchers get a bad name in policy circles, but this is unfair because they are only doing their job; the point is, it is a different job from delivering results in a government programme.

Similarly, ministers and those responsible for delivery in government often get a bad name among researchers – 'Why didn't they wait until we'd finished our study?' This is unfair too – people trying to deliver government priorities have to get on and do that, which often means, in practice, taking decisions with incomplete information. There can also be incompetence on both sides – poor research or poor policy and implementation – but that is a different issue altogether.

Reports undertaken by a government audit or inspection regime are a rather different category, and those involved in these kinds of study have a responsibility to provide insight and comment as close to real time as possible because part of their mission is to ensure good outcomes for citizens and good value for taxpayers – not simply to publish 'I told you so' reports after the event. The Audit Commission in the UK, before it was summarily abolished, produced beautiful reports, but too long after the event; the Government Accountability Office in Washington has a similar track record.

The Office for Standards in Education (Ofsted) in England used to cause me similar frustration. They would write a report on some education policy I was responsible for and explain to me the key criticism just before it was published. Often the messages were pertinent, and either we had already discovered the problem and sought to fix it, or occasionally we hadn't and would have benefited from knowing sooner. They defended the degree of confidentiality on the grounds that it was part of their jealously guarded independence. For my part, I respected (and valued) their independence, even when it meant being in the firing line of their critique, but I wanted to know sooner what problems they had uncovered so that we could address them and the citizens – in this case children and their parents – could benefit. It was as if Ofsted was sometimes more interested in the headlines they could generate than in their impact on implementation.

The main point here is that neither research studies nor reports from auditors or inspectors address the need those responsible for implementation have for good, close-to-real-time data. And without data of this kind, it is impossible to manage a system or check progress.

A couple of examples will illustrate the point. In 2007, the Minister of Health in Namibia and his cabinet colleagues were concerned about the poor health outcomes in the country – everything from the devastating impact of HIV on the population to performance of the health services themselves. They made Kahijoro Kahuure, an agricultural economist with a reputation for getting things done, the government secretary (top civil servant) at the Ministry of Health and Social Services.

He inherited an organization with a lack of strategy, a lack of leadership and coordination and a track record of failure in implementation. At the heart of the problem, a review of the health system at the time noted, was totally inadequate data. There were 'no clear performance indicators or tracking systems to give feedback on how goals were met'. In short, the ministry did not know what the problems were or whether they were making progress towards solving them.

The lack of data was something the new government secretary focused on and, as a result, had a remarkable impact. Here is one example. Most of Namibia is rural and dispersed. Apart from Mongolia, it is the emptiest country in the world, with just 2.5 people per square kilometre, but its capital city, Windhoek, nevertheless has all the problems of urban areas, one of which at that time was that ambulance response times were notoriously slow. No one knew how long they were exactly, but everyone knew that if you called an ambulance, even in an emergency, you shouldn't hold your breath (even assuming you could).

Data changed everything. Once they knew the average response time was two and a half hours (the average!), they started looking for solutions. An obvious one made all the difference. For non-emergencies or routine transport, they could send a bus. Immediately, actual ambulances were freed to deal with actual emergencies. Within a few weeks, the average response time was down to twenty minutes. There's a key lesson here – once there is good data, checked regularly, it drives action. By making a problem transparent, you create the conditions for solving it. Those who dismiss data analysis as 'bean-counting' and a burden on the system miss this fundamental point.

Here is another example. The Delivery Unit took on responsibility in 2002 for reducing road congestion on Britain's motorways. Anyone who has driven on them, especially around the large conurbations such as London, Birmingham or Manchester, knows what a challenge that is. Small, crowded island; not enough roads, insufficient public transport and too many cars. Add to that – in 2002 – the tenth consecutive year of economic growth, and you have a motorway system under severe strain. 'What was the plan?' we asked the relevant officials, and in reply came a collective shrug, 'What can you do?' So we asked a simpler question to try to generate a conversation: 'How do you measure road congestion anyway?' It turned out not to be as simple as we thought.

The Department for Transport had invented a bizarre system of paying thirteen people in the country to drive various routes at different times of day and calculate an estimate of congestion. This data was then aggregated once every two years (and revealed that the problem got worse!). On the day I happened to ask this innocent question, the officials responsible felt obliged to apologize for the fact that one of the thirteen had had an accident the day before, so the system was even less effective than usual. I felt there was something faintly biblical about this and wondered whether the thirteenth man had been paid thirty pieces of silver, but I didn't say so. Instead, with the appropriate degree of hesitancy and humility, my colleagues asked a killer question: 'Haven't you heard of GPS?'

It turned out they had, but it had never crossed their minds that they might use it to monitor congestion on Britain's motorways – at least until that moment. Several months later, all objections overcome ('It'll be expensive'; 'Not remotely as expensive as the road congestion we're unable to manage at present', etc.), the GPS-based system was – as it were – ready to roll. We piloted it on the motorways around Birmingham with the newly enthusiastic team at the Highways Agency. The six weeks of monitoring revealed a mass of precise data about what caused congestion and – just as with ambulances in Windhoek – a creative search for solutions. The most common causes of congestion were accidents – how could the operation to clear the highway be speeded up? – and breakdowns – how could the recovery services get there faster? The least common cause of congestion in that period (it only happened once) was an elephant crossing the motorway, and we suggested they need not worry about this at all. More importantly still, they began to know precisely at which junctions and which times congestion was most likely. And most importantly of all, they knew what was happening as it happened, in real time, not two years after the event.

Just as with ambulances in Windhoek, the data made the system manageable. Officials who had sat shamefacedly in headquarters, dreaming up excuses for why nothing could be done about the remorseless tide of road congestion, suddenly found that they could after all make a difference.

In the years afterwards, road congestion in Britain remained a problem, but management of it improved. Each accident caused less delay; drivers were warned by signs above the motorways when there were delays ahead; and hard shoulders became available for use on urban motorways during rush hour.

> **RULE 29**
> DATA MAKES A JOB
> DO-ABLE
> (until then, all you can
> do is make excuses
> and hope for the best)

LEAD INDICATORS

Where I live in Devon, you sometimes get those early mornings shrouded in fog. Branches of trees look like ghostly arms. Sounds are muted. If you climb a hill, you rise above the fog. You can look down on the blanket of fog stretched across the magnificent Taw Valley.

'Foggy at seven,' they say, 'fine by eleven.' And if you wait and watch, as the sun rises and warms the land, the fog lifts and it is indeed fine by eleven.

The knowledge of country people, developed when livelihoods depended on the vagaries of the weather, often turns out to be soundly based. In the language of the science of delivery, 'foggy at seven' is a lead indicator of 'fine by eleven'. If you just tracked the main indicator – fine weather – you'd be depressed at seven because it's anything but fine; but if you know that fog at that hour is a lead indicator, it's a reason to be cheerful. Technically a lead or leading indicator is 'a metric that helps to predict future performance on a target metric'. Fog predicts fine weather.

Lead indicators are very useful indeed, because if you get them right they will tell you *before* your target metric moves that you are on track. Or not, in which case you can begin to make adjustments to your plan. It therefore makes sense in the planning phase to identify what might be lead indicators. Often there is research which can help inform you.

As with other indicators, lead indicators can raise ethical issues which you need always to keep under consideration. Charles Duhigg tells one powerful cautionary tale in *The Power of Habit*. Target, the US drugstore chain, knew that new parents often became the most loyal customers. They asked researcher Andrew Pole to see whether he could identify from their purchasing patterns which of the women who shopped at Target were pregnant. These patterns would be lead indicators of becoming parents and Target could start ... well ... targeting such women with marketing even before the baby was born.

Pole cracked the problem analytically, but it raised ethical questions, especially when an outraged man in Minnesota complained at his local Target that they were mailing material about baby clothes and cots to his daughter who was still in high school. Shockingly, it turned out Target knew more about this man's daughter than he did; she was indeed pregnant. Being right about the lead indicator in a technical sense, though, did not make what Target had done right in an ethical sense.

Lead indicators don't always involve such dilemmas. For example:

- A lead indicator of reduced infant mortality? See what's happening to vaccination patterns.
- A lead indicator of student graduation? Check how many credits they got in the first semester.
- A lead indicator of performance in a failing school being turned round? Order in the corridors.

And so on. They are always there, like the canary in the coal mine. And the fog on those mornings in Devon.

THE PLAN ITSELF

Once you have understood the problem, decided what will drive change, made sense of the delivery chain, produced a trajectory (which isn't a straight line) and identified some lead indicators, finalizing a plan should be plain sailing. In fact, the planning – in Ike's terms – as opposed to the plan, is done. Still, there might be someone demanding a plan for accountability purposes and for the sake of thoroughness it is worth completing the task.

This is where templates come in. In any large organization, ask for a plan and in return you'll get asked for a template. In the early phases of the Delivery Unit, we refused to produce one, partly because we wanted to see what people would do without one, but also because we knew if we produced a template, next thing it would be called 'a form' which had to be 'filled in', after which it would be a short step to accusing us of creating bureaucracy. Whereas no one could object to being asked for a plan since they already had responsibility for achieving a goal.

Later, in dialogue with other governments (where I was advising rather than instructing), I relented. We produced a template.

A good delivery plan should:

1. Articulate its purpose. (What's it for?)
2. Set out the key actions and make clear for each one who is responsible and when it is intended to happen. (Who will do what when?)

3. Set out leadership and governance and how performance will be managed. (Who is in charge?)

4. Show the delivery chain, with its strengths and weaknesses and how, where necessary, it will be strengthened. (How will you make this happen?)

5. Incorporate benchmarking – what comparisons will be made of progress, both with implementation and against trajectory. (What are the reference points?)

6. Explain how key stakeholders will be managed. (What relationships matter most?)

7. Identify the resources necessary to deliver. (How will you pay for it?)

8. Anticipate and prepare to mitigate key risks. (What might go wrong?)

It is just a question, in other words, of being thorough. There are hundreds, perhaps thousands of books about planning and about programme and project management on the market, some better than others. This is not one of them – but the list above is a summary of what they say.

Helmuth von Moltke, the German field marshal who created the much admired (and much feared) Prussian army of the mid-nineteenth century, made the point that 'No plan survives contact with the enemy',[15] but it didn't stop him from planning thoroughly.

On D-Day, things did not go according to plan for Ike either, and over the next few weeks – at the Falaise Gap, for example – some things went horribly wrong, but the value of the planning paid off handsomely. Paris itself was liberated on 25 August 1944, less than three months after D-Day.

Implementing a government programme may not involve quite the same drama (and certainly won't involve the degree of force), but however good the plan, it won't survive contact with reality. The planning should, though. It ensures the resilience and the foresight to persist.

The key then is how those responsible know whether the facts on the ground are changing in the way that was anticipated and hoped for. More than anything else, that is about building routines into the way government works. This is the subject of the next chapter.

5

Routines

One of my favourite walks is to climb England's highest mountain, Scafell Pike, from Langdale. This is not the shortest ascent, but on a fine day is surely the most glorious, a walk which demands serious, persistent effort over several hours and which offers magnificent rewards in return: panoramic views of rugged mountains, glacial valleys and the distant Irish Sea.

A. Wainwright, whose incomparable guides to the Lake District mountains make wonderful companions, summarizes the walk thus:

> The walk falls into four distinct and well-contrasted sections.
> 1. To Mickleden Sheepfold – easy, level walking, Gimmer Crag on the right and the Band rising on the left.
> 2. Rossett Gill – gradual climbing. Bowfell's crags well seen on the left. Rossett Pike on the right.
> 3. Rossett Pass to Esk Hause – undulating grass shelf with two descents where streams flow to Langstrath, right . . .
> 4. Esk Hause to the Summit – easy gradients, but becoming very rough across a lofty plateau; two more descents before the final steep, strong rise.

He adds, 'This is a splendid walk, depending for its appeal on a wide variety of scenery and on the elusiveness of the Pike [the summit], which . . . remains concealed until the final stages.'

He has a pencil-and-ink drawing of the moment when, after many hours, the summit finally comes into view, and comments:

> Many hearts have sunk into many boots as this scene unfolds. Here, on the shoulder of Ill Crag, the summit comes into sight, at last, not almost

within reach as confidently expected by walkers who feel they have done quite enough already to deserve success, but still a rough half mile distant with two considerable descents and much climbing yet to be faced before the goal is reached.[1]

I love this walk and Wainwright's description of it because it is such a perfect representation in genuine landscape of what it takes to achieve any major goal in life – the sense of endeavour, the challenges (such as Rossett Gill, which is much tougher than Wainwright suggests) on the way, the persistence when your muscles ache, the moments when you think success is within grasp but it's not, it's half a mile distant with two descents and significant climbing still to do.

It is a metaphor for life, and it demands, like much of achievement in life, steady, relentless effort – the walk may be in four distinct phases, but in the end what gets you to the summit is putting one foot after another, however rough the terrain might be, again, again and again.

This chapter is about building the resilience into government that enables that persistence. This resilience is partly a question of leadership and partly one of building the right processes – routines – into the way government operates. There is a whole section later (in chapter 7) about the leadership delivery requires; this chapter focuses first on the specific aspects of leadership required to get implementation started, and then on those crucial routines that can be built into the way government works to enhance the likelihood of success, once delivery is under way.

THE LAUNCH

September 24 2010. Oprah Winfrey: 'So, Mr Zuckerberg, what role are you playing in all of this?'

'I've committed to starting the Startup: Education Foundation, whose first project will be a one hundred million dollar challenge grant . . .'

Oprah again, interrupting, 'One. Hundred. Million. Dollars.'[2]

Thus Mark Zuckerberg, founder of Facebook, announced his $100 million investment in Newark Public Schools. Why Newark, New Jersey? Because Zuckerberg 'believed in' the mayor of Newark,

Cory Booker, and the governor of New Jersey, Chris Christie, who were there with him on Oprah's show.

Now that was a launch that had the 'wow' factor! The most famous chat show host in the world, the most famous face of the new generation of social media innovators. An up-and-coming African-American mayor, willing to take on the vested interests in his own Democratic Party. And the larger-than-life Republican governor, willing to challenge orthodoxy on his side of the aisle too. That set everyone talking; talking about the disaster that was Newark Public Schools; talking about the spectacular rescue to come; talking about the exciting new alliance of leaders of the new America. Just one problem – no one had done anything yet. With a launch like that, expectations are raised sky high, but until someone starts work, the ground reality is unchanged. The gap between the two is vast. The result is a greatly increased risk.

Rhetoric. Reality. Many a great idea has fallen through the gap between them. As Dale Russakoff put it in the New Yorker, Cory Booker, Chris Christie and Mark Zuckerberg had a plan to reform Newark's schools. In fact, 'They got an education.'[3]

In this case, it would be wrong four years later to say there has been no progress – Cami Anderson, who runs the School District, points to increases in achievements, enrolment and physical infrastructure.[4] However, even the celebrities involved would admit the outcomes are far short of the aspirations set out that day on Oprah. There has been effort and struggle and conflict, and some eked-out progress, but not yet transformation. It is certainly worth considering whether they might have made more progress had they quietly got started and sought attention on Oprah only once they had some results to show. As Denisa Superville wrote, 'the road from now to 2017 [in Newark] could be extremely bumpy'.[5]

As this example shows, a launch is both an opportunity and potentially a moment of risk. There are many ways to screw them up, as I have discovered myself. When my political masters made the mistake of allowing me to launch Education Action Zones (in January 1998) and I slipped up in briefing journalists, we ended up with front-page headlines roaring that privatization of the education system was at hand. A senior figure in government rang David Blunkett and asked him to 'fire the mad professor'. Fortunately for me, David declined to do so.

The problem is that launch and delivery are integrally related. Get it right, and those involved feel informed and excited to be part of it. You have a fair wind. You can get on with the job. Get it wrong, and people are confused. They don't know what the story is and they may very well feel ill-disposed towards your agenda. Added to that those politically and administratively responsible for the policy are now on edge, fearful of making another blunder and on the defensive, constantly having to explain what they really meant. Meanwhile, the media, having smelt one rat, are actively looking for others.

All of which is to say, before a launch there are some tough questions you should ask yourself:

- Do you really need a launch?
- If so, how much do you want to raise expectations?
- What form will it take?
- Who will make the announcement? Is he/she a seasoned professional? Do you really need that celebrity?
- What's the message? Will the reality bear it out? When?
- How does it connect to the big strategic themes?
- What will the critics say?
- What is the one-line (hopefully memorable) summary?
- What is the policy's name?

Indeed, giving your policy a name is not to be underestimated. In business you'd call it getting the brand right. Muhammad Pate was a remarkably successful health minister in Nigeria, whose mission was to improve health outcomes by taking preventative approaches and especially by ensuring more effective immunization campaigns. He set up a delivery unit in his health department and drove the agenda relentlessly for three years until he left office in 2013. In a country where delivering in government is notoriously difficult, he made impressive progress. The president loved the policy, partly because of its intrinsic merit, but partly also because Muhammad Pate branded it brilliantly. He called it 'Saving One Million Lives'. He had heard about a programme led by the American healthcare expert Don Berwick called 'Saving 100,000 Lives'. 'We added a nought and then [to plan it] worked backwards from there,' he explained to me.

THE LULL

You have established your goals (chapter 1); you have set yourself up to deliver them (chapter 2); you have decided your reform strategy (chapter 3); and you have done your planning (chapter 4). Now, if you haven't already, you need to get started. This may be the moment when, in von Moltke's terms, your plan does not survive contact with the enemy, but the most likely response at the outset is something much worse – a deafening silence. A lull. The doldrums.

I remember the awful feeling in September 1998 when the literacy hour – the daily literacy lesson – was supposed to go live in all the classrooms in 19,000 primary schools across England. After all the planning, all the preparation and all the controversy, this was the moment of truth. Would there be a boycott? Would there be demonstrations? Or, worse still, what if, in spite of all the training that had already taken place, the primary teachers of England just carried on doing what they'd always done? What would government do then? How powerless would I be? To be ignored: surely a worse fate than to be resisted.

I'm sitting at my desk on the fourth floor of the Department for Education with a view of Hawksmoor's magnificent west front of Westminster Abbey, wondering . . .

Nothing.

Are they doing literacy hours out there, or not? I visit a couple of schools, and they are! Good – but obviously they are going to do literacy hours when I visit. I summon the relevant top people from Ofsted, which inspects roughly 500 schools per month. Surely they'll know? They tell me they'll produce a report for me next spring. Fine, I say, but I want to know what's happening now. Could I meet some actual school inspectors who've been in classrooms? Yes, I can, but not until October. By then, I'm thinking, six vital weeks will have gone by, what if there is no momentum by then? I talk it through with John Stannard, my wonderful director of the Literacy Strategy. He is calmly optimistic, as are his fifteen regional directors . . . but maybe they are too calm, too patient?

Then, out of the blue, from a source I hadn't expected, at the end of

September, I get the feedback I want. Conor Ryan, David Blunkett's special adviser, had been at the Labour Party Conference and all the MPs he met had been telling him what a marvellous advance the literacy hour was; parents loved it! Now, at last, after a month, I know something is happening out there because constituents rarely approach MPs at all, still less often with positive stories. By the same token, I know that if there had been a campaign of opposition to it, the MPs would have made absolutely sure David Blunkett heard about it.

Experience helps too. I knew a wonderful school principal from Kentucky who was asked to turn around, in short order, a failing school in Pennsylvania. She told the superintendent that she would do so on one condition. She expected that for the first two months after she started at the beginning of September, the superintendent would hear a series of complaints; the condition was that every single complaint should be studiously ignored. Then, by November, the principal promised, the school would begin visibly to improve . . . which is what happened.

> **RULE 30**
> DON'T BE SPOOKED
> BY THE DEAFENING
> SILENCE
> (but keep listening)

The lessons for leadership are clear – hold your nerve, trust experienced people and keep looking for a sign, like Noah waiting for the dove to return with a twig in its beak.

THE IMPLEMENTATION DIP

You get your planning and early implementation right. Everything is new and exciting. After the lull, the early feedback is positive. There is a sense of celebration – it's working! Then there is the implementation dip. I remember vividly explaining this concept to the cabinet in Colombia shortly after Juan Manuel Santos had been elected president in 2010. At the time, he was enjoying positive poll ratings of over 80 per cent. The meeting took place in the grounds of a beautiful villa outside Bogotá. No sooner had I mentioned that however well they were doing at that moment, the implementation dip lay ahead, than

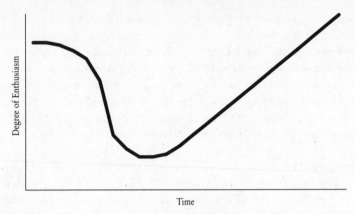

Time

Figure 20

the blue sky turned dark, thunder followed bolts of lightning and the rain became torrential. The symbolism was not lost on any of us.

This is a moment of high risk. Celebrating success too early is, as John Kotter points out, a very easy mistake to make. It can have two problematic consequences. One is that the opponents of the change celebrate with you because they hope that you'll stop paying attention. Whereas a few months ago they were saying 'It's impossible', now they are saying 'We're already doing it.' The second is that you will think the job is done. After all the preparation, the euphoria. And in government there are always many other issues clamouring for attention: if this is going well, why not turn to the rest of the agenda?

A huge error! This is a moment when serious leadership is required. Not only would it be a mistake to turn away – and play into the critics' hands – the truth is, the state of affairs is probably about to get worse before it gets better. The euphoria of 'the new' wears off; suddenly it's about grinding out results. It is a hard slog; there are new, perhaps difficult, skills that now have to be mastered, not just understood. There are new, perhaps demanding, management arrangements. The excitement of a new boss wears thin when it turns out she is human too; and this is happening a thousand times across a system. Worse still, the new arrangements, with all the skills and management, don't seem to work. The real world proves stubbornly resistant to change and for a while things may seem to go backwards.

This is because there are four stages of learning* which everyone has to go through. Before the change was introduced, most of those due to be involved were *unconsciously incompetent* – they didn't know what they couldn't do because no one had asked. Oblivious, and happy about it.

Then, when they realized whatever it was was coming and new skills were required, they discovered they had a problem. They were going to be asked to do something they couldn't yet do. They were now *consciously incompetent*. Beginning to learn this new set of skills was exciting at first; then it dawned that whatever it was was harder than expected to learn, so it would be much easier to retreat to the old ways of doing things.

If the leadership doesn't prepare for this moment, not only will the reform fall into the implementation dip, it will probably also never come out of it. A huge waste of time and energy; a huge missed opportunity. We might call this the Grand Old Duke of York problem – he marched them up to the top of a hill and he marched them down again. Except in this version they straggle down.

However, if the leadership anticipates the implementation dip, those involved can be taken to the next stage, *conscious competence*. As with the child who has just learned to ride a bicycle, the new skills begin to work, to make a difference, but each aspect of applying them requires conscious effort. Remember driving home that first time after passing your driving test? Everything from looking in the mirror to signalling left feels so self-conscious until eventually it becomes habit.

And still, persistence is required until the new skills, the new arrangements, become the new normal: we used to do it that way, now we do it this way. Why didn't we do this years ago? This is *unconscious competence*, the highest level of skill.

Think about this from an individual level for a moment. You want to lose weight. You sign up for the gym and feel proud of yourself for taking this first step. You have that induction session in which the

* Concept originally attributed to Noel Burch of Gordon Training International: *Four Stages for Learning Any New Skill*

trainer shows you how to use all those machines – the rowing, the running, the cross-trainer, the weights. Very exciting. After a couple of sessions, you get the hang of them. You are now consciously competent ... and then it dawns on you that everything so far was the easy bit. You go regularly for a while, but your weight stubbornly refuses to go down; then comes that cold, winter morning when it's barely light outside and you've got a pile of work waiting for you in the in-tray at the office. Maybe the right thing to do today is skip the gym and go straight to the office ... yes, absolutely right ... and the routine begins to crumble.

Imagine that psychology working across a system such as Britain's National Health Service with 1.2 million employees, or Punjab's schools with 300,000 teachers, or New York City's police department ... To take a change through the implementation dip requires an act of leadership. You've done the planning, you've survived the lull, now you have to cross the gap.

On that walk up Scafell Pike, this is the moment when the glorious glacial valley of Mickleden is behind you. You have covered the ground in great strides, listening to the gurgling of the running brook – or 'beck' as they call it in those parts – chatting with your friends. And now Rossett Gill rises ruggedly, even brutally, before you. It's still easy to turn back ... Scafell Pike from Langdale is not a walk for the faint-hearted, believe me, and neither is any major reform of a government or public service.

> **RULE 31**
> ANTICIPATE THE IMPLEMENTATION DIP (and demonstrate the leadership required to get through it)

DISTRACTION

In June the monsoons come to Pakistan, Northern India, Nepal and the Himalayas. Rivers such as the Kali Gandaki flowing down between Annapurna and Dhaulaghiri turn into broad, raging torrents crashing out of the mountains into the floodplains below. The huge rivers – the

Brahmaputra, the Ganges and the Indus – sluggish before the monsoon, become vast and swirling as they head to the sea.

In 2010, the monsoon rains were unusually heavy, not just in the high mountains, but across the Indus basin. They were the heaviest for eighty years – and it kept on raining. The ensuing flood covered one fifth of the land area of Pakistan. Over 20 million people were affected and around 2,000 lives lost. Estimates of the economic impact vary, but some suggest the cost to the country was over $40 billion. Ban Ki-moon, UN General Secretary, called it the worst disaster he had ever seen. Not any flood. The Flood.

For just under a year before The Flood, I had been trying to encourage Pakistan's leaders at federal and provincial level to take education reform seriously; to stop simply writing reports about how awful it was and actually do something. I had been due there that August, but with the country underwater and everyone understandably distracted by the inundation, I postponed my visit. The waters were receding by the time I came to Islamabad in September. Forty or so of the country's education leaders assembled as planned in a small, somewhat tacky hotel in the outskirts of the capital for a two-day session on the implementation of education reform. What I found – maybe I should have expected this, but I hadn't – was forty people who were utterly shellshocked. Most had been pulled off their education duties to tackle the flood and its consequences. In effect, what they said to me, led by an influential adviser to the prime minister, was, 'We can't do education reform any more; we've had a flood.'

For me, this was a make-or-break moment. I could have been understanding and sympathetic. The flood had been devastating. I *knew* that, though I hadn't *felt* it as they clearly had. I could have accepted their plea, in which case there would have been little point continuing my efforts. (It would actually have been a relief from a personal point of view – I had too much to do and it was demanding to visit Pakistan every month.) What I did, though, was the opposite. Something in me made me seize this moment. I chose to be ruthless. 'Did the flood make your schools better?' Silence. 'Did the flood make your schools better? You agree you had an education problem before the flood . . . you've still got one after the flood.' Silence.

Crises will come and go in all countries, more often in some than in others; at these moments, someone has to lead, has to make sure that while the crisis is addressed, it doesn't overwhelm the pre-existing agenda for change. Allow that, and failure beckons. Hence Harold Macmillan's famous lament about why he had not achieved more: 'Events, dear boy! Events.'

That ruthless moment in the tacky hotel was my leadership moment. Exactly a month later, we had the breakthrough in Lahore that led to the Punjab Education Roadmap which resulted in improved education for millions of children.

> **RULE 32**
> DEAL WITH CRISES
> (but don't use them as an excuse)

STANDARDS

They say that in Kyoto, the former capital of Japan, 'If you throw a stone it will hit either a Buddhist monk or a university student.' It is an ancient place of religion and learning. I loved visits to the Golden Pavilion and the Nijo Palace, but the most important learning for me – bordering on the religious, in fact – came from the journey there.

I travel from Tokyo to Kyoto on the 9.10 a.m. Shinkansen or bullet train. At 8.45 a.m., the train arrives at the platform having come from Kyoto. Four women in pink wait at the door of each carriage. They bow to disembarking passengers. As soon as the carriage is empty, they climb aboard and clean it. They make it spotless. Then the seats, which were all facing forwards as the train came from Kyoto to Tokyo, are reversed so that on the journey back to Kyoto we'll all face forwards too. The driver walks past, in immaculate uniform, proud to be about to drive this magnificent train.

And it is magnificent. The engine looks more like a rocket than a train and the white carriages are low and sleek. At 9.05 a.m. the women in pink have completed their work and we embark. The seats recline. There are footrests and hooks for jackets. Later I discover the toilets are spotlessly clean too. The wifi works. On time (needless to say) the train begins to move. There is no jerk or clank. Just smooth acceleration. The engine doesn't roar, it purrs. It's not far to the first stop at Yokohama, but thereafter you feel the sense of acceleration and then the genuine speed. On the right, views of Mount Fuji, snow-capped, rising above the clouds; on the left, the coastline. There are three stops before Kyoto, where the train arrives on time (needless to say), having completed 285 miles in just over two hours. Since it first came into service the Shinkansen has transported 5.6 billion passengers. There has never been a serious accident, and the average delay is under a minute.

Travelling up and down from London to Devon as I do, I experience First Great Western (FGW) trains often. FGW are not a bad train-operating company by British standards. Often their trains are on time, sometimes they aren't. In Britain, being within ten minutes of the advertised arrival time counts as on time anyway – inconceivable in Japan – and sometimes we drift inexplicably. The lost time accumulates. There is often a puzzling congestion at Reading (don't they know we're coming?), where we lose more time. Meanwhile, the toilets are often dirty, the water in the basin doesn't always run, and the windows are grimy.

Yes, I know the Japanese invested in infrastructure back in the 1970s and 80s when we in Britain chose not to, and that makes a difference. I know too that however hard FGW tried, they couldn't provide a view of Mount Fuji (White Horse Hill isn't quite the same) but – and this is the point – they could do something about the small things: the cleanliness, the pride of the staff, the explanations when things go wrong ... and they could show a greater sense of intent rather than, as it often feels, just shrugging their shoulders when delays occur. In short, they could set higher standards.

The key word in this account is 'standards'; not bad by British standards, but by Japanese standards, awful. Now, there is a key point about standards: it's not just the provider who is responsible, it is the customer too. The reason why First Great Western standards are as they are is that we allow them to be. The standards are embedded in culture, the organizational culture and the wider culture.

However clear your priorities, however good your strategy and your planning, it is really important to remember that, if success depends on setting new standards, you are embarking on culture change. That will take time. And the only way to succeed, therefore, is to build those new standards into your routines, into what you do all day every day. You have to change expectations at every level.

Such rigour creates resilience. My colleague Denise Todd was in Japan when the terrible tsunami and earthquake hit. She was in Tokyo, so not at the epicentre, but for everyone there it was still a major trauma. The following day she travelled from Tokyo to Kyoto on the bullet train; it left on time and arrived on time. That is what setting high standards does for performance.

DILIGENCE

After standards comes diligence. *Chambers Dictionary* defines 'diligent' as 'steady and earnest in application' and 'diligence' as 'steady application; industriousness'. Diligence matters because however the standards are set, the key is that they are steadily applied on every occasion. For some government programmes this is not just desirable but essential. Eliminating hospital-acquired infections, for example, depends on everyone washing their hands every time. Eliminating polio, the same attention to detail applies. Many health and safety procedures, ditto. When it comes to children learning to read, the issue may not immediately put lives at risk, but diligence there matters too. Or policing – the recording of a crime or taking down a witness statement; done shoddily it can lead later to the collapse of a case.

Diligence and reliability go together. Reliability isn't very exciting, but it is really important if you are to succeed. Too often, public officials contrast reliability with creativity or imagination. They imply reliability is somehow beneath them; what's needed is an act of brilliance instead. This is self-deception. The opposite of 'diligent' is not 'creative', it is 'shoddy'. The opposite of 'reliable' is not 'brilliant', it is 'unreliable'. And standards, once set, change the lives of citizens only if they are diligently applied. This requires a cultural shift in the professions, as set out in Table 12. In its school system, Singapore comes close to illustrating what this shift looks like.

Atul Gawande, the wonderful writer on largely medical issues, puts it this way:

The Required Cultural Shift

Comfortable	Demanding
• Hit and miss	• Universal high standards
• Uniformity	• Diversity
• Provision	• Choice
• Producers	• Customers/citizens
• Inputs	• Outcomes
• Generalization	• Specificity
• Talk equity	• Deliver equity
• 'Received wisdom'	• Data and best practice
• Regulation	• Incentives
• Haphazard development	• Continuous development
• Demarcation	• Flexibility
• Look up	• Look outwards

Table 12

People underestimate the importance of diligence as a virtue. No doubt this has something to do with how supremely mundane it seems ... There is a flavour of simplistic relentlessness to it. And if it were an individual's primary goal in life, that life would indeed seem narrow and unambitious.

Understood, however, as the prerequisite of great accomplishment, diligence stands as one of the most difficult challenges facing any group of people who take on tasks of risk and consequence.[6]

The point could not be better made. In his later book *The Checklist Manifesto*, Gawande builds on this theme. Mistakes will happen, he argues. Sometimes this will be because we don't know enough; sometimes it will be because we didn't apply what we did in fact already know.

The solution, Gawande goes on to argue, is simple. Experts, including top professionals, need checklists. The checklist, seen from this perspective, is not something reductive or limiting. It is a prompt for diligence and an underpinning which allows professionals to be both reliable and creative. This argument is fundamentally important and undeniable. Checklists underpin professionalism; and the opposite of 'professional' is 'amateur'.

If delivery is to become a science, therefore, we need standards, diligence and checklists, applied with that 'simplistic relentlessness' to which Gawande refers. In short, we need routines.

ROUTINES

In the past few years, there has been an outbreak of excellent books on the subject of popular social psychology. One of them, by Charles Duhigg, examines *The Power of Habit*. He looks at the challenges we all face in breaking bad habits and establishing good ones – neither task is easy, as we all know. Early in the book, a major in the army tells Duhigg how becoming conscious and systematic about habits has changed his life.

> Understanding habits is the most important thing I've learned in the army. It's changed everything about how I see the world. You want to fall asleep fast and wake up feeling good? Pay attention to your night time patterns and what you automatically do when you get up. You want to make running easy? Create triggers to make it a routine . . . My wife and I write out habit plans for our marriage. This is all we talk about in command meetings.[7]

I keep wondering whether the major's marriage is going well – maybe he is taking the idea too far – but, more significantly, I see the connection between the psychology of habits and what I was trying to do in Downing Street in the early days of the Delivery Unit – build good habits and break bad habits.

Later in the book, Duhigg himself makes this connection between personal habits and organizational ones by telling the story of Paul O'Neill. After a career in the government bureaucracy, O'Neill became a successful businessman, and in 1987 was approached to lead Alcoa, America's leading aluminium company. To the surprise of the markets and the workforce he had inherited, he built his entire strategy around a single indicator – and it wasn't sales or profits per unit of aluminium. In fact, it was not a commercial goal at all. It was, in his words, 'to make Alcoa the safest company in America. I intend to go for zero injuries.'[8]

His insight was simple:

> I knew I had to transform Alcoa. But you can't order people to change. That's not how the brain works ... If I could start by disrupting the habits around one thing [safety], it would spread throughout the entire company.[9]

Suffice to say, his strategy worked. Under his leadership, Alcoa's safety record became exemplary and its commercial track record enviable. By changing working habits, he changed effectiveness and motivation, and as a result profits soared.

Interestingly from our point of view, O'Neill had learned about the importance of habit during his seventeen years in government. I wish I had met him back in 2001 when I was establishing the Delivery Unit, because by then I was starting to arrive at exactly the same insight. I had spent four years in the Department for Education, and had seen that where we had built systematic routines to check progress, as with literacy and numeracy, we had been successful; where we had not, as with Education Action Zones (an attempt to improve schools in tough locations), we had failed. So much of government seemed haphazard – another new idea here, a media story there, a crisis in the making on the horizon ... As a result one often simply tried to get through the day. And yet we in the Department for Education were seen by the rest of government as *the* success story, and we had results to show for it: fewer failing schools, more children able to read and write and do sums.

Early in 2001, before the election and the establishment of the Delivery Unit, I was asked to present to the top team at the Home Office, where they were struggling to satisfy Blair that they had a grip on crime. In a meeting at No. 10 that became legendary, the Home Office officials had attempted to convince the prime minister that crime rose in a recession because there was greater poverty and rose in a period of prosperity too because there was more stuff to nick. This had not gone down well.

In my presentation, I see that I was struggling towards the idea of habits and routines but had not quite got there yet; I talked about 'continuous monitoring and problem-solving' and 'maintaining the focus even when it gets boring'. I was almost there, but a conversation with O'Neill would definitely have been enlightening.

In Downing Street they were nowhere near. They were responding to the media, asking for new ideas, summoning ministers haphazardly to explain, and on the lookout, as Blair said in that infamous note that leaked, for 'eye-catching initiatives'.

It was in these circumstances that I started urging Downing Street to change the way its Policy Unit worked so that it pursued implementation. Then, when that seemed too complicated, I proposed instead that they set up a separate delivery unit, which, eventually, is what came to pass. At the heart of this idea, I put routines – routine reporting, routine data collection, routine monitoring, routine problem-solving. Later, when I looked back at what had been happening and what we eventually put in place, I drew a contrast between 'government by spasm' (the old way) and 'government by routine' (the new way). I turned it into a PowerPoint slide (Table 13).

Government by spasm	Government by routine
• Everything matters	• Clear priorities
• Vague aspiration	• Specification of success
• Crisis management	• Routine oversight
• Guesswork	• Data-informed
• Post-hoc evaluation	• Real-time data
• Massaged impressions	• An honest conversation
• Remote and slow	• In touch and rapid
• Present-focused	• Future-focused
• Hyperactivity	• Persistent drive
• Soundbites	• Dialogue
• Announcements	• Change on the ground
✖	✔

Table 13

I've used this slide now on a number of occasions with people from governments all around the world. They 'get it' immediately. The first panel all too often describes their daily experience; the second, they see, would be so much better, if only they could change their bad habits for good ones. The rest of this chapter is about how to do that through establishing routines that work.

> **RULE 33**
> GOVERNMENT BY ROUTINE BEATS GOVERNMENT BY SPASM (it's not even close)

The whole point of routines is that they are dull. Predictable by definition, they are the opposite of a surprise (which we call a break in the routine). As Charles Duhigg points out, routines should become a habit and the whole point about a habit is that you don't have to think about it. 'Boring' might be a problem in many walks of life – such as sport, art or writing – but in government it is quite simply necessary.

There is no shortage of surprises in government – in fact, there are far too many of them. Few presidents or prime ministers leave office complaining that they have been bored. Far from it. Listen to James Callaghan, who had a very tough time: 'It is never a misfortune to be Prime Minister ... it is absolute heaven.'[10] He doesn't sound bored. And then there's Churchill's famous (perhaps apocryphal) answer to a young woman who sat next to him at a dinner shortly after the war: 'But you don't understand, my dear, I loved every minute of it!' Certainly not bored. And countless leaders around the world would say the same.

When I ran the Delivery Unit for Blair, my task could be defined as having responsibility for bringing the dull, the boring and the predictable to the heart of government. This might be why one journalist described a presentation I gave as 'comparable to a lecture from the speaking clock'.[11] Some people might have been offended by such denigration, but for me it was confirmation that I was doing my job, which was, in common parlance, to grind stuff out. Somebody has to if results are to be delivered, especially in a world defined by volatility, uncertainty, complexity and ambiguity.

And here's the secret: you have to find ways to make the dull, the predictable and the boring absolutely riveting, not to journalists, but to the key figures inside government. In what follows, I'll do my best to pull off the same trick for the reader.

Monthly Notes

Years ago, the *Economist* ran an advert that proclaimed 'It's lonely at the top, but at least there's something to read.' There certainly is something to read, above and beyond the *Economist*. Even the most assiduous prime minister, president, governor or minister couldn't possibly read everything presented to him or her. So when, early in my time in No. 10, Jeremy Heywood, the prime minister's private secretary, suggested I wrote a regular monthly note for Tony Blair on each priority area, I wondered how on earth I'd get him to read it. I debated the idea with my team and they were cautious – why write a monthly note, they asked; much better to write a note when there's something to say. I was tempted to agree with them, but that just shows I had not yet fully learned the importance of routines. With Heywood constantly reminding me that monthly notes updating Blair were vital, both to make sure I got noticed and to make sure the prime minister kept paying attention, eventually I insisted. And we began sending them; once a month, a note on progress towards the health targets; the same on crime, on education and on transport. The routine had begun.

Four aspects of the notes were designed to make them interesting. First, it was vital they were well written. They came to me late on a Friday morning and I personally edited them if necessary, to try to give them life. Second, there was the fascination of waiting to see what the next update of the data will reveal, which is why football fans love league tables and why baseball fans are data geeks. We would do the same with the monthly data on health or crime. Once we had a clear, elegant way to present the data, we could simply update it each month – the prime minister would be waiting to see whether the data was going the right way or the wrong way. It wouldn't quite be true to say he was on the edge of his seat, but there was certainly an element of suspense. Third, the iconography of the note – the way it looked – became familiar, so the prime minister could find what he wanted to know rapidly. (As with the newspaper you like, you know your way around it.)

Finally, I wrote a brief covering note of just a paragraph or two, highlighting what I thought were the key points and – always, always – suggesting a solution wherever we identified a problem. Often I would add at the end in bold a question such as 'Do you agree?' Blair could then just say 'Yes' or 'No', but the key from my point of view was that it made it more likely he would read the note.

Similarly, we have designed beautiful charts for the chief minister of Punjab. For him, we also provided monthly updates of what we call 'heatmaps'. These are stunning maps of Punjab and its thirty-six districts: a district that is on-target on the indicators is green; a district way off-target is red, and there are of course the two shades in between. This information is gold dust for the chief minister.

I know he shares the sense of suspense about what the data will say. A 2014 email from him says, 'I'm really glad to know the improvements in Roadmap data; however I would be equally interested to know the trends in enrolment data which I believe is a stepping stone for advancing the reforms . . .' I had to tell him he'd have to wait another week for that; another leader on the edge of his seat.

At the time Jeremy Heywood and I hit upon the monthly note concept, I assumed that we had invented something new – but that was hubris. Long after I had left No. 10 I discovered, reading Christopher Andrew's monumental history of MI5, that its leaders had had almost precisely the same debate in relation to Churchill during the war. As Andrew explains: 'Duff Cooper proposed that the Security Service send the Prime Minister a monthly report of two or three pages.' Given that Churchill had just expressed fascination with the incredible story of Agent ZIGZAG, they were a bit worried he'd get overexcited. Guy Liddell wrote cautiously, 'There are obvious advantages in selling ourselves to the PM, who at the moment knows nothing about our department. On the other hand, he may . . . go off the deep end and want to take action, which will be disastrous to the work in hand.'[12]

They knew their Churchill, but decided to take the risk of a monthly note because, as Sir David Petrie explained, 'It is only fair . . . that the good work of the Service . . . should be brought to the notice of the

Prime Minister.' There is only one thing worse than being noticed, and that is not being noticed.

So their first monthly note was prepared and submitted to Churchill on 26 March 1943. It has to be said it was easier for them to make their notes riveting for the prime minister than it was for me when updating him on the punctuality (or lack of it) of trains. Here is an extract from that first note:

> In all 126 spies have fallen into our hands. Of these, eighteen gave themselves up voluntarily; twenty-four have been found amenable and are now being used as double-cross agents. Twenty-eight have been detained overseas and eight were arrested on the high seas. In addition twelve real, and seven imaginary persons have been foisted upon the enemy as double-cross spies. Thirteen spies have been executed and a fourteenth is under trial.[13]

It may lack graphs and maps, but it has everything else, including data, clarity and telling detail, including the brilliant 'seven imaginary persons' and some real executions.

Churchill added a comment at the bottom of the note: 'Deeply interesting.' An understatement, I think. Certainly Blair never wrote anything quite so complimentary at the bottom of one of our notes.

One minor digression is required here because it is so astonishing. Just as with us, the MI5 leadership were determined to make sure the note was well written. They naturally asked their best writer, who was also handsome and loved by everyone, to draft it. He was Anthony Blunt, who many years later was revealed to have been a Soviet spy. As a consequence, Andrew points out sardonically, 'it is highly probable they [the monthly notes] went to Soviet intelligence as well – and quite possibly to Stalin personally.'[14]

So, the lesson for the science of delivery is that while matching MI5 for sheer riveting detail will probably be impossible, it is hard to beat the value of a good monthly note. It keeps the leader informed and interested, means you know what he or she thinks, and demands the discipline of regularly updating the data.

RULE 34
PREPARE MONTHLY NOTES FOR THE LEADER (and make them 'deeply interesting')

Crucially too, it requires a synthesis of the big picture on a regular basis. The narrative is constantly being updated. This creates a sense of momentum. I told you it was possible to make the dull, the predictable and the boring absolutely riveting. Well, deeply interesting at least.

Routine Meetings or Stocktakes

It would be hard to write two words together more likely to induce a yawn than 'routine meetings'. We have discussed routine already; meetings are the dread of leaders in almost every sphere, and their diaries get crammed full of them. In his witty and poignant account of four years as Labor Secretary in Clinton's cabinet, Robert Reich comments at one point: 'I'm scheduled to the teeth.' He then lists his commitments for that day (2 March 1993), which begins at 6.45 a.m. and finishes at 9.00 p.m., and in between has two conference calls, two media interviews, a speech, a reception, forty-five minutes of 'telephone time' and eleven meetings! 'No one gives me a bath, tastes my food or wipes my bottom – at least not yet. But in all other respects I feel like a goddamn two-year-old.'[15]

Many leaders through the ages have felt similarly overloaded and infantilized. The Audit Commission in Britain once entitled a brilliant report they wrote on the ineffective use of time in local government *We Can't Go On Meeting Like This*.

In this context, when a fan of the science of delivery arrives on the scene suggesting routine meetings, he or she risks being run out of town. As with the routine notes, the trick is to convince the relevant leaders that these routine meetings will be different, that they may even be riveting and actually save time. Such claims will surely be met in the first instance with a sceptical raised eyebrow. The only counter to this is to ensure that the meetings, when they do happen, really are different. What does different look like? Implicitly everybody knows – just ask a group of top people what the characteristics are of the (few) meetings they actually look forward to ... The problem is that meetings like this are the (rare) exception, not the rule.

For the science of delivery to work, the meetings related to it have to have these characteristics. In truth, it's not that difficult. It is simply

Eleven Characteristics of a Good Meeting
• A well-planned agenda with major focus on just one or two items.
• Enough time but not too much, and a clear endpoint.
• The right people in the room, not too many hangers-on and no one who drones on and on.
• Well-chaired, with a clear opening and a strong, action-oriented summing up.
• Good, sharp briefing materials in advance.
• A shared acceptance of any data to be used (so time isn't wasted arguing about the validity of the data).
• A brief opening presentation. (No more than five minutes. Really.) This is in case someone, perhaps a prime minister, hasn't read the briefing.
• A collaborative atmosphere that allows – encourages even – divergent views.
• Live theatre, not over-planned ceremony.
• Genuine deliberation.
• Start and finish on time – or even early.

Table 14

a matter of being conscious of how the meetings should unfold and planning them carefully in advance. It is a question, in other words, of replacing bad habits with good ones.

There are two pitfalls with the planning of a meeting. On the one hand, if there is insufficient planning, all kinds of unsatisfactory consequences can follow – too much time spent on early, unimportant items and then rushing through the items that matter; a rambling, unfocused debate about whether the data is valid or the briefing adequate ... and so on. On the other hand, over-planning can kill a meeting too. The biggest fear most civil servants have about a meeting is not that it will reach a bad decision, but that there might be 'a scene'. They want 'orderly' and 'smooth', and fear surprises and disruptions. As a result, civil servants over-plan, which means they are brilliant at state funerals, but less good at ensuring meetings are genuinely open. Planning for an open, productive meeting paradoxically takes more time and imagination than over-planning does. Hence the emphasis in Table 14 on live theatre, not over-planned ceremony.

The fundamental issue is that the success of a meeting on delivering outcomes requires genuine deliberation. All too often in governments around the world this is what is lacking, and the lack of it can have the direst of consequences.

When I picked up *The Blunders of Our Governments* by Anthony King and Ivor Crewe in a bookshop just off Trafalgar Square, I did so with some trepidation. I knew it was a book about thirty years of blunders in British government and that a significant number of those it focused on were during the Blair years. I knew that the first thing I'd do once I got out of the store would be to look myself up in the index. (Yes, I know what that says about me.) However, given the title of the book, on this occasion I hoped *not* to be in the index, and discovered that that was the case.

Even more valuable than the accounts of the blunders were the lessons King and Crewe drew from their research. Perhaps the most important, and certainly the most relevant to the science of delivery at this point, was what they called a 'deficit of deliberation'. They write:

> 'Deliberation' is not a word one hears very often in connection with British politics – for the good reason that very little deliberation actually takes place. British politicians meet, discuss, debate, manoeuvre, read submissions, read the newspapers, make speeches, answer questions, visit their constituencies, chair meetings and frequently give interviews, but they seldom deliberate.[16]

This sentiment is startlingly similar to how I saw the routine stocktake meetings on delivery under Blair. I didn't use the words, but I think it would be fair to claim that, through the stocktakes, we were addressing the deficit of deliberation which King and Crewe rightly identify.

Helpfully, King and Crewe go on to describe the characteristics of good deliberation.

1. Careful consideration, weighing up.
2. Not being over-hasty, taking one's time.
3. Conferring, and taking counsel.

This reinforces my view of a good stocktake too – that there is a shared evidence base, that the right people are in the room or have been consulted and that, above all, there is an honest conversation (a 'weighing up' in their terms) in which difficult issues aren't avoided and divergent views are welcome.

On the face of it, stocktakes generally would not have met King and Crewe's second rule to take one's time. We were usually in a hurry, and indeed trying consciously to counteract an inbuilt bureaucratic tendency to delay. However, the value of routine stocktakes – not each one, but the regular series – is that you make a provisional decision in each one knowing that you can come back to it in the next. You can decide to try something at one meeting, see whether it works, and refine or not as the case may be, in the next. Sounds obvious, but fundamentally a series of stocktakes focused on achieving a goal becomes a learning process, and once you get that going major blunders are much less likely. Mistakes, on the other hand, will be common, and welcome because they provide an opportunity to learn.

Let me give an example from Punjab. Following the May 2013 election, the chief minister and his party were committed to the introduction of District Education Authorities across Punjab. These would provide a new, elected tier of government responsible for education in each of the thirty-six districts. This was a long-standing party aspiration and, given that Punjab is a province of 100 million people – bigger than most countries – it does not make sense to try to run everything from the centre in Lahore. However, the Education Roadmap, which the chief minister loves, depends on the province keeping hold of certain vital responsibilities – data collection to enable benchmarking of districts, setting overall strategy and targets, insisting on merit-based appointments rather than patronage and, perhaps most important of all, holding district-level leadership to account and being able, in the last resort, to intervene. As we have seen in chapter 3, these are vital ingredients of an Awful to Adequate strategy.

In short, two good ideas – DEAs and the Roadmap – in tension with each other. In the normal course of events, without stocktakes, these two ideas would have been developed separately, moved towards realization independently and collided, causing some kind of crisis, one possible outcome of which would have been the demise of the Roadmap.

With stocktakes, a different course of events was possible. Before the DEA legislation became something more than a gleam in the eye, I raised the potential conflict. The chief minister enjoyed it when I said that just as the British had lost an empire in 'a fit of absence of mind', he risked doing the same with his Roadmap. He also got the point. Then, at successive stocktakes, we refined our collective thinking about how these two ideas might be made consistent with each other, or better still might combine to strengthen our capacity to deliver at every level. Because we had all the right people in the room – the chief minister, chief secretary, chairman of planning and development and finance secretary as well as the schools secretary – all the relevant interests were present and we could have a rounded discussion. We established a small working group to go through the details before the next stocktake, at which point we could further refine our thinking. That, in short, is true deliberation. It did not mean there would not be problems. It did mean there wasn't a crisis. It also meant that there were opportunities we would otherwise not have considered.

There is one other massive advantage of planning a series of stock-takes into the future, and it is so obvious it is easy to miss: each stocktake provides a deadline. It might not be a real-world deadline like the go-live data on President Obama's healthcare website, but a false deadline – one that is a simple construct of the leader's calendar. Nevertheless, it creates a huge opportunity for those responsible for delivery to set deadlines for others to meet. In conversation, Martin O'Malley calls this 'the circle of inevitability'.

My friends and colleagues Katelyn Donnelly and Saad Rizvi, who were the beating heart of my team on the ground during the early days of the Punjab Education Roadmap, couldn't help noticing how, in the week just after a stocktake, the Punjab officials always claimed to be 'busy' and were hard to pin down, whereas in the week before a stocktake those same officials were clamouring for advice and work-ing late to complete tasks in time. Once they saw that the stocktake would be an honest conversation and the chief minister would know whether or not a task had been successfully completed, they realized that the only way to impress him was to actually get things done. Warm words and excuses would no longer get them through a meeting.

Perhaps not quite so visibly, the same thing happened during my time in No. 10, and in every other place where effective routines have been established. After all, it's no more than human instinct, the same instinct which means we revise much more rigorously in the last week before an exam than we did earlier; and that has us rushing to tidy up before mother arrives.

Looking back at my diary, written at the time, it is notable how my accounts of stocktakes focus on the quality of the relationships as much as on the content. This is partly because I knew the formal minutes would capture the content and data, but it is also a key insight into delivery – if the relationships are strained, delivery is much less likely to occur than if relationships are good. Delivery is a soap opera as well as a documentary.

The importance of priorities, data and routines is clear too – otherwise the meetings would have defaulted to the media stories of the day.

Just reading my account of a random week in January 2004 – a week which began with a meeting on Monday morning with Blair and finished with an awayday at Chequers on Friday, at which I was expected to open proceedings, and in between included two stocktakes on Tuesday and Wednesday and a visit to Canada leaving on Wednesday evening and returning in time to get to Chequers on Friday – makes me exhausted, and reminds me of the commitment I made to Blair early on: delivery never sleeps. It also reinforced the fact that that a focused, well-briefed leader makes a big difference.

Sometimes the initiative for routine meetings will come from the political leaders themselves; there are those who know they need order and routine to succeed. One such was President Calvin Coolidge, who succeeded to the office in August 1923 on the unexpected death of Warren Gamaliel Harding. Coolidge rarely makes the experts' lists of the top American presidents, but in his own terms he has a case. He set out to cut the budget and unleash American business, and all the indicators suggest that on those terms he was a tremendous success. Not everyone, of course, agrees with his goals, and soon after his term of office finished America was plunged into depression, but he certainly delivered on his promise. And, as Amity Shlaes makes clear in her excellent biography, routine meetings were absolutely vital to his success.

> The [budget-cutting] meetings took place once a week. He scheduled them at 9.30am on Fridays before the session with the full Cabinet at eleven ... Together, the president and his budget director [Herbert Mayhew Lord] cut, and then cut again ... there was a sense of awe and duty to their meetings.[17]

At one of their early meetings, they decided to send 'a stiff letter to all government departments, warning that they needed to remember to spend less – $300 million less in total'. Soon afterwards, to prove their determination, they agreed to take one-fifth out of the budget of the District of Columbia (which was then controlled by the federal government). They used their routines to look at every detail. Soon enough, civil servants were told that to be issued with a new pencil they would have to return the stub of the old one, to prove they really had used it up. The *Los Angeles Times* summarized the new president's approach in a headline: 'President To Be Own Watchdog'.

Five years later, in the last three months of his presidency (and after his successor Herbert Hoover had been elected), Coolidge was still at it. In December 1928, when he might have been expected to be winding down, incredibly, he had five meetings with Herbert Mayhew Lord, and the following month Lord himself took the opportunity to celebrate the budget surplus: 'The pruning knife fell here, there and everywhere in the grim fight for a balanced budget,' he said.[18] Perhaps not everyone's idea of triumph, but undoubtedly a triumph for relentless focus and the disciplined use of routine meetings. Sometimes, particularly after a period of hyperactivity in government, such as the First World War had been, leaders such as these are perhaps a necessary corrective.

> **RULE 35**
> ROUTINE MEETINGS OR STOCKTAKES CREATE FALSE DEADLINES (and solve problems before they become crises)

REVIEWING THE DELIVERY AGENDA

'Deeply interesting' monthly notes and regular stocktakes, perhaps every quarter, help establish a rhythm and the effective use of time, but periodically something deeper is required. It is necessary to review not just each priority in the delivery programme, but the programme as a whole. Is it broadly on track? Where should overall strategic focus of the president, prime minister or governor and his or her delivery unit be in the next few months? What lessons can be learned from across the programme that could be applied generally to accelerate and deepen progress? What has happened elsewhere in the world that we might learn from?

These are big questions with immense potential to strengthen a government's capacity to deliver, but they are not the sort of questions that will arise in the preparation of a monthly note or a routine stocktake; still less in the kind of weekly meeting Coolidge favoured. For questions such as these, a six-monthly rhythm makes most sense. A year could work, but it is a big chunk of a term of office so adds risk, while anything less than six months doesn't give enough time to do the analysis and learn the lessons. This is a good moment to reinforce a point made in a previous chapter: a major advantage of having a delivery unit or equivalent is that it can prioritize these big, strategic delivery questions as well as the day-to-day driving of progress. The rest of the bureaucracy, whether at the centre of government or in the departments, is unlikely to have the time, inclination or capacity to do so.

Najib Razak, the prime minister of Malaysia, whom we have met before, favours an annual review. He is an ardent fan of the science of delivery and has perfected the art of routine meetings. He has six priorities and sets aside time each Monday to review progress on one of them – so each priority comes round every six weeks. Every week, on a Monday, 9.30 a.m.–12.30 p.m. is delivery time. His head of delivery, Idris Jala, sits in the cabinet and so is able to report regularly there, but once a year the prime minister wants something more substantial. Is the programme really working? And how should it be developed? So he established an International Advisory Committee

(IAC) which meets once a year. Idris Jala explains the benefits: 'We have a view that is inside-out and I really want an outside-in view, a fresh view. [The IAC] usually tell us, this is how other countries do it . . . they give us a lot of pointers on how to make performance better the subsequent year.'[19]

The committee is sent extensive documentation and asked to submit comments in advance, both on progress on each of the priorities and on the overall strategic challenges ahead. (In 2013 all the material came not on paper, but on a beautifully pre-prepared tablet device, demonstrating Malaysia's tech-savvy edge.) The committee involves international experts from the World Bank, for example. It includes me too. I have always submitted comments and suggestions for the future, such as urging independent checks of the data systems and stressing the importance of not letting early success distract the PM and his cabinet from the task ahead.

I haven't always been able to attend the meetings in Kuala Lumpur, but when I did, what I saw was a PM and his delivery unit head willing to give extensive time to listening, learning and thinking, and then strengthening their approach. Obviously there is a public relations benefit to the government of having an international panel express support for the programme – but this is a side benefit and indeed, if the programme wasn't delivering, it would be a risk.

In the Blair administration, we ultimately developed two of these more strategic routines; the first was a six-monthly exercise undertaken within the Delivery Unit, largely by my staff and their counterparts in departments. This led to a comprehensive report to the prime minister on what was going well and what was going less well across the programme. As part of this process, the plans for each priority for the next six months were agreed with departmental heads and then shared with their ministers and with Blair. The lessons from the programme as a whole were drawn out too, and these were shared with the cabinet.

The second routine, which began in July 2002 and became an annual highlight for me (and an hour of torture for the world's media), was my joint appearance with Blair at one of his monthly press conferences. Here I made public my report on where we had got to on delivering the domestic policy priorities. The next two sections look at each of these two routines in turn.

The Assessment Framework and the League Table

It was one of those windows you'd never notice unless you looked for it. Although it was large and gave out onto Parliament Street – just across from No. 10 and the Cenotaph – it was grimy and, if you bothered to peer through the grime, your view of the room would be further inhibited by the heavy, dingy net curtains. We were told these were 'bomb' curtains designed to prevent flying glass in the event of an explosion, and you could tell they would work! Once, 53 Parliament Street had been the offices of Britain's greatest engineer, Isambard Kingdom Brunel.

In the early autumn of 2001, in this meeting room (known as the Westminster Room) behind the grimy window and the unwashed net curtains, a small team from the new Prime Minister's Delivery Unit invented a very beautiful thing. It served the Delivery Unit and the prime minister extraordinarily well for four years, since when it has been sadly neglected, for which I blame myself more than anything. If I had to choose just one technique on which to found a science of delivery, this would be it. We called it (blandly) the Assessment Framework.

This is the problem we were seeking to solve: we knew the data, once it started flowing on each of our goals, would tell us whether we *were* making progress and, once we had trajectories in place, whether we *were* on track. What it wouldn't tell us was whether, ultimately, the goals would be delivered on time and on standard. What a political leader wants to know, more than anything, is not whether things are on track, but whether the ultimate objectives will be delivered at the relevant point in the future. In the Westminster Room we were wrestling with how to predict the future – at least in relation to Blair's delivery agenda. Crucially too, we wanted to be able to compare progress on very different goals – railway performance with crime, maybe: this meant that what we were judging departments on was 'Likelihood of Delivery'.

We arrived at a good-enough version of the Assessment Framework in October 2001 and then unveiled our judgements using it, generating a storm of controversy inside the upper echelons of the civil service. For the first time, someone had sought to benchmark departments' performance – they could see how well they compared with each other. One permanent secretary rang me in a rage; he hadn't been consulted, and what was more, he added, 'Bloody hell! You've even traffic-lighted it!' I knew that if we had consulted him and his colleagues, we would have been prevented from doing it, or at least its cutting edge would have been lost, so I made no apology. I responded by offering a home truth or two about how government functions. Since time immemorial, political leaders have turned to their close advisers and asked, 'How is so-and-so doing?' and the advisers always reply on the basis of whatever they happen to know about so-and-so, which most likely is based on a media report or one of the ugly rumours that circulate all the time in big bureaucracies. So-and-so never finds out what was said, or on what basis he or she was judged. The judgement, however, might have massive consequences for a programme or a career. So I explained to this permanent secretary that at least now he could see what the judgements were and the criteria on which they were based. Bluntly, I said, this was a step forward for evidence-based policy and performance management. And, if he could provide me with different evidence that would show his performance in a better light, I would correct the judgements that the prime minister had seen. He couldn't, of course . . . and over the next few years we became firm friends.

By December 2001, we had revised the Assessment Framework and the process, in part in the light of this angry conversation, and over the next few years we honed it into a powerful and accurate tool of prediction.

At this point, it is important to remember first my predilection, shared with the handful of colleagues who developed the Assessment Framework, for four-point scales; and second that, prior to setting up the Delivery Unit, I had begun to tour Whitehall with a presentation called 'How to Implement Absolutely Anything', which, for me at any rate, was the founding text of 'deliverology'. This presentation established a set of guiding principles for each of the four stages of implementation (Fig. 21).

Four Stages of Implementation

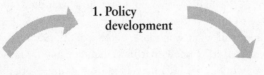

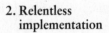

Figure 21

I gave a copy of this to my chief number-cruncher, Tony O'Connor, and a small team of colleagues and asked them to develop the Assessment Framework. The key was to be able to do the benchmarking and the rank-ordering. The work developed from there, ultimately being tested, as we've seen, with the prime minister and top civil servants.

Tony and his colleagues came up with a chart that set out the four things you need to know to assess the Likelihood of Delivery (Fig. 22).

First, the *Degree of Challenge*: how ambitious is the goal? If it's very ambitious, it makes it much harder to deliver. If it is merely an incremental step, it makes it much easier, so we have a four-point scale.

VH – very high challenge

H – high challenge

M – medium challenge

L – low challenge.

Given that we were examining Blair's top priorities and these had been set in the first flush of a spectacular election victory that summer, needless to say most of our agenda was either H or VH.

The PMDU Assessment Framework

Likelihood of delivery

Department ....
PSA Target ....

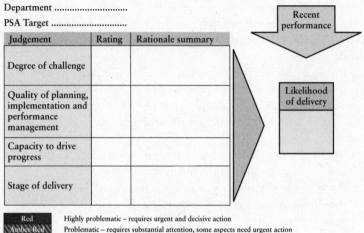

Judgement	Rating	Rationale summary
Degree of challenge		
Quality of planning, implementation and performance management		
Capacity to drive progress		
Stage of delivery		

Red	Highly problematic – requires urgent and decisive action
Amber-Red	Problematic – requires substantial attention, some aspects need urgent action
Amber-Green	Mixed – aspect(s) require substantial attention, some good
Green	Good – requires refinement and systematic implementation

Figure 22

Second, the *Quality of Planning, Implementation and Performance Management*. Once you know the degree of the challenge, you then need to know whether the planning of those responsible is good and actionable; whether they already have experience of implementation and whether they have a process for managing performance across, for example, twenty-three train-operating companies, 300 hospitals or 23,000 schools. The more of these features that were in place, the more you would be willing to believe they could deliver. Another four-point scale here, the familiar one:

- Green
- Amber-Green
- Amber-Red
- Red.

Third, the *Capacity to Drive Progress*. This has some overlap with the second aspect, but is nevertheless quite distinct. This is about every level in the system, all the way out along the delivery chain. Do they know what the priority is, do they even know that it is a priority? Do they have the skills to do what they need to do to make it happen? Do they have the relationships among them to drive the agenda forward or is there conflict between unions and management, local and central government or different departments in the centre whose collaboration is essential? Again, we used the traditional four-point scale.

Finally, in addition to measuring ambition, planning and capacity, you need a measurement of progress in time. You might be making good progress but running out of time to hit the target. So again we arrived at a four-point scale, based on the presentation mentioned above.

1. *Policy development* – you are still working up the policy and approach, and implementation has barely begun.
2. *Early implementation* – you've got going, but it's only the start.
3. *Late implementation* – you are well on the way, but the process is not yet complete.
4. *Irreversible progress* – the target has been met, the structure of the system changed as necessary, and the culture is now such that no one wants to go back to how it was before (this, by the way, is a high bar – see chapter 7).

Having reached a judgement on each of these four aspects, the latest data (see top right of Figure 22) should be reviewed, as a kind of reality check. Several available data sources could be looked at – reported crime, recorded crime and crime surveys, for example. And with all that done, it is possible to reach a combined judgement on Likelihood of Delivery, again using the familiar four-point scale. To guide teams to a decision, the Assessment Framework has a detailed rubric with questions and descriptions of Green and Red.

We never pretended this was wholly scientific – far from it. The framework provided the basis for an informed conversation leading to an informed judgement. The first time, we had this conversation purely among ourselves in the Delivery Unit; thereafter we involved the relevant departmental officials too. They inevitably knew more about their area of responsibility than we did – but we knew more about what characterized successful delivery; the result was a rich and meaningful dialogue which was as important an outcome of the process as the colour judgements. More practically still, in reaching the judgements, it became abundantly clear what needed to be done to advance progress in the six months ahead, so delivery plans could be updated and refined.

To top it all off, we then reached agreement between the department and ourselves about what they needed to do and what we would do to assist and ensure that progress actually occurred. We called it a Joint Action Programme.

Just in case there is any danger that the reader is finding this a little boring, let me say simply this: what I have just described is the engine room of delivering results in government. It will never make the news, and most journalists would have no inclination to understand it, but the crucial (and prosaic) truth is that if this process, or something like it, is working, delivery is highly likely; without it, much less so.

It has to be one of the classic tales of defeat snatched from the jaws of victory. In the autumn of 2013, President Obama faced down the Republicans who had forced him to close government. He refused to buckle to their blackmail; he would not concede on his vaunted health reform, popularly known as Obamacare. After all, he pointed out, Congress had passed Obamacare into law; to allow a congressional minority to overturn it through a blackmail threat would undermine American democracy and future administrations of whatever party. Polls showed that the American people were behind the president, leaving the Tea Party no option but to beat a shame-faced retreat. Political victories don't come much bigger than this. Unfortunately, behind the scenes the president was just becoming aware – and very soon America would become aware too – that his victory would be snatched away, not by a competing issue of major political principle, but by, of all things, a website.

At a meeting in the White House on the evening of 15 October 2013, the president was briefed by a small team of advisers that HealthCare.gov, the online insurance market at the centre of his health reforms, was about to crash. With the deadline for Americans to register under the new legislation just a few months away, the website on which everything depended was riddled with problems. The meeting inevitably and rightly focused on crisis management – what to say to the media and how to fix the problem. The president prepared himself to take responsibility: better to humiliate yourself than be humiliated by others. Jeffrey D. Zients, troubleshooter and former chief performance officer, was put in charge of sorting out the mess. As the story unfolded in a blaze of talk shows, the president's political victory disintegrated. Trust in Obamacare unravelled as his personal promises turned out to be unfulfilled.

Jeffrey D. Zients, an extremely competent operator whom I had met previously and come to admire, made good progress, but the president suffered excruciating months of delay and took a blow to his credibility from which he may never recover. And in spite of Zients's excellent efforts, the website remains, shall we say, suboptimal, and the timetable has slipped. Not just Obamacare, but the Obama presidency had been damaged, perhaps irreparably, by what in this book we would call a 'delivery failure'. The president himself realized this in that fateful meeting on 15 October: 'We created this problem we didn't need to create . . . it's of our own doing, and it's our most important initiative.'[20] As the president understood, it did not need to be like this. The damage was self-inflicted and, with the right disciplines in place – the disciplines of delivery – it could and should have been avoided. After all, the legislation on which Obamacare is based had been approved by Congress and signed into law in 2009, a full four years earlier.

By the spring of 2014, the news was somewhat better for the president. Thanks to Zients's efforts, the website was up and running, registrations were increasing and the debate was about whether enough young, healthy people would register to cover the costs of others. 'The increase in medical enrolments across the country is encouraging but more work is left to do,' said Health Secretary Kathleen Sebelius, shortly before she stood down, in effect carrying the can for, and drawing a line under, the débâcle.

I conclude simply that the catastrophe of the HealthCare.gov website would have been inconceivable if, from 2009 on, the routines set out in this chapter had been applied. How could it have if the president had been receiving and reading monthly notes, if stocktakes had been data-informed and deliberative and if the White House and the department had collaboratively reviewed progress every six months, really getting beneath the surface? The problem would have been identified ahead of time and solved. There might have been delays, but they would have been planned. And some of the earlier grand claims might have been toned down, but how bad would that have been? There would not have been a catastrophe. There may be something close to gridlock in modern Washington, but that is no excuse. As Governor Martin O'Malley put it at a seminar in London in 2014, 'Failure to drive delivery contributes to gridlock, not the other way round.'

Profound, generational reforms such as Obamacare are too import-ant to be left to government by spasm. They depend on government by routine.

If the Obama administration had put the routines in place, not just on Obamacare but across, say, four or five priorities of personal import-ance to the president, they would also have developed the capacity to learn from delivery in one sphere lessons applicable in others. Arne Duncan, for example, has been the most successful education secretary in US history, a point acknowledged across the political divide in Washington. His understated tone, ability to listen and persistent focus on results are exemplary. His team put in place routine processes to drive delivery and, by 2013, the results in states such as Tennessee and Delaware, which were prioritized by Duncan, were coming through. The entire federal system could learn lessons from this approach. In the bowels of the Office of Management and Budget, Shelley Metzen-baum battled away at this kind of thing for four years but, though she would not say so herself, her work never received the priority it deserved and eventually she was tempted away from the administration.

In the Blair administration, once we had completed applying the Assessment Framework to each of the twenty-odd priorities, we were able to benchmark them against each other. In fact, we could rank-order for the prime minister his top twenty priorities on the basis of their Likelihood of Delivery. The result was surely the best one-page summary of a government programme any British

Progress on the PM's Priorities

Dept	July 2004	Degree of challenge	Quality of planning, implementation and performance management	Capacity to drive progress	Stage of delivery	Likelihood of delivery	Rank (out of 21)
			Assessment Criteria			Overall Judgement	
A	PSA1	L	G	G	3	G	= 1
B	PSA2	L	G	AG	2	G	= 1
C	PSA3	H	AG	AG	3	G	3
D	PSA4	H	G	AG	3	AG	4
A	PSA5	VH	G	AG	2	AG	5
B	PSA6	H	AG	AG	3	AG	6
C	PSA7	H	AG	AG	2	AG	= 7
D	PSA8	H	AG	AG	3	AG	= 7
A	PSA9	H	AG	AG	2	AG	= 7
B	PSA10	VH	AG	AG	2	AG	= 10
C	PSA11	VH	AG	AG	2	AG	= 10
D	PSA12	H	AR	AG	3	AG	12
A	PSA13	VH	AR	AG	2	AR	13
B	PSA14	VH	AG	AR	2	AR	= 14
C	PSA15	VH	AG	AR	2	AR	= 14
D	PSA16	VH	AR	AR	2	AR	= 16
A	PSA17	VH	AR	AR	2	AR	= 16
B	PSA18	H	AG	AR	3	R	= 18
C	PSA19	H	AG	AR	2	R	= 18
D	PSA20	VH	AG	AR	3	R	20
A	PSA21	VH	R	R	2	R	21

Table 15

prime minister has ever had. Table 15 shows how it looked in July 2004.

At a glance, the prime minister could see which priorities (PSA = public service agreement target) were on track and which weren't. I could make sure that, in the ensuing six months, effort was focused where it was needed most, on those slabs of Red in the bottom half of the table.

More importantly, this league table (or ranking) would be shown both to the cabinet and to a meeting of permanent secretaries. They could all see what was working and what wasn't. This needed some careful handling in a number of respects. Take the risk of leaks, for a start – had it become public at the time, the league table would have been dynamite, perhaps costing a minister or two their jobs.

Perhaps, too, undermining our approach altogether since, had it leaked, the pressure to massage future judgements would have been substantial. So, at Blair's suggestion, we put the league table up on a PowerPoint screen at these meetings, but we didn't print it out or circulate it.

You must consider the sensitive question of the egos involved, and how those whose responsibilities are a sea of Red will feel and respond. An important point to re-emphasize is that Red is not necessarily a judgement on someone's performance; simply a statement that whatever it is, for whatever reason, is not on track to deliver in future. And you need to prepare people so that they are not humiliated out of the blue in front of their peers. Take the case of the permanent secretary responsible for the priority at the bottom of the league table shown above. I had dinner with him the night before this was presented to all his colleagues, briefed him on the issues and then hammered out with him what action he needed to take so that he could respond positively to my presentation the following day. There is no doubt that a ranking of this kind is a spur to performance, as the evidence in chapter 1 shows. This permanent secretary drove real progress over the next six months so that the priority concerned was no longer bottom of the pile by December.

Perhaps more important than any of the above is the ability to learn generalizable lessons across the agenda. My staff and I used to debate this thoroughly in the run-up to my presentations to cabinet. The idea was to make the lessons sharp, clear and memorable. Here are two examples, one from 2003 and one from a year later.

2003

Lesson 1 – A week may be a long time in politics but five years is unbelievably short.

Lesson 2 – Sustained focus on a small number of priorities is essential.

Lesson 3 – Flogging a system can no longer achieve these goals: reform is the key.

Lesson 4 – Nothing is inevitable: 'rising tides' can be turned.

Lesson 5 – The numbers are important but not enough: citizens have to see and feel the difference and expectations need to be managed.

Lesson 6 – The quality of leadership at every level is decisive.

Lesson 7 – Good system design and management underpin progress.

Lesson 8 – Getting the second step change is difficult and requires precision in tackling variations and promoting best practice.

Lesson 9 – Extraordinary discipline and persistence are required to defeat the cynics.

Lesson 10 – Grinding out increments is a noble cause ... but where progress is slow, it's even more important for people to understand the strategy.

2004

The right mindset	Effective performance management	Bold reform
• 'Guiding coalition' • Shared vision • Ambition • Clear priorities • Ministerial consistency • Urgency • Capacity to learn rapidly • Collaboration across goverment	• Targets • Sharp accountability • Good real-time data • Best-practice transfer • Transparency • Management against trajectory • Capacity to intervene where necessary • Incentives to reward success	• Choice • Personalization • Responsiveness to the community • Contestability • Vibrant supply side • Serious investment • 3-year funding for frontline • Flexible deployment of staff

Table 16

What a delivery unit is able to do through a process such as this is connect the detail to the big picture and the frontline to the centre. We were often accused of being top-down (as anyone working for a prime minister or president is likely to be) and sometimes we were, but more often this missed the point – we were the connection, and the impact was two-way.

Press Conferences

A delivery unit or equivalent is better placed than any other part of the machinery of government to summarize the government's underlying progress towards its goals. In Blair's first term, he and Peter Mandelson had tried to do this by preparing an annual report as a company would do. They failed to get the tone right and the media received it with howls of derision. When Blair asked me to report for the first time in July 2002, it was simply to explain to the media how we approached delivery and to tell a story or two, but in the following years we turned it into a report on progress and found a way to get the tone right. At the insistence of Blair himself and his media people, I was to be deadpan and to make the report as plain-speaking about failures as about successes.

So I'd do my presentation with its beautiful graphs in a monotone. Throughout one of them, the *Sun*'s political correspondent responded to each new graph by muttering, under his breath, 'Bullshit'. (He wasn't aware that the person on his immediate right was Tony O'Connor, who had drawn the graphs.) Once I had finished, Blair would ask the journalists if they had any questions for him or me, and they would respond by asking their usual questions for that night's news and ignore the whole thing. No journalist ever asked me a question. The following morning, I would be mocked in the comment pieces for my dullness, but in fact the strategy worked. The handful of more serious journalists absorbed the messages. In July 2004, Peter Riddell of *The Times* noted that my 'update tends to be ignored by journalists as a slightly tedious ten minutes before they can get on to the red meat of politics', but, he argued, 'The most important words came not from Tony Blair, but from Michael

Barber.' Why? Because I had summarized the situation of the government:

> Last year I said to you that there was demonstrable progress in most areas, but it was not yet irreversible. This year I am more optimistic. There is widespread and significant progress which is becoming irreversible.[21]

> If the routines are in place, the political leader can move from crucial detail to big picture, from nuts and bolts to overall design, from individual to nation because he or she, or at least the head of delivery, really knows what's happening now.

> **RULE 36**
> A FULL-SCALE REVIEW OF THE PROGRAMME AT LEAST ONCE A YEAR PROVIDES DEEP LEARNING (which can be acted on immediately)

There is another walk in the Lake District that I love, this one less rugged, less dramatic and less hard work, not least because Rossett Gill is not involved. Even so, it is achingly beautiful and it has a personal connection because it involves crossing a wooded hillside once owned by my great-grandfather. His son, my grandfather, built a log summerhouse up there some time in the early twentieth century. It was still there when I was a boy, with its stained-glass windows, wooden benches and large jugs with which we fetched water from the stream below. Once, I'm told, my grandfather was there looking, as he always did, for the distinctive summits of Langdale Pikes in the distance, only to discover that, in the year since he had been there last, the view had been obscured by a far-off pine tree which had inconsiderately grown taller. He went striding off through the wood with an axe and, after a good walk, chopped down a single tree before returning to the summerhouse. Miraculously, the view was now clear, and his beloved Langdale Pikes stood out gloriously against the sky. How had he known so precisely which tree to cut down? Here was someone who could connect detail to big picture and back again. That is what delivery routines make possible for a political leader.

You become able to see both the wood and the individual trees – and the view beyond.

The next chapter examines how to solve problems as they arise. Notwithstanding my grandfather, you cannot take an axe to everything.

RULE 37
UNDERSTAND THE WOOD AND THE TREES (and the view beyond)

6

Problem-solving

In my diary I noted:

> Blair rang me at 9.00am on Saturday morning. Fortunately I'd been up for 10 minutes by then. He was worrying away about illegal asylum applications. I gave him the very bad news about the figures in this week's report – a big jump in applications due to the 'closing down sale' before the tougher benefits arrangements came in. He asked me to check the figures, but also suggested we went into 'Cobra' [Cabinet Office Briefing Room where emergencies are handled] mode on the question. I consulted Jeremy [Heywood] and then rang Blair back.

On the Monday, Blair cleared his diary for the entire morning and proceeded to spend the next five hours – yes five – going through the asylum process forensically, finding out how it worked, what had happened, what was being put in place and what more could be done. This was a prime minister trying to understand in great detail what precisely was going on. I realized at the time that between his phone call to me on Saturday at 9.00 a.m. right over the weekend he had been focusing on asylum. He had even read the 1951 UN Convention Relating to the Status of Refugees.

This weekend in February 2003 reveals a lot about how a politician at the height of his powers – a few weeks before the war in Iraq began, as it happens – goes about solving a very big problem on the brink of becoming a crisis. Blair demonstrated mastery of the key elements:
* *Focus*: he had been working on it the entire weekend.
* *Prioritization*: he cleared his diary.
* *Data*: he asked me to check the figures.

- *Details*: he wanted to be sure himself that he understood exactly how the process worked and spent five precious hours on it.
- *Confronting facts*: I gave him 'the very bad news' and he didn't rant, he got to work.

And he suggested the COBRA process, used in times of crisis, because he had seen how it galvanized the entire system and he knew how it worked.

In fact, the asylum issue had not yet become a national crisis, but the prime minister treated it as a crisis to prevent it from becoming one. He knew the steady stream of illegal asylum seekers was politically damaging; more fundamentally, he knew that if the asylum system lacked legitimacy, if it was easier to get into the country by breaking the rules than by following them, then his vision of a diverse, open, modern Britain was threatened.

The following day, Blair summoned to COBRA all the ministers from departments with influence on the asylum issue including, crucially, the Home Office, which oversaw immigration policy, and the Foreign Office, which issued visas. Previous meetings of this group had been chaotic, tense and acrimonious, but this one wasn't. Instead, there was a hugely authoritative performance from the prime minister. At the end of the meeting, I suggested we convene again in two weeks' time so as to keep the pressure on.

Because the leader had done his detailed homework, he could dominate the meeting and give instructions. Because he had a delivery unit, he knew the agreed actions would be followed up. Because by then we knew the importance of routines, we set a (false) deadline of two weeks for the actions to be taken. The moral is that dealing with a major problem often just requires the science of delivery to be applied with greater intensity. Deliverology on steroids, perhaps.

By 2003, in No. 10 we had tried to bring clarity to the management of problems. We had arrived at what we described as four levels of intensity. The first level was straightforward: we called it the 'timely nudge'. We in the Delivery Unit would notice a problem – maybe this month's data is off trajectory, or perhaps there's a problem in one locality that we've visited. Or maybe we had doubts about the effectiveness of a particular official. Usual civil service practice in such circumstances would be to shrug, assume it's nothing serious and wait and see. Delivery Unit obsession suggested an alternative – could we dig a little deeper into the data? What had caused the deviation? If one locality was off track, perhaps we should check another couple to see whether there was a pattern. It may be true that one swallow doesn't make a summer, but what about two or three? In each or any of these circumstances, we would raise the issue with the relevant department, probably with a top civil servant just to make sure they were aware and, incidentally, knew we were watching.

Here's an example from Punjab, Pakistan. It is all too common in the Pakistan civil service for officials to be appointed and then moved on within months. People can be transferred for all kinds of reasons – for being corrupt, for being honest; for being effective, for being hopeless; for being well-connected or for not being well-connected enough. The result is that it becomes impossible to achieve any kind of consistency in strategy or implementation, and therefore little or no progress is made. In 2011, for the education reform in Punjab, the chief minister put a stop to the revolving door. He insisted all officials would be appointed on merit and that, subject to performance, they would stay in post for two to three years. It took a while for the new norm to be established, but once it was, the effect on performance was dramatic. At last, basic management was in place and the system could learn, refine and improve.

After the election of 2013, a new challenge arose, however, because the new prime minister of Pakistan, brother of the chief minister of Punjab, inevitably needed good new officials in Islamabad and just as inevitably turned to Punjab, the country's best-run province. In February 2014, with an excellent new post-election team of officials in place to oversee the education reform, the Secretary – Schools heard that two of them were to be transferred to federal government. He contacted me, I emailed the chief minister, the transfers were blocked. That is a typical timely nudge.

The second level of intensity occurs where a problem is significantly affecting delivery but the cause and solution are not obvious. Perhaps performance is plateauing or dipping, perhaps one part of the country is underperforming and no one is quite sure why. In a situation such as this, again the tendency in bureaucracies is to wait and see and hope it gets better, just as football managers sometimes hope a player will run off an injury. This might work occasionally, but more often than not it is an excuse for avoiding action – and the hard work entailed – as a result of which the problem is likely to get worse. In the year 2000, we in the Department for Education intervened in the Education Authority in Liverpool. In spite of huge hostility in the city to intervention from London, we threatened the use of our power to contract out the city's deeply ineffective Education Authority. The chief executive of the city, David Henshaw, acted with vigour and commitment; new leadership of the Education Authority was put in place; the entire staff was moved to bright, modern offices; and a radical improvement plan was put in place. I made six visits to the city in the course of the next few months to persuade headteachers and teachers that this was not an attack on them, but a matter of ensuring that they received the support they deserved from the city and the children got the education they needed to succeed in the modern world. It worked: the next few years saw real progress.

A few months later, a report revealed that Bristol had similar problems. This time the leaders of the city argued that the report was harsh, that they were making progress behind the scenes and that all that was needed was an advisory group to oversee progress. I was tired after four years of relentless reform and didn't have time for visits to Bristol on top of those I was already making to Liverpool (and Leeds) and so decided to give the city the benefit of the doubt. Big mistake. Bristol's education system continued to underperform for another decade.

That was when I invented for myself the rule, 'If you are about to give someone the benefit of the doubt, why are you so doubtful?' In short, with a Level 2 problem, if in doubt, act. And act with rigour. Investigate the cause of the problem – we'll come to means of doing so later in this chapter – and search for solutions. Look at what worked elsewhere. Create the circumstances in which those responsible see the benefit of being open about the problems and imaginative about solutions. Don't fall for the oldest excuse in the book (as I did with Bristol): 'We're already doing it.'

Also, if at first you can't see the cause of the problem, don't assume there isn't one – after all it was the fact that the data was off-track that prompted you to act in the first place. Look beneath the surface. In his poetic book *The Old Ways* Robert Macfarlane gives a perfect example when he goes to sea in the Western Isles with an experienced sea captain.

> I was realising that Ian had two simultaneous states on the water. One was quietly and simply joyful to be at sea. The other . . . was analytical: his mind gathering data from sources and of types that I barely knew existed; from subtleties of wind, wave and waymark, from smells, from what he had called in a poem, 'the bounce of light from incidental land' and the 'elaborate counter-physics' of tidal water . . . 'You need to look for disturbances to the expected,' he told me, 'be alert to unforeseen interactions.'[1]

Level 2 problem-solving involves expertise, insight and clarity; perhaps a team combining knowledge of the relevant frontline, expertise in the relevant areas and the leadership of a persistent problem-solver who does not accept superficial answers or glib assertions that 'it'll be all right on the night'. We called Level 2 Standard Problem-solving.

Level 3 problems are similar to Level 2 but more complex, less amenable to the normal problem-solving techniques and reflect more severe challenges to delivery. In public systems they often also involve significant political complications – differences of view between leading political players in the government, for example, or maybe the issue is at the heart of political confrontation between parties, which inevitably brings with it greater media scrutiny or intrusion, making it much harder to admit failure; leaders clam up, troublemakers leak, the storm is whipped up.

With a problem at Level 3 – Intensive Problem-solving – therefore, what is needed is similar to Level 2, but it will also require greater political and leadership input from a trusted minister, for instance, and from whoever leads on delivery. And it may need either a longer time period or greater intensity. What is unlikely to work is the standard bureaucratic solution: the establishment of a 'high-level' working group or committee that meets occasionally and, whatever the intention, allows things to drift between meetings.

Level 4 is Crisis Management. Delivery is seriously threatened, the public is screaming with frustration and the newspaper headlines are, from the government's point of view, a horror story. In my time in the Delivery Unit we used this approach twice, once with street crime in early 2002 and again a year later in relation to illegal asylum seekers (the story with which this chapter begins). After that, with the Delivery Unit in full stride and on top of the data, we avoided these major crises because we saw them coming and could resolve problems using Levels 1 to 3.

Crises will always beset governments, and understanding how to manage them is a vital skill. In the winter of 2013–14, the British government found itself almost overwhelmed by a series of storms off the Atlantic – wind brought down trees and rain caused the rivers to flood, especially across southern England. At first, quite understandably, the government assumed that the storms would die away after a week or so, or a month . . . but when they kept on coming every few days for three months, the level of intensity rapidly shifted from Level 2 to Level 3 to Level 4. As a detached observer (living under the path of the Atlantic storms), I thought the government and the relevant department (the Environment Agency) were handling the situation pretty well while it was at Level 3. When it shifted to Level 4, public frustration understandably went up a gear and headlines reflected that the government was too slow to react and suddenly sounded complacent. From that moment on, the government was chasing the game. This illustrates a key issue: when a crisis reaches Level 4, what you say matters as much as what you do. Much better to overreact than to underestimate; much better to sound sympathetic and decisive than to defend a record, however good.

Overreact yes, but that does not mean panic, because panic makes good judgement less likely. Listen to Mark Cavendish, the great cyclist:

> A sprint isn't a chaos bomb exploding in your sightline, it's not bedlam on fast forward – it's a multiplication of problems to be solved quickly . . . but at the same time rationally . . . I generally have more energy and move faster than anyone else because I am staying calm and clinical.[2]

Worse still in a crisis is any attempt to pass the buck. In November 2013, following Typhoon Haiyan, one of the most devastating weather events ever known, President Benigno Aquino of the Philippines, who until then had an excellent track record and good ratings with the public, sought to pass the buck for the ponderous response to the crisis on to the local authorities. There was a tangled web of family and party politics behind this, but it made him look unsympathetic and defensive, and undermined his credibility. Soon, other problems, such as corruption among some of his cabinet colleagues, began to pile up, and he was under pressure. There is a reason why one crisis often seems to be followed by another. It is simply this: while things are going well, much else is forgiven; once you are on the run, the public and the media are on the lookout for other blunders or sins. Trust is broken and a downward spiral becomes a distinct possibility. All the more reason to ensure an effective response when faced with a Level 4 problem.

By contrast, Shahbaz Sharif handled a major outbreak of dengue fever in Punjab in 2011 excellently. He held daily meetings at the crack of dawn with all the relevant officials. They hated it – they told me so – but not only did it ensure that Shahbaz Sharif looked in charge – telling the story – it ensured much more rapid action than would otherwise have been the case. The innovative Punjab Information Technology Board mapped each case of dengue fever, which enabled the government to target its response more effectively, and to identify and deal with the specific pools of stagnant water in which the dengue mosquitoes were breeding. A massive publicity campaign took place in parallel – both telling a story of a government in charge and increasing the effectiveness of the action against the outbreak.

Yes, there was some duplication of effort. Yes, there was some loss of impact elsewhere (including for a month or so on the Education Roadmap) and yes, maybe more resource was thrown at the problem than strictly necessary ... but that is with hindsight. With a Level 4 problem, efficiency is rightly sacrificed for effectiveness. Many lives were saved – by definition, you can't count them – and the government's credibility was unscathed, perhaps even enhanced. The contrast a couple of years later when a similar outbreak in another

Levels of Intensity

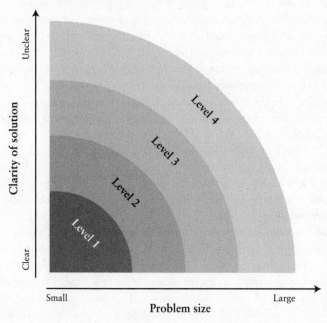

Figure 23

province, Khyber Pakhtunkhwa, caught an inexperienced government unawares was stark. There, the epidemic got out of hand, and for the new government the honeymoon period came to an abrupt end.

Figure 23 illustrates a simple way to think about the four levels of intensity. Over time, if you become effective at Levels 1 to 3, you won't need Level 4, except for those crises known as Acts of God – which you cannot predict but still have to deal with.

RULE 38
CATEGORIZE PROBLEMS BY THEIR INTENSITY (and act accordingly)

*

Shortly after completion of the Trans-Siberian Railway, Russia found itself at war with Japan. There was a problem for the Russians. As Christian Wolmar explains in his excellent history of the great railway, it ran uninterrupted from Moscow to Irkutsk, close to Lake Baikal, one of the world's largest, deepest lakes. And beyond Lake Baikal it ran uninterrupted through Manchuria to Port Arthur or Vladivostok. In between, though, everything carried on the railway had had to be detrained and taken across the mighty lake in a steamer, the SS *Baikal*, and a couple of its sister ships. This created a significant challenge in peacetime; in war, with the mass of men and matériel headed for Port Arthur, the problem greatly intensified.

Winter made things worse. Lake Baikal freezes solid in January and doesn't unfreeze again until April or May. Unfortunately for the Russians – perhaps no accident, given Japanese competence – the war began in February 1904.

They tried to run a railway across the ice, but early on a locomotive fell through it and sank. After that they had to rely on horses and carts. The result was chaos. The men and supplies rushed to Siberia from Moscow piled up on the shores of Lake Baikal. Thousands of soldiers kicked their heels while cases and bales of weapons, uniforms and the other essential supplies stood uselessly on the station platforms in Irkutsk and on the lakeside. Crossing the lake in the other direction were the inevitable refugees fleeing the conflict, bringing with them hunger and disease.

A year later, the Russians found themselves facing a calamitous defeat, which in turn stoked revolution. There was no single reason for this defeat, but the logistical challenge of the immensely long supply lines and the bottleneck at Lake Baikal were without doubt major contributors.

The lesson of Lake Baikal for the science of delivery is to be forensic about logistical issues. They may seem dull in the grand scheme of things, but they make all the difference. There is a wider point too. In the first section of this chapter, we categorized problems by their severity and the response by its intensity. In this section, the intention is to categorize problems by their nature because the nature of the problem will determine the approach to problem-solving.

Given the number of problems and crises governments face, you might think that they would by now have become expert in knowing how to respond. After all, when things go horribly wrong there are often inquiries designed to ensure that whatever it is 'never happens again'. I always shudder when I hear that commitment, because while an identical problem is extremely unlikely, there is a high chance that a related problem will recur and the 'never again' commitment will come home to roost. Moreover, in my experience government bureaucracies are not terribly good at learning. Collective memory is selective and haphazard, and systematic knowledge management usually absent altogether. Furthermore, there is almost no learning across departmental boundaries, so the chances of a lesson learned, say, in the health department being applied to a similar situation in education are very low indeed.

The result is that mistakes are repeated, and each problem or crisis is responded to as if it is something entirely new. In the slow-moving years of the early and mid-twentieth century, the consequences were less severe, partly because the pace of change was slower and government activity was less, and partly because senior civil servants tended to stay in place longer and thus had their experience to draw on. The first head of MI5, Sir Vernon Kell, held the post for over thirty years. When R. A. Butler became education minister in 1941, aged thirty-eight, almost all of the top civil servants in his department had been there since he himself had been a schoolboy.

At the moment, governments around the world too often fail to learn from their mistakes – simply because their bureaucracies are not set up to do so. Indeed, the instinctive reaction of a bureaucracy to a problem or a crisis is to become more cautious, more risk-averse. Ironically, in an era when change is as rapid as it has become in the early twenty-first century, this reaction ultimately adds to the risk of failure rather than reduces it.

A delivery unit or the equivalent can step into this void and make a significant contribution. After all, the whole point of a delivery unit is to learn what works in delivery and then apply those lessons systematically to challenges across the government's various delivery priorities. To give an example, once the Department of Health really got going on reducing wait times in Accident & Emergency departments, they set up

Type of Problem

Characteristic	Symptoms	Do	Don't	Message
Policy design failure	• Overenthusiastic small group • Reaction to media storm • Friendly critics are losing faith • Poor data	• Cut your losses • Radically redesign if required	• Persist in spite of the evidence • Take it personally	• We need a rethink • Yes, it's embarrassing, but politics is about learning
Policy implementation failure	• You never come out of the implementation dip • People start telling you that it's not a good idea after all	• Review leadership, system and delivery chain • A priority review	• Give the benefit of the doubt • Abandon the policy	• We're learning the lessons and applying them • Yes, there are problems, but we're onto them
Logistical	• Bottlenecks • Pile-ups	• Learn process re-engineering • Delivery chain analysis	• Abandon the policy • Buy off interest groups who are screaming	• Demand is higher than we expected, which is good news • We're ironing out the problems
Bureaucratic conflict	• Briefings and counter-briefings • Confusion at the frontline	• Put someone of authority in charge • Remove bureaucratic game players • Remember the mission	• Assume it will just get better • Simply take sides	• The mission is clear; it's taking time for the bureaucracy to catch up
Leadership failure	• Criticism of leadership from enthusiasts • Defensiveness from the leadership	• Change of leadership	• Complain about the leadership without acting	• The issue needs a fresh pair of eyes • Implementation is a new phase and requires new leadership
An 'epidemic'	• Rapid increase in a problem • It's a fashion	• Treat it as an epidemic, not a remorseless rise • Address symptoms and cure	• Watch it get out of control	• We are taking charge, and the public can help by x, y and z
A resistance problem	• One or more stakeholders dig in in defence of the status quo • They issue threats and make it a trial of strength	• Stick with the mission/moral high ground • Build public support • Avoid implementation errors • Make concessions on symbols, not substance	• Compromise at the first whiff of grapeshot • Believe the amount of noise represents the quality of the argument	• This is the right thing to do and we will not be deterred • We never said this was going to be easy
An Act of God	• Obvious – weather, earthquake, etc.	• Take charge • Go to the problem • Overreact rather than underreact • Sympathize	• Start allocating blame during the crisis • Sound complacent	• Our first responsibility is to those affected • We can address the immediate challenges • We will come to the lessons we can learn later

Table 17

a 'war room' which examined the weekly data promptly, learned the lessons from it and followed up immediately with those A&E departments that appeared to have underperformed the previous week. The effect, as with the New York City Police Department and Compstat, was a significant improvement in performance. From a delivery perspective, we saw this as a model of best practice which we then recommended to the Home Office in dealing with its multiple challenges, and to the education department in dealing with truancy. In short, we were becoming a centre of expertise in delivery rather than policy.

It therefore makes sense to try to categorize problems by their nature so that systems can improve at diagnosis and learn systematically what the options are for solving different types of problem. Table 17 illustrates, as a start, what could be done. It is just a sketch, but as Nassim Nicholas Taleb's 'black swan' argument makes clear, unexpected events of one sort or another will recur. How much more effectively could government work if it was systematic in identifying the type of problem and the intensity of the response required?

Of course, any given problem may involve a number of these characteristics – for instance, poor leadership and poor implementation are likely to go together. Using real examples, here are some considerations about how to respond.

> **RULE 39**
> DIAGNOSE PROBLEMS
> PRECISELY (and
> act accordingly)

Cut your losses if you can

The well-known saying 'When you're in a hole, stop digging' has a point, and not just when your apology for an insult simply exacerbates it. In government, while a determination to honour commitments and follow through on delivery is rightly highly valued, there are times when simply cutting your losses, apologizing and then abandoning whatever it is, is the best thing to do. And it takes significant courage because accusations of pusillanimity or incompetence are almost inevitable.

The London Olympics of 2012 were recognized the world over as an unqualified success. Even in cynical, muddling-through Britain,

83 per cent of the population thought they were a success, and just 2 per cent a failure – remarkable figures by any standards. My own recollection is that the period of the Games was the only time when, for several weeks even London cab drivers, who had consistently moaned about it for the previous year, suspended their cynicism. Bill Bryson memorably said that the British are the only people in the world who, when asked 'How are you?', reply 'Mustn't grumble.' For those glorious weeks, no one grumbled.

Such was the triumph, that a series of disasters not many years before was forgotten. London had won the right to host the 2005 World Athletics Championships, but we were so far behind with building a stadium in 2003 that disaster was looming. Tessa Jowell, the new Secretary of State for Culture, Media and Sport, inherited responsibility for the World Athletics Championships from her predecessors and when, in a meeting with the officials responsible, no one could tell her who was in charge, decided to cut her losses. Embarrassing? Yes, absolutely. Better than a fiasco at the Championships themselves – or pulling out just before? You bet. Not only did that searing experience help Tessa Jowell become the minister for the Olympics and play a leading part in delivering those spectacular Games, but if she hadn't abandoned the flawed plans for the 2005 World Athletics Championships, the 2012 London Olympics would probably never have happened. As Churchill said, 'I have never developed indigestion from eating my words.'

Remember Relationships

'*Kto vinovat?*' One of the first phrases I learned in my (largely failed) attempt to master Russian. It means 'Who's to blame?' The other phrase I learned at the time was '*Sto delat?*', Lenin's favourite question, 'What is to be done?', except that in Russian it would be better translated – accompanied by a shrug – as 'What can you do?' One Russian friend went so far as to say that if I mastered these two questions it would be enough to get me through most conversations with government. Hello, please and thank you would do the rest.

The more you think about it, the more you realize my friend has a point – and not just in Russia. When there is a problem in government, and still more so when there is a crisis, these are indeed the only two questions that matter. The problem is that they get asked in the wrong order. As soon as a problem becomes apparent in government, both politicians and bureaucrats reach for 'Who's to blame?' Some try to vanish, some begin wiping their fingerprints from the crime scene, and others start pointing fingers. The effect is corrosive; as everyone tries to mind their own back while burying a knife in someone else's, it becomes almost impossible to solve the problem. Meanwhile, more often than not, the media is screaming that 'heads should roll', adding to the tension. For the public, though, while 'Who's to blame?' is clearly of interest, 'What is to be done?' is both more urgent and more important. Jim Collins puts it succinctly: 'Conduct autopsies without blame.'[3]

From our Delivery Unit perspective, we sought always to answer 'What is to be done?' first, and allocate blame – if it needed to be allocated – later. For this to happen, the relationships inside government have to be constructed so that the relevant people have an incentive to be plain-speaking and to take responsibility. No yelling. No threats. No blame (at this stage). Instead, thoughtful questioning, a focus on the facts, a sifting of myth from reality and a determination to confront the brutal reality. In the PMDU, we learned from Benjamin Zander, the great conductor, to respond to a blunder or reports of failure with the phrase 'How fascinating!' That way, we could get people to talk openly about the causes of the problems as well as the symptoms. Crucially, we could persuade them that there was a problem and it needed fixing. Our next line was simple: 'We're not going away until it's fixed.' Once people realized we meant it, we could establish a collective focus on solving the problem, whatever it was.

Sometimes you can supplement the evidence that comes from the key officials with other sources. At any given moment when implementation of a major change is in progress, there will be people complaining about it. The question is, how do you know when this standard rumble of complaint is being exceeded? And when it is, how do you separate out the signal from the noise? If you have time, you can do surveys or investigations. If you don't, though, one crude but effective means is to ensure you have in place a network of people at the frontline – such as headteachers, GPs or police officers – whom you know well enough to be sure they will tell you what they think rather than what you'd like to hear. A headteacher from Cumbria stormed out in the middle of one of my speeches twice in six months. When I called him after the second time – my assistant had gathered his name badge from him – he was impressed (once he'd got over the shock) and told me what he really thought. People such as this are gold dust in a crisis.

At the government end you have to have leaders who are willing to listen too. Again, a delivery unit can help make the connection between the frontline and the leader. In the weeks immediately before the 1917 February Revolution in Russia, Tsar Nicholas II was out of Petrograd at one of his palaces when Rodzianko, the head of the Duma (the Russian Parliament), sent messages to him warning that the trouble on the streets of the capital was getting out of hand. Nicholas dismissed them in his diary: 'More rubbish from that fat slob, Rodzianko.' If you don't listen, you won't hear the noise or the signal.

The Tools of the Trade

In a crisis – Level 4 – you have to act fast and drive hard. At Level 2 or Level 3, you may have more time to analyse the problem. What you don't have time for, ever, is a major inquiry or the commissioning of an independent review. It is not that these are never worthwhile for other purposes – of course they are – but they are not fast enough to provide solutions in anything like real time.

We developed tools of analysis which helped us, and the relevant government departments, to understand rapidly and effectively the nature of the problem that confronted us. In fact, in the case of both street crime and illegal asylum, the two Level 4 problems we faced, we had applied these tools in the preceding weeks – before a serious problem had become a crisis – and as a result, when the crisis culminated we were able to both explain the problem and suggest practical solutions. The most important tool was the Priority Review, which incorporated another, the Delivery Chain Analysis.

My colleague and friend Richard Page-Jones, a distinguished

former school inspector, played the leading role in the invention of the Priority Review. It is a rapid analysis of the state of delivery in a high-priority aspect of the government agenda, with a firm focus on identifying action that needs to be taken. It can be done in a month from start to finish and results in a short report to the prime minister and relevant ministers. Once we decided to do one, we would put together a team of four or five people from the Delivery Unit and the relevant department. We would add an acknowledged expert in the field and one or two trusted people from the frontline of the relevant service. For the next month, this review would be, if not their full-time role, then most definitely a major part of their work; not one of those committees that meet monthly and, in between, drift.

In the first week, the team would pull together all the relevant data on the issue, with the assistance of our statisticians, and then generate some hypotheses about the state of play. As a result, they would have provisional answers to questions such as: Are we on track to deliver the goals? If not, how far off track are we? What are the causes of this problem? And how might it be fixed?

In the same period of time, the team would decide on field visits and set them up. Thus, by weeks three and four, they were ready to get out to the frontline. In effect, what they did, starting at the frontline and working back, was to interview people at every level in the delivery chain – this is the Delivery Chain Analysis – and ask the same set of questions: What is working? What isn't? How strong are the links in the delivery chain? What could be done to improve performance? And finally (always motivational), what advice do you have for the prime minister? The team would promise to pass advice on.

By asking these questions at each level, the team rapidly gained insight into where the problems were and whether they were logistical or human. A key twist that clinched the effectiveness of the process is that they would carry it out in two separate locations, one where the data was on the whole good and you could test out solutions, and one where the data was poor and you could accurately diagnose the problems. By the end of week three or four, the team would therefore have tested its hypotheses from week one and refined its understanding of what the problem was and how it could be solved. That just left the preparation of a brief, compelling report, usually in PowerPoint, with some killer charts and clear recommendations. Again and again, these Priority Reviews proved their worth. So much so, that after a while instead of applying them only when we had a problem, we applied them routinely, even where the data looked promising. The result was that we anticipated and avoided serious problems and therefore moved from cure to prevention.

The biggest challenge in most cases was not carrying out the review, but persuading the relevant officials at the outset that it would be a good use of their time, given that they were busy already, albeit sometimes responding haphazardly to the problems the review would enable them to solve. The other reason they had for resisting the idea was less honourable, but understandable nevertheless – they were worried about what they might discover out at the frontline. Once we had their commitment, though, they almost always found the process genuinely riveting. It had pace, energy and insight. Above all, once it was done they could do their jobs better.

Any government in the world can do this with virtually any problem. The secret lies in the urgency and the positive can-do tone. Idris Jala and his Pemandu colleagues in Malaysia invented a variation on Delivery Chain Analysis called, memorably, the Putrajaya Inquisition. Putrajaya is Malaysia's striking Islamic capital in the jungle, not far from Kuala Lumpur. When Pemandu identifies an official or group of officials who are the block to progress in the delivery chain, it issues those officials with an invitation to come and see the prime minister in Putrajaya about three weeks hence. Miraculously, by the time the officials arrive for the meetings, the blockage has been unblocked, the problem solved. This leaves the prime minister with the simple task of thanking them for resolving things.

The Value of a Crisis

'Why is it that when we have a real crisis ... we get the job done?' Blair to me on 11 March 2002. Good question. The answer is that in a real crisis, solving the problem is prioritized and everything else on the agenda takes a back seat for a while; if money is required, it is found; above all, the normal constraints of the day-to-day are lifted.

As Blair discovered, the military in particular are very good in a crisis. Alastair Campbell once exclaimed, 'The only people who deliver in this country are the spies and the soldiers.' The military are pre-eminent in a crisis because that is what they are trained to be. Sir Kevin Tebbit was the permanent secretary at the Ministry of Defence from 1998 to 2005. Though a civil servant through and through, Sir Kevin had that upright military bearing and clipped, lucid way of explaining things that you might expect to find in a top army officer. In his role, he had more opportunities than he might have wanted to see the military handle a crisis, including wars in Sierra Leone, Kosovo, Afghanistan and Iraq, as well as civil emergencies such as the fuel crisis of 2000 and the outbreak of foot-and-mouth disease in Britain's cattle in 2001.

Once asked to take something on, he explained when I interviewed him, the military just get on with it. They may not even be conscious of how they go about it, it's just what they do. 'What you see as a detached observer,' he continued, 'are clear lessons in how to handle a crisis.' Watching them, Tebbit identified four key factors.

1. Preparation and improvisation

The military combine the boring detail of routines, preparation, training and drill – everything from square-bashing to table-top planning – with mission commands; officers are trained to extemporize within their delegated area of responsibility so they can act promptly. In other words, the military don't choose between routine and improvisation. They do both (as Nelson taught them long ago).

2. The Red Team

Drawing on an idea which originated in the US, for each mission British military commanders establish a Red Team, a small group whose job it is to criticize the way the mission is being run, to try to identify flaws in the planning and action and to identify potential risks or circumstances where the mission might go wrong. In short, they are authorized to be frank, blunt and critical. Dissent and critique are legitimized and incentivized. This makes groupthink, identified by

Anthony King and Ivor Crewe as a major cause of blunders in government, much less likely.

3. Battle rhythm

The military, says Tebbit, start with the assumption that they will dominate the crisis and solve the problems once they establish a battle rhythm. Every morning and evening promptly at a fixed time, all the relevant military players – logistics, intelligence and the battle commanders as well as the Red Team – assemble to assess the state of play and make decisions about what to do next. This establishes a rhythm (or routine) of review, decision-making and action which drives progress and, if done well, means that problems are addressed promptly rather than neglected.

4. Command centre

At the centre, the military make sure they have sufficient capacity – erring on the side of overdoing it – to get the job done. Commenting on the foot-and-mouth crisis of 2001, Tebbit said that the Ministry of Agriculture, Fisheries and Food (MAFF), with veterinary surgeons in the lead, simply didn't get its arms round the crisis. They consistently underestimated the capacity required to solve it. Only when the military took charge was this problem rectified. As he explained to me, 'The vets didn't know the difference between consultation and discussion on the one hand and command and action on the other.' The military clearly did.

Once you've seen a crisis solved by applying these techniques, it's a short hop to looking at a problem which is just shy of a crisis and deciding to utilize the crisis techniques.

This is what struck Blair so forcefully in early 2002. The previous year, the outbreak of foot-and-mouth had threatened the livelihoods of countless farmers and the state of the British countryside. It had also threatened the reputation of Blair's government in the run-up to a general election. Blair postponed the election for a month and, frustrated by the ponderous response of the MAFF, brought in the military. He himself led the emergency response. Cattle were slaughtered and smoke rose from piles of their carcasses. People were banned from their beloved countryside walks for a while. Terrible though it was, it was clear that the government had 'gripped' the problem at last and was on the way to a solution. Blair's respect for the military was enhanced further. The following February, when the prime minister summoned the Home Secretary and me to his office in Downing Street to discuss the growing epidemic of street robberies – muggings for mobile phones mainly – the foot-and-mouth precedent was clearly in his mind. He knew that it would be inappropriate to involve the military, but surely we could learn lessons from the way they had responded. Blair's solution? We should call together COBRA and deal with robbery through that mechanism. In short, we haven't quite got a real crisis yet, so why don't we create one?

We did exactly that. It took a while for the Home Office officials to catch up. At first, their minds still worked within the tramlines of business as usual, but the whole point of a crisis is that business-as-usual is suspended. Within a few months, the number of muggings had been halved. The problem was under control and business as usual – now better informed – returned.

Needless to say, you cannot create a crisis too often because you would then undermine the entire government machine. This book is mainly about making sure that the machine becomes more effective at delivering for the citizens, but, just occasionally, when a problem is at Level 4 or heading that way, it is worth remembering the phrase that became ubiquitous after the collapse of Lehman Brothers in 2008: a crisis is a terrible thing to waste.

To summarize, as it becomes apparent there is a problem – you can see it in the data, for example – step one is to acknowledge its existence, step two is to decide what kind of problem it is – both its intensity and its nature – and step three is to do something about it – and to do so without giving the benefit of the doubt. Err on the side of rigour. While a delivery unit might prompt each of these steps, the responsibility for solving the problem lies squarely with the relevant minister and department. There is a difference between solving a problem and ensuring that it is solved. The delivery unit might pitch in to inspire and assist, but the responsibility is clear – as is the attribution of credit once the problem is solved.

Problem-solving Approach

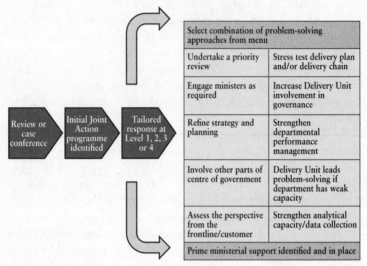

Select combination of problem-solving approaches from menu	
Undertake a priority review	Stress test delivery plan and/or delivery chain
Engage ministers as required	Increase Delivery Unit involvement in governance
Refine strategy and planning	Strengthen departmental performance management
Involve other parts of centre of government	Delivery Unit leads problem-solving if department has weak capacity
Assess the perspective from the frontline/customer	Strengthen analytical capacity/data collection
Prime ministerial support identified and in place	

Review or case conference → Initial Joint Action programme identified → Tailored response at Level 1, 2, 3 or 4

Source: Deliverology 101, p. 57

Figure 24

EXCUSES, EXCUSES

We all know the tendency in our own lives. So it is with bureaucracies. In your heart of hearts you know there is a problem that needs solving, but at the same time you don't want to confront it and you can think of plenty of excuses for not doing so, or at least for postponing facing up to it. In such situations, many of us find our willpower wanting, which is why having a coach, a teacher or a mentor can be useful; someone to stiffen your resolve, to tell you to do what you know you ought to.

As problems arise, a delivery unit or equivalent can play exactly this role: prompting action that otherwise might be postponed – or as I used to put it to top officials in departments, part of our job is to help put steel in your spine. For the delivery unit team, what this implies is that you have to recognize the excuses as you hear them and take them off the table. Once you start accepting them, you are well on the way to 'going native'. Here is a guide to the most commonly heard excuses and how to counter them.

EXCUSE 1: *We're already doing it.*
RESPONSE: How come we have a problem then? If you are already doing what is needed, where's the evidence it is working? Are you doing it with enough intensity? Maybe you're doing whatever it is on paper in the department, but it's not biting out there in the system. To put it bluntly, you may be able to fool yourself, but you can't fool me.

EXCUSE 2: *You're asking the impossible.*
RESPONSE: It may look impossible to you, but they've done it before in France/the US/China (delete as appropriate). If the other 90 per cent of your system performed as well as the top 10 per cent you'd exceed what I'm asking. You just need a little bit of courage. Three departments last year told us the same thing and now look – they're flying!

EXCUSE 3: *It's impossible and we're already doing it.*
RESPONSE: I promise you I've heard this combination of excuses 1 and 2 more than once from the mouths of officials. The response is that they can't both be true – get real!

EXCUSE 4: *It's very risky.*
RESPONSE: Agreed, but not as risky as doing nothing. And if this doesn't work we'll try something else.

EXCUSE 5: *There will be unintended consequences.*
RESPONSE: Of course, there always are. Some of them might be positive, incidentally, but either way we'll check. The inevitable consequences of not acting look a good deal worse.

EXCUSE 6:   *By intervening you are distracting us from delivering.*

RESPONSE: If you were delivering, we
              wouldn't be intervening!
              We'll help you deliver
              once the way forward is
              clear but understand we
              are not going away until
              the problem is solved ...
              at which point we will
              want to congratulate you.

> **RULE 40**
> TAKE ALL THE
> EXCUSES OFF THE
> TABLE

LEARN FROM FAILURE

Ernest Bai Koroma was elected president of Sierra Leone in 2007 on
a platform of delivering improvements in energy, transportation,
health and education. In a country which not long before had been
embroiled in a brutal civil war which left 50,000 dead and 80 per cent
of the population living on less than a dollar a day, Koroma's commitment was a tall order. He published his Agenda for Change in April
2008, but as Michael Scharff comments in his account of this work,
'Koroma quickly found that implementing his agenda was far more
difficult than writing it.'[4] Beautifully put.

He established a Strategy and Policy Unit (SPU) to oversee implementation, in part on the advice of Tony Blair's Africa Governance
Initiative (AGI). The idea was right, but somehow it did not quite
work out. Governance in Sierra Leone was genuinely difficult; many
of the nation's most talented people had left the country during the
war and as a result many key posts were filled by people who were
not up to the job. The ministries themselves were often without power
for hours or even days on end. Moreover, the first version of the SPU
had problems of its own. Its five key staff did not work effectively
with the ministries. Relationships were confrontational. Partly this
was because they were too senior – a former minister and a former
attorney general. Also, they were much more interested in thinking
'out of the box' than about the nitty-gritty detail of ensuring things

got done. Added to that, no one was clear what the unit's mission was – was it really delivery or, as its name implied, something much more to do with long-term strategy? As we've seen, one of the key lessons of the science of delivery is that if you combine strategy and delivery, more often than not the former trumps the latter in priority – in Sierra Leone they learned this lesson the hard way. Finally, and crucially, the SPU failed to establish the routine stocktakes.

By 2009, though there were some successes, the SPU experiment had failed. As in life and sport, so in government. What marks a leader out is not whether they experience failure – of course they do – it's how they respond. It must have been a temptation to President Koroma simply to close the SPU down and move on, but he didn't. Instead, identifying the problem correctly as one of implementation rather than design, in 2010 he reconstituted it, having learned the bitter lessons of the previous three years. The remodelled SPU, again taking advice from Blair's AGI, set out, in Scharff's words, 'to reduce the number of priorities on the agenda, develop a stronger rapport with ministers, rework the monitoring system … and improve the quality of information provided to the President'.[5]

The new SPU also hired a different kind of people, candidates who combined management experience with vital interpersonal skills, supported by a bigger team of more junior analysts. Crucially, too, they established monthly stocktakes which the president chaired and at which SPU officials led the discussion. This gave ministry officials working on the priorities access to the president. Meanwhile, the president, with an excellent memory, was able to remind officials that decisions taken months before ought by now to be implemented.

Sierra Leone began to make progress. The director of the SPU, Victor Strasser-King, appointed following his success overseeing a dam-building project, put this progress down in part to the sharper accountability and in part to the people. 'You have to be very particular about the people you hire. You don't want people who come in with their own agenda.'[6]

Miatta Kargbo, who played a key role in the SPU's health work, put it this way:

If a ministry is just told to 'set targets and implement them and we'll get back to you later', it's not going to get done. But the monthly updates, the advisers being in ministries and engaging as partners, the whole change model that you're not just there to monitor ... but there to partner, drive change, remove bottlenecks and facilitate getting the work done, that's really important.

Only someone who deeply understood the science of delivery could express those sentiments so succinctly. As a result, she said, 'together we are transforming our great nation'.[7]

It is important to remember that had they not chosen to learn from failure and try again, the chances are they would never have succeeded.

> **RULE 41**
> LEARN ACTIVELY
> FROM EXPERIENCE
> (failure is a great teacher)

RESISTANCE

The French love a good revolution. The tradition of opposing government on the streets of Paris, established in 1789, is alive and well. No sooner does a government embark on any major reform of government or the public services, than members of the relevant interest groups pour out onto the streets, shut the service down and wait to see whether the government has the courage to take them on. Invariably it doesn't, which is why France spends such a large proportion of GDP on its public services without the stellar results such lavish expenditure might be expected to deliver.

Not every nation has the same revolutionary tradition as France, but in most countries, when radical reforms are proposed, there are significant and powerful vested interests which will seek to defend the status quo. Often they have been beneficiaries for decades of the kind of failed Trust and Altruism discussed in chapter 3, and reform for them is likely to be at best uncomfortable. Thus the problems that occur with implementation are often associated with managing or facing down resistance. There is a fondly held notion among civil servants, the public and public sector workforces, that the way to avoid resistance is to get 'buy-in'. If the government consulted more and conceded more to bring their opponents onside, all would be well – that is the theory.

And yes of course government should consult, but it is totally unrealistic to believe that buy-in will inevitably result. The fact is that at least some of the opponents of a government reform are probably determined to try to resist it successfully, and any concessions you make to them will only encourage them to come back for more. In these circumstances, delivering successfully depends not on getting buy-in but on anticipating where the resistance might come from and applying some proven techniques to ensure the best chance of success. Here are some guidelines.

1. *Implement well*

The widely held view that the way to bring about change is to 'win hearts and minds' and then proceed is largely a myth. In fact, the reverse is true: you need to proceed, and if you do so well – a very big and important 'if' – hearts and minds will follow. This is because beliefs follow behaviours. Think about it at a practical level – you might hope that a new piece of software for your computer will enhance your performance, but until you try it, learn how to use it and see that it works, you are unlikely to believe in its power. The behaviour – using it – leads the belief. So it is with a government reform: it is a journey into the unknown, leaving a safe haven behind. Why take the risk? Can I hold onto as much as possible of what I've got? No amount of persuasion, least of all from politicians, who are rarely trusted, is likely to change your mind. However, if you embark on the journey and find it goes well – so much better than expected – then your beliefs will follow.

That 'if', of course, applies in spades. Implement badly and the sceptics will have a field day; a brave departure will become a débâcle. I saw this close up, long ago, when I represented a sceptical vested interest group, the National Union of Teachers, at the time when John Major's government in England was introducing tests in English, mathematics and science for eleven- and fourteen-year-olds. The objective behind the tests was two-fold: check that the children were learning so that parents could be informed; and hold the schools to account for their performance. Such a mix was unlikely to appeal to union members who only a year or two earlier had questioned the idea of a national curriculum, never mind national testing.

Had the government proceeded with due care and attention, it could probably have imposed the tests in spite of the scepticism of most teachers and the downright opposition of some, but it didn't. Instead, it made one blunder after another. While it piloted the maths and science tests for fourteen-year-olds, it failed to do so thoroughly for English, the very subject where there was the most opposition. Then, at the last minute, the hapless minister John Patten decided that the tests would include a paper on Shakespeare – a good idea (which I secretly supported) had the ground been prepared, but inflammatory in the circumstances. As the opposition began to mount, the government's examinations chief bizarrely claimed that these tests were the best-prepared in the history of education. (Bold claims need to have a foundation in fact.) Meanwhile, the government refused point blank even to meet representatives of teachers, thus adding fuel to the fire.

The result of this incompetence was that in the summer of 1993 all the government's tests were successfully boycotted, not just the controversial English one. John Patten lost his job. I watched all this with incredulity, having drafted the motion for the NUT which set the profession on the road to a boycott. I also absorbed the lesson for government – there is no greater gift to a government's opponents than poor implementation. This was a lesson I took to heart when a few years later I found myself in government and responsible for the implementation of education policy (including the controversial tests).

2. Remember Achilles and Odysseus both have a point – and so does Pericles

Lawrence Freedman's magnificent history of strategy explains that Ancient Greece provided us with two archetypes of strategy. There is Achilles, who depends on force or strength, and Odysseus, who depends on cunning. For much of the Trojan War, they depended on Achilles, but in the end it was Odysseus' idea of the Trojan Horse which brought them victory. Bearing both of these perspectives in mind makes sense for a government embarking on a major controversial reform, which is why Theodore Roosevelt used to say, 'speak softly and carry a big stick'. As far as possible, government needs to build its strength, but it also needs to be tactically aware and imaginative.

In old-fashioned conflicts, strength came in part from reserves of funding or physical material – such as the Thatcher government famously stockpiling coal before the 1984 miners' strike (and the miners playing into the government's hands by going on strike as summer began). More often, though, it is a question of political capital, and here other factors come into play. What else in the government's portfolio, other than your conflict, might be draining its reserves of political capital? If that is happening, you risk losing even if you play your hand well. (I remember seeing Blair's political capital leaking away in the aftermath of the conflict in Iraq.)

Furthermore, ultimately political capital derives from legitimacy – or in cruder terms public support – and this is where Pericles comes in, because in a Greek city-state, just as today, public support was fundamental in a conflict. Having sought to negotiate a settlement with Sparta to avoid war, Pericles became an advocate of it: 'If you yield to them you will immediately be required to make another concession, which will be greater, since you will have made the first concession out of fear.' As the war began, he continued to insist on restraint as well as firmness. In the conflict itself he sought to avoid a land battle, in which Sparta would be superior, and to wear the enemy down. As Freedman comments, 'Pericles' success lay in his authority and ability to convince people to follow strategies developed with care and foresight.'[8]

This is a statement about political capital, and the point is that it comes not just from what you do, but how you do it and how you explain it. Some people may support you, others might be persuaded by the rhetoric. Still others will express doubt, but perhaps concede that at least 'he knows what he's doing' (or she, of course).

3. *Think of the whole bell curve and don't be dragged into mud-wrestling*

There is a famous bell curve – attributed to Everett Rogers[9] – which illustrates how you might expect a population of stakeholders to respond to a proposed reform.

Bell Curve of Adoption

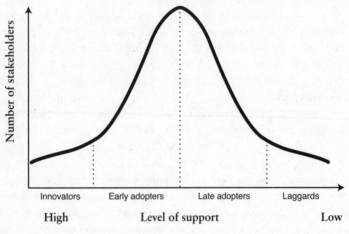

Figure 25

If you are Pericles, the innovators will be with you, and may be even more enthusiastic than you are yourself. The early adopters, if not initially convinced, will soon come with you. They may not want war with Sparta, but they will readily see that you have acted with restraint and that it would be wrong to make concessions out of fear. The late adopters will be more sceptical, but since you are Pericles, they probably think your insights are better than theirs and that means, reluctant though they are, they'll come on board so long as the proposed conflict goes well.

With that much support, Pericles doesn't really need to worry about the laggards; they've got nowhere else to go and can be left ineffectually whingeing on the sidelines. The problem is that not everyone is Pericles. Plus the modern world is a good deal more open and diverse than it was back then. Maintaining or strengthening political capital therefore involves not just effective implementation, but effective implementation combined with a clear, consistent, convincing message about why the reform is needed, how it is going to work and what the benefits will ultimately be. As Governor Martin O'Malley says, you need the techniques of delivery *and* a convincing story.

As the message is crafted, it is worth thinking consciously about how it will impact on each segment of the bell curve. The ideal, from the government's point of view, is that the innovators are ahead of government, urging you to go faster; they then provide a counterweight to the much larger groups who would prefer delay. The key target group of the communication should be the early adopters, who can become allies but first need to be convinced that this really is going to happen. Put another way, they don't want to be marched up a hill only to be marched down again. The late adopters are also significant. For them, the message is: 'We understand your concerns and we've taken them into account. We've thought about what you said and have made adjustments on a practical level.' But they too need to believe it is really going to happen. As long as this is in doubt, they have every reason to act (or not act) on their scepticism.

The key group not to target is the laggard group. They are unlikely to be persuaded and will seek to make a lot of noise to draw attention to themselves. Some of the media will love them because controversy makes a good story. This means they do have to be answered sometimes, but the answer needs to be targeted to keep the early adopters onside and bring the late adopters round.

What the laggards want, above all, is to drag you into a mud-wrestle in which you and they become equivalent, the early and late adopters start tearing their hair out at the spectacle, and the public conclude 'a plague on both their houses'. In short, Pericles' combination of firmness and restraint has much to be said for it.

Since Pericles' time, the means of communication have changed. Even in the past decade, since I was in No. 10, they have done so dramatically. Social media have become ubiquitous. The days of the controlled announcement are over; or, more accurately, the controlled announcement is only a small part of the story.

In this context of the explosion of social media, the communications company Brunswick suggests it is better to think less about making announcements and more about joining conversations. 'It is said that there are only seven plots in drama. We think there are 11 big conversations about the challenges facing the world today – and that

corporates [and governments, I would add] need to join these conversations.'[10] To win arguments these days, governments need to engage
continuously in these conversations rather than relying on set-piece
speeches and announcements.

The Keys for Dealing with Resistance
• Don't rush to compromise at the first sign of resistance.
• Address fears of change – don't give way to them.
• Deploy evidence.
• Point out the risk of inaction.
• Constantly emphasize the moral purpose.
• Tell a convincing story.
• Remember the bell curve.
• Join the conversation and stay engaged.

4. *Apply the methods of principled bargaining*
There have been major advances in recent decades in approaches to
negotiation. What is surprising is how little effect they've had on the
way government and key stakeholders, including unions, negotiate
with each other. Here I am referring not just to formal negotiations
but also to all those interactions with stakeholders in relation to a
major change which are in effect a negotiation.

Though the literature on the subject is vast, the impact on government and its relationships is still limited. This is a pity because the
potential is significant – better results could be achieved at less cost in
damaged relationships. The diagram below (Fig. 26) is the best way to
summarize the basic ideas.

It is simple really. In a negotiation, if you have little concern for
yourself and your point of view and not much for the other either
(bottom left), you might as well withdraw. If you have high concern
for yourself but not much for the other (bottom right), you will no
doubt take them on. If you have low concern for yourself and your
own position but high for theirs (top left), you will yield. Why not?

Meanwhile, your opponents are thinking about the issues from
their perspective. If you and they both decide to contend, a collision is
inevitable. As a result, what generally happens, depending on the outcome of a trial of strength, is that the solution is found somewhere

Negotiating Strategies

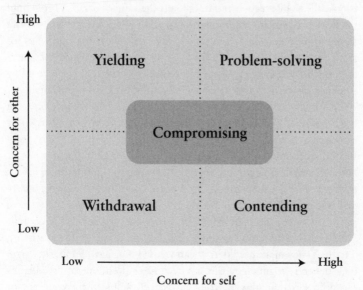

Source: Ramsbotham, Woodhouse and Miall, *Contemporary Conflict Resolution*

Figure 26

in the middle, usually a messy compromise (middle box) that often satisfies no one, and everyone knows that sooner or later it will be necessary to come back to the issues. Relationships are frayed, perhaps permanently, and the suppressed conflict often festers beneath the surface. Paradise postponed, perhaps indefinitely.

The top right-hand box is different. Here you have high concern both for yourself and the other. If you are a government, this is in fact where you should almost always aim to be. You may be at odds with doctors, nurses or the police, but in the end you know you depend on them for success. They might not reciprocate your concern for them, but if they are part of a publicly funded service they really ought to, because they share an interest with government in convincing taxpayers that theirs is a service worth investing in. This last point often gets forgotten in the war of words, with the consequence that the public despair.

Once the negotiation is pushed up into the problem-solving box, it is possible to be creative and to take off the blinkers that so often limit the field of vision in a traditional negotiation. Once the parties establish a shared purpose – improving the quality of service and outcomes for the citizen while maximizing the value of every tax pound or dollar – then the potential is huge. If in addition the negotiation is informed by evidence rather than merely taking positions, progress can be made.

This might sound idealistic, but in my experience simply creating the possibility of a more principled negotiation – whether formal or informal – opens up new options for solving the problem. In any case, I'm not recommending it as an alternative to Achilles, Odysseus or Pericles, which is why I introduced them into the chapter first. Power matters, so does guile and so does persuasion; but to depend purely on these may be to miss the point. Also, as Lawrence Freedman makes plain, if you overdo the exercise of power you risk achieving compliance rather than collaboration. (In the words of another ancient, Tacitus, 'They made a wilderness and called it peace.') Similarly, if you over-depend on guile you risk losing trust. Indeed, one of Freedman's big points is that playing your cards well helps to fill your pot of political capital in a conflict, whereas playing badly drains it.

There are sometimes some blockheaded and unreasonable people – in among the laggards – whom you may never bring round and there is no point being unrealistic about that. But the lesson is that for the most part you are more likely to solve more problems more effectively if you appeal to 'the better angels of our nature', as Lincoln put it, or at least start there.

> **RULE 42**
> NEGOTIATE ON THE BASIS OF PRINCIPLE
> (but don't depend on it)

AVOIDING FOLLY

Philip II, king of Spain, was also at various times before his death in 1598, also king of Naples, Sicily and Portugal and duke of Milan. Briefly, as a result of his luckless marriage to the ill-fated Mary I of England, he was king of England too. During his long reign, silver from the Spanish Empire in South America came across the Atlantic from Cartagena to Seville in vast quantities. You might think this would have made Spain rich, but keeping the sprawling empire together was a constant drain on Philip's resources, especially once the Netherlands – also part of his empire – revolted and refused to buckle.

Philip took ruling seriously. He insisted on seeing every document of significance and many more that weren't. In his rambling Gormenghast of a palace – the Escorial outside Madrid – Philip sat in the gloom commenting endlessly in his spidery script. What's more, he had an obsession. His dead English wife's sister, Elizabeth, was now on the throne in England and had two serious faults as far as he was concerned – she was Protestant and she was aiding the Dutch rebels.

Philip planned her downfall: a vast armada would sail from Spain, pick up the flower of the Spanish army from its base in the Netherlands and overthrow both Elizabeth and the English Reformation. Endless planning. Endless spidery script. When eventually, in 1588, after a decade or more of agonized planning, the armada sailed, it proved luckless. More nimble English ships disrupted its progress. Then they launched fireships in among it when it moored on the French side of the Channel; and finally an Atlantic storm blew it beyond England into the North Sea. A few stragglers made it back to Spain, having sailed home the long way, round the north of Scotland and the west coast of Ireland.

Many of Philip's advisers had warned consistently of disaster ahead; the logistical challenge was simply too great, especially against the English, who were already becoming masters of the sea. Barbara Tuchman, the wonderful American historian, had this to say about Philip: 'No experience of failure of his policy could shake his belief in its essential excellence.'[11]

That is folly in a nutshell.

Five years before her death, Tuchman published *The March of Folly: From Troy to Vietnam*, a sumptuous history of the follies of government, including Philip II's, freewheeling across the centuries. She starts with a reflection:

> Mankind, it seems, makes a poorer performance of government than of almost any other human activity . . . 'While all other sciences have advanced,'

confessed [America's] second President, John Adams, 'government is at a stand; little better practiced now than three or four thousand years ago.'[12]

Tuchman identifies four forms of misgovernment: tyranny, excessive ambition, incompetence or decadence and folly. Her book, she says, is just about the last of the four. Helpfully for our purposes, she defines folly:

> ... the pursuit of a policy contrary to the self-interest of the constituency or state involved. Self-interest is whatever conduces to the welfare or advantage of the body being governed; folly is a policy that in these terms is counterproductive.[13]

She then says that for her enquiry folly must meet three criteria:

1. It must have been perceived as counterproductive in its own time, not with hindsight.
2. A feasible alternative course of action must have been available.
3. It must have been the policy of a group and sustained over a period of time.[14]

She makes special mention of 'woodenheadedness, the source of self-deception' and claims it plays a large part in government. 'It consists in assessing a situation in terms of preconceived fixed notions while ignoring or rejecting any contrary signs.'[15]

It will be immediately obvious how this is relevant to delivery. Folly is all too likely and woodenheadedness all too common in government circles. King and Crewe, cited earlier, identify some classic recent British examples. The science of delivery, if it is to have any credibility, must reduce or eliminate the risk of folly and identify and challenge woodenheadedness wherever it occurs. Conducting the routines rigorously, as argued in chapter 5, and solving problems systematically, as outlined in this chapter, should in fact do so. In the routines, the focus on data and the insistence on an honest conversation make folly less likely. Bringing to bear on problems the views of outsiders as well as insiders has a similar effect. Identifying problems early and solving them before they become intractable also prevents folly.

Still there is a special kind of problem that the science of delivery needs to be alert to; and it may come upon you so gradually that you don't notice from one stocktake to the next and therefore may not seek to apply the problem-solving techniques to it. As on an English summer evening when the light fades imperceptibly and you notice far too late that the darkness is upon you, so with a policy. You might see all the indicators looking OK – a dip here, a dip there, but nothing to worry about – and then far too late you find you have a massive failure on your hands. Darkness has fallen. Or to take a phrase from politics long ago, the Fabian Society used to talk of 'the inevitability of gradualness'. For them it was a good thing; slowly everything would improve, so socialism – to which they aspired – might arrive without the need for revolution. But what if the inevitability of gradualness was a process of slow decline? Would you notice before it was too late?

History is littered with examples of well-intentioned programmes that turn out to be disastrous. At any given moment, the argument for carrying on outweighs the argument for turning back, but the cumulative effect of each incremental decision is catastrophic. The slide into war in Vietnam, which Tuchman examines in depth in *The March of Folly*, is a classic of the genre. Robert McNamara, Secretary of Defense under Kennedy and Johnson, and thus closer to the disaster than almost anyone else, waited nearly thirty years to publish his reflections on the searing experience.

What began as an understandable (in the context of the Cold War) attempt to prevent the expansion of Communism across Vietnam, became a metaphorical swamp into which the US was sucked deeper and deeper. McNamara, a highly intelligent and successful former head of the Ford Motor Company, wanted performance indicators of progress as any businessperson might (and as the science of delivery would recommend). But what indicators could you use to show progress in such a war?

McNamara explained his thinking in his 'unsparing' (as the *Wall Street Journal* called it) account of his experience, *In Retrospect*.

> I was convinced that, while we might not be able to track something as unambiguous as a frontline, we could find variables that would indicate our success or failure. So we measured the targets destroyed in the North, the traffic down the Ho Chi Minh Trail, the number of captives, the weapons seized, the enemy body count and so on.

The body count was a measurement of the adversary's manpower losses; we undertook it because one of Westy's [General Westmoreland, the US commander] objectives was to reach a so-called crossover point, at which Vietcong and North Vietnamese casualties would be greater than they could sustain.[16]

One recoils morally even to read this. Did no one on the inside question the ethics involved? Even if you assume the war was justified, surely winning it with the fewest possible deaths should be the goal? Whereas here McNamara chose 'body count' because, as he almost says, they couldn't think of anything better. And, once that choice was made, success presumably was defined by increased body count.

So one oft-repeated lesson of the science of delivery that may help prevent folly is to remember the moral purpose. Even if you leave this aside for a moment, McNamara's indicator looks like folly because that war in a distant corner of a foreign field could not be won simply by killing more and more of the enemy. History taught that. The situation did too; the war was in Vietnam, to state the obvious.

And then, to make matters still worse, McNamara explains that in any case 'often reports [on body count] were misleading'. Westy stated in the spring of 1967, as McNamara tells us, that the crossover point had been reached but the CIA had a different view: the enemy were increasing their numbers.

Even almost thirty years later, McNamara was complaining how 'hellishly difficult' it was to know what to believe. Surprisingly, he does not point out that in wars the army will usually have an incentive to exaggerate its impact, while the intelligence agencies have an incentive to find out uncomfortable truths. In this case, they probably both had a point; the body count may well have been rising, but this was simply provoking more and more Vietnamese to join the defence of their homeland. To be brutal about it, therefore, if body count was an indicator at all, it was a lead indicator of future Vietnamese strength.

The second lesson in avoiding folly is never to lose sight of the big picture, which is what was happening to McNamara. Incidentally, if this can happen to McNamara, surrounded as he was by very talented people – 'the brightest and the best' – it's worth remembering that being clever is no guarantee against folly. Indeed, since being clever and being arrogant often go together, it may make things worse.

Many other lessons of earlier chapters apply too – confront facts, however brutal, address the deficit of deliberation, don't rely on any single indicator, avoid endlessly giving the benefit of the doubt and be prepared, from a position of leadership, to challenge yourself and everyone around you.

In the end this is what McNamara did. In May 1967, he opposed Westy's request for an additional 200,000 men and called time on the downward spiral to folly they had all found themselves caught up in. He wrote a brave, even moving, note to President Lyndon Johnson, whom he revered.

> The picture of the world's greatest superpower killing or seriously injuring 1,000 non-combatants a week, while trying to pound a tiny backward nation into submission on an issue whose merits are hotly disputed, is not a pretty one.[17]

McNamara stayed in office, though, for another nine months, leaving on 29 February 1968 after a warm exchange of letters with the president. On the way to the formal departure ceremony in his honour, McNamara and the president got stuck between floors in a lift. McNamara's story is a cautionary tale of a once good man marching with the wrong indicators to the kind of folly described so vividly by Barbara Tuchman. The result? Irreversible failure.

RULE 43
GUARD AGAINST FOLLY (it has been common throughout history)

The next chapter examines how to ensure irreversible success.

7

Irreversibility

LEADERSHIP

There was a bit of clamour outside the hotel, with lots of taxis picking up or dropping off for a function. I said to my Toronto friends that they could drop me and I'd walk the last 100 yards. They laughed at me, but, when I persisted, let me get out. In that 100 yards I realized how people die of cold. With windchill it was minus 30° Celsius that January evening, and I was very relieved to make it back into the hotel.

The event I had attended had been anything but chilly, though. I had spent the afternoon and evening with Dalton McGuinty, the newly elected premier of Ontario, and his cabinet. After years in opposition, they had won a great victory in November 2003 and now had a full term (at least) ahead of them to transform Ontario. They had been following the progress of the Blair administration from afar and asked me to present on how we drove delivery. I set it out for them, found they were riveted by the details of what it would take, and somewhat overwhelmed as well as excited by the opportunity the voters of Ontario had given them.

Overall, I was impressed. While maybe not classically charismatic, McGuinty came across as a leader with a quick wit, a willingness to learn, a thoughtful manner with people and, perhaps above all, a fierce determination to seize his opportunity. He was one of those politicians who gave you the sense, like Clement Attlee after the war in Britain, that they had qualities better suited for governing than campaigning, though of course he was good at both. I left the following morning wondering whether I'd seen the early days of a major success or something that would soon enough end in tears. And I stayed in touch especially, but not only, with their education reform, which McGuinty had marked out as his top priority.

In this chapter, we will take it as read that you have mastered the content of the previous chapters, and that you are a fully paid-up deliverologist. The question now is: will you see it through? Will the change to which you aspire become irreversible?

It turned out Dalton McGuinty really was in it for the long haul. He won three election victories and stayed ten years as premier, during which time he resolved an energy challenge, fostered innovation in the economy, responded to the financial crisis and its consequences, made good progress on health and saw the Ontario education system rank consistently as one of the best in the world, with high standards and high equity. In September 2010, tempered by seven years in office, McGuinty reflected in a keynote speech in Toronto on what he had learned about the kind of leadership required to drive through reform, as he had done by then in education. Without the kind of sustained leadership he demonstrated, a major reform programme is unlikely to become irreversible.

Early in the speech he recognized the improved results and the top-five placing of Ontario in the global rankings. 'So are we excited about our progress? You bet ... Now are we satisfied with our progress? Different question ... I'm reminded of that Belgian car that broke the world land speed record in 1899 when it went 100km per hour. The name of the car was "La Jamais Contente", the "never satisfied".' Then, encouraging the audience of educators to keep learning and improving, he set out the eight lessons for political leadership. They are an excellent exposition of the leadership required from a head of government who really wants to drive profound change in a major field. I've summarized and generalized from them below.

Lesson 1 – The drive to make progress can't be a fad. It has to be an enduring government priority backed by resources and an intelligent plan.

Lesson 2 – A reform is not important to your government unless it's important to the head of your government – personally.

Lesson 3 – It doesn't matter how much money you invest, it doesn't matter how much you want change, you won't get results unless you engage the workforce.

Lesson 4 – To succeed, you need to build capacity among staff and to empower the right people in the right way.

Lesson 5 – Settle on a few priorities and pursue them relentlessly.

Lesson 6 – Once you start making progress, you've got permission to invest more.

Lesson 7 – The job is never complete.

Lesson 8 – The best way to sustain your effort to improve is to keep it personal. You yourself, as a leader, have to care.

McGuinty finished the speech by talking about the role education had played in successive generations of his family. So it's personal, political and persistent. No amount of science of delivery can succeed without sustained leadership, ideally, as in McGuinty's case (or Shahbaz Sharif's in Punjab), from the head of the government.

If McGuinty is a role model at head-of-government level, then at ministerial level it is hard to find anyone more effective than Andrew Adonis, who first in schools and then in transport drove significant progress in the Blair and Brown governments. Andrew and I were colleagues in No. 10 before he became an education minister following the 2005 election. Andrew had been pursuing education reform for years from Downing Street, so he knew what he wanted to do. His priority was to create a large number of independent state secondary schools called academies which would deliver in the state sector what Britain's great independent schools were delivering in the private sector. Above all, he wanted to be sure that these academies would transform educational opportunity in the most deprived areas in England, especially in its big cities. This wasn't all he wanted to do, but it was his passion and his priority. He was close to deserving that accolade: 'a single-issue fanatic'.

As he put it himself, 'The challenge was simple. It was to create successful all-ability secondary schools, absolutely no-nonsense about standards and results ... and making it possible to bridge the debilitating divide between state and private education.'[1] Later he brought the same focus and drive to ensuring there would one day be a high-speed train service from London to Manchester, perhaps of the same quality as the one from Tokyo to Kyoto.

Soon after he had become a junior education minister, I asked him how he was going about pursuing his passion for the academies. He had discovered what countless ministers before and since have discovered: your day gets filled up with stuff! And if there isn't quite enough paperwork coming down the pike, your private office can always fill another slot with a futile meeting or two. 'I spend fifty hours or so a week just keeping the work ticking over,' he said, 'and then I really drive change in the other twenty-five hours.'

Eventually, when the academies policy had become successful and, indeed, irreversible (because the coalition government that succeeded Blair and Brown adopted it), Andrew had time to reflect on what it takes to be a reforming minister. His thoughts, set out in *Education, Education, Education*, are consistent with McGuinty's perspective, but go deeper. Here they are:

1. Address the big problems.
2. Seek the truth and fail to succeed.
3. Keep it simple.
4. Be bold, but go with the grain as far as possible.
5. Lead and explain, lead and explain.
6. Build a team.
7. Build coalitions not tabernacles.
8. Champion consumers not producers.
9. On important issues, micromanage constantly.
10. Keep calm and carry on.
11. Remember that reform is a marathon, not a sprint.
12. Always have a plan for the future.

Eisenhower, whom we met at the beginning of chapter 4, offered advice on leadership very similar to that given by our two modern politicians. He was referring to leadership in the military, but might just as well have had politics in mind.

> All of us are human and we like to be favourably noticed by those above us and even by the public. An Allied Commander-in-Chief, among all others practicing the art of war, must more sternly than any other individual repress such notions. He must be self-effacing, quick to give credit, ready to meet the other fellow more than half way, must seek and absorb advice and must learn to decentralize [we would say delegate now]. On the other hand, when the time comes that he feels he must make a decision, he must make it in a clean-cut fashion and on his own responsibility and take full blame for anything that goes wrong whether or not it results from his mistake or from an error on the part of a subordinate.

Everything depends, he added, on 'your personality and good sense'.[2]

There is nothing difficult conceptually about McGuinty's, Adonis's or Eisenhower's advice; the challenge, as with delivery in general, is being disciplined about following it when there are so many potential distractions and pitfalls. To realize the difficulty, you just have to look around the world and see how few leaders and ministers are able to pursue their agenda over the long run. In some cases, they don't have the personality and good sense, but in many they simply don't have the single-minded discipline.

Sometimes this is also because they are not around very long. The same is true all too often of officials in Pakistan and India. Some British prime ministers – Blair and Brown both, for example – reshuffled their ministerial teams so often that some unfortunate ministers rarely spent more than a year in a post before the kaleidoscope was shaken and they emerged in another role, only for the cycle to be repeated. To take just one example, Kim Howells MP held six different roles during Blair's ten-year premiership. I saw a good deal of him when, at Transport, we were enjoying collaborating on the brave effort to ensure that the trains ran on time. We were just getting some traction when, for no reason I ever understood, he was gone again, this time to the Foreign Office to deal with the Middle East.

In other cases, the temptations of the office seduce ministers.

Perhaps they become unable to resist the comforts of the role and allow the civil service to mollycoddle them. Perhaps they would rather announce initiatives, make speeches and open buildings. There is a career to be made in this line of business – but it is not a career which delivers improved outcomes for citizens, and certainly not irreversible change.

> **RULE 44**
> THERE IS NO SUBSTITUTE FOR SUSTAINED, DISCIPLINED POLITICAL LEADERSHIP

IRREVERSIBILITY

Before coming to the definition of irreversibility, it is worth pointing out that it is different from a word that has become fashionable, especially in development circles – sustainability.

Often the first question I get asked when I tell the story of the Punjab Roadmap is, 'Is it sustainable?' Part of the problem with this question is that the word has become so hollowed out it is in danger of losing its meaning. Indeed, it is now widely used to oppose anything radical – 'it won't be sustainable' – and thus to undermine ambition. When the Roadmap began to deliver significantly improved outcomes, its critics said, 'Yes – but it won't be sustainable.' The truth is that, at any moment with any ambitious programme, whether or not something is sustainable depends on what people do – will they see it through or not? This is a statement of the blindingly obvious, but is too often missing from the debate.

And if people do see it through, by applying the disciplines of delivery, what they will achieve ultimately is not just sustainability, but irreversibility. Irreversibility means not being satisfied merely with improvement in outcomes but asking whether the leadership, structures and culture are in place that will guarantee the right trajectory of results for the foreseeable future.

This definition is tough. It's a high bar and it should be the objective for any major reform. See it through. Persistence cubed. And don't get bored on the way. The next section explains how to avoid that fate.

OVERCOMING BOREDOM

'Boredom is . . . a vital problem for the moralist, since half the sins of mankind are caused by the fear of it,' Bertrand Russell once said (perhaps self-reflectively). Not just for the moralist, I should add, but also for the deliverologist. Much of the excitement in politics, whether for the politicians or the civil servants who work for them, lies in the new: the new strategy, the new crisis or the new state of affairs, or in the public: the speeches, the media and, if you're lucky, the celebrity or semi-celebrity status.

But irreversibility depends on persistence, as both McGuinty and Adonis make plain. Stick at it, get into the details, oil the engine, whatever it takes. It is, as Adonis says, a marathon not a sprint. There are some people who have the right kind of mindset to grind out a change over time (I discovered I was one of them), but the evidence suggests that in politics they are relatively rare, which means the challenge is to mitigate the boredom somehow, or even better to find ways of making it interesting.

This is not as hard as it sounds. The potential for boredom can certainly be mitigated if the political leader takes a continuing interest in the issue, as McGuinty with education or Blair with health. Regular access to a political leader is like gold dust, and if they value persistence, it makes it much more interesting for you too. And a delivery unit can reinforce this – the steady round of data, routines and problem-solving makes it much harder for a minister or department to deviate from the chosen path, even if they'd like to. This is why the routines described in chapter 5 are so important.

But mitigation may not be enough. As McGuinty points out, at least for himself, the fact that it is a major aspect of public policy may not be enough to sustain a focus. It also needs to be personal, and to have deep meaning at that level as well as the system level. This means constantly reminding yourself of the purpose and the benefits to citizens.

Then again, the best way to overcome the boredom is to turn it around. Beneath the surface of the data there is always plenty to fascinate – the contrast between one hospital and another, the geographic variation, race or gender differentials and occasionally the bizarre, such as the elephant crossing the motorway (in England) to delay traffic. Better still is if you can achieve that 'anorak' or 'geek' mentality where minor changes in the data become fascinating and each week or each month as you wait for the next set of data the tension mounts. As Adonis says, undisputed truths are rare in the field of public policy, so there is always a need to debate and understand the meaning of changes in the data. Here what matters most is the people you spend time with, which is why any successful leader, whether in politics, bureaucracy or business, should ensure they have a team around them that will challenge and question without fear. Being surrounded by yes men and women simply adds to the boredom, whereas constant challenge from within the team keeps things vibrant (and reduces the risk of folly).

Finally, from the data and regular visits to the field, which McGuinty and Adonis both emphasize, you can always go deeper into a problem. It is one thing to understand national trends in reading performance, another to know what motivates Bangladeshi eleven-year-olds in London and their parents to succeed. It is one thing to track rail performance over time, another to understand why leaves on the line are a problem in New York City but not in Warsaw. Moreover, as time progresses, there are new allies (and perhaps new enemies) to keep you entertained.

And at the end of the rainbow there is that crock of gold called credit, or even a legacy. This, needless to say, often turns out to be more elusive than you might think. For one thing, as the proverb has it, success has many parents and failure is an orphan. The truth is that, at the outset of any proposed reform, almost certainly there were several people who could lay a claim to having originated it, although at that time (particularly if the idea is ambitious and/or controversial) it is likely that there were many more people questioning it. Through the implementation dip, a number of sympathizers probably peeled off too. But then, as it gathered momentum and began to deliver, those who peeled off, and indeed the original sceptics, begin to come on board. Some of them even discover that they were 'always' in favour of it after all. So it is not just that success has many parents; it acquires even more as time goes by. In terms of managing the boredom, therefore, it's as well to prepare for sharing the credit with a larger group than you might have expected.

Then there is the media. Maybe at the beginning, when you announced the change, you got some good headlines, but after that chances are the critics got more airtime and column inches than you did. As you went through the implementation dip, it got worse. You held your nerve, but it was no fun. At least, when momentum is generated and the results are coming through, you will be rewarded for your courage and persistence . . . or maybe not.

Good news barely registers. 'Government Success' is not much of a headline (at least in countries with a free press; and where it isn't free, the headline won't be believed). Having paid the heavy price earlier, you now struggle to get a story on page 17. Worse still, the media, unforgiving as it is, does not just avoid reporting the good, it also changes the story. Even if you do get your good news onto page 17, the chances are it will be drowned out by some other story, related to your area and on page 1 or 2, which is bad news. I remember vividly the fact that, as we reaped success in reducing health wait times in 2004 and 2005, the media moved the focus onto hospital-acquired infections (we reduced those as well later, in the teeth of opposition from the health service, but that success too was drowned out).

And then there is one last twist to the diminution of credit. Somewhere along the way, the validity of your data – the currency in which your success is measured – will be questioned, and however robust it might be, because it is government data the chances are you will not be believed. I recall all too clearly a press conference I did in Lahore with the Secretary – Schools on the latest set of positive data from the Education Reform Roadmap. I set out the figures and then there was a question to me (in English) about how valid and reliable the data was. Before I'd finished answering, the rest of the room was engaged in vigorous argument with the secretary. They were sufficiently polite to the outsider not to yell at me; the shouting match was in Urdu.

The truth is that for any major reform, you have to win the battle twice: once on the ground to make the change real, and once on the airwaves to convince people that it is real. It is indeed a vital part of the change programme to take on the battle in the media as well as in the real world, because the two are integrally linked, but don't imagine that as a result, in return for the boredom and persistence, you will be rewarded with credit. The crock may be smaller than you think and its contents might not necessarily be gold.

Julio Frenk, the highly successful former Minister of Health of Mexico who now leads the School of Public Health at Harvard, has a nice line on how to achieve a legacy. The wrong (but all-too-common) way, he says, is to claim, as they say in Mexico, that 'My predecessor was an idiot and my successor is a traitor.' The right way is to take care first of two things: don't make big mistakes, especially of the personal scandal variety; and don't ruin something good that you inherited even if it was from a government of a different political persuasion. Get these fundamentals in place, he says, and then embark upon successful reform; then and only then do you have a chance of substantial legacy.

Years after the event, when the media is focused on the latest hapless government attempting the latest hapless reform and you are enjoying your retirement from politics, someone somewhere might publish some academic papers proving that you did make a difference. And later still, with a bit of luck, it may get written into a history book. In this way, legacy is often a pale and distant echo. Which means that

> **RULE 45**
> PERSIST (but don't expect the credit)

the only certain way to alleviate the boredom and handle the pressure is to do what you are doing because it is the right thing to do. Moral purpose trumps all the rest every time.

THE UNVARNISHED TRUTH

Both McGuinty and Adonis emphasize the importance of continuing to learn, and there are plenty of opportunities to do this, whether it's through debating the latest data with officials, reading reports, or getting out on the frontline and seeing for yourself. With the right kind of curiosity, each and all of these can be genuinely fascinating. But there is a deeper question – how do you get the unvarnished truth about what is happening at any given moment and how you are doing?

Grigory Potemkin, as well as serving Empress Catherine the Great as a general and governor of a region, was her lover. When he won a great victory at Ochakov, he received the kind of praise that must be unusual from a monarch or political leader of any kind. 'I take you by the ears and kiss you in my thoughts,' the empress wrote. As a result of his various campaigns, Russia acquired swathes of territory from the Ottoman Empire in the Crimea and around the Black Sea. He was rewarded by being made governor of this New Russia. When the empress came to visit for an extended period, he erected temporary villages along the banks of the river Dnieper to impress her. Once the royal party had moved on, the village would be dismantled and rebuilt downstream to impress Her Majesty once again. Hence one of Russia's greatest military leaders has become famous in history not for what he actually accomplished, but for having these fake villages named after him – the Potemkin villages. (Another way to achieve legacy is to have something named after you.) Not everyone has pulled off such a massive deception of a visiting dignitary (and historians debate whether Potemkin himself did), but what we might call the 'Potemkin Syndrome' is alive and well.

The chief minister of Punjab was shocked by the photographs we showed him of Punjab schools, not because he hadn't ever visited schools, but because, whenever he had done so, the authorities had done the equivalent of a Potemkin village makeover in advance. Even for a minor celebrity like me, if they knew I was coming they tidied up and made sure the teachers were present. This is not just a syndrome in the developing world; it was the same for Blair. Everything would be meticulously planned in advance. The twenty-first-century need for security simply adds to the air of unreality. The visits are still important and an opportunity to learn, but they are not real. And the same applies to visits by ministers, civil servants and other dignitaries.

The unannounced visit is hard to achieve, but much more revealing. On my trips to Punjab, I'm only rarely able to escape the security people (and the truth is mostly I don't want to because I value their advice). But I do want to visit schools unannounced. To give one example, in 2012 I was able to do so out by the Indian border in the district of Kasur. You could see the barbed wire and the armed watch-towers, beyond which lay India. The river Sutlej, broad and slow, wound its way past. Local farmers pulled a ferry laden with hay across it. A kingfisher put on a show over the river and the cattle wandered freely. At the boys' school some students were present and the water ran from the handpump, which was good. The boys were outside though, some sitting on the dusty ground, others on a rickety bench. The teacher was doing suspiciously little teaching, and while the boys had textbooks, they were tattered and torn and all open at different pages. There were some classrooms, but they lacked furniture and one of them was full of military equipment, presumably for the border guards. Meanwhile, the girls' school was locked up and the teachers were said to be on 'World Bank training'. Maybe, but the lock had a suspiciously permanent look.

In late 2013 and early 2014, I made further unannounced visits and mostly I was impressed by the visible impact of the Roadmap, but I did stumble across one school where thirty or more children aged from four to ten were locked in a school compound but out of the classrooms. There was not an adult in sight and no water ran from the pump. Soon enough the headteacher came running; he had been relaxing in his house nearby. Such a visit doesn't tell you everything, but it is a reality check. Importantly, too, it affects your emotions. It redoubles your energy and commitment; the need to change the facts on the ground.

The master of the unannounced visit was Theodore Roosevelt. His stellar career, which catapulted him to the presidency by the age of forty-two, saw him appointed police commissioner of New York City in his mid-thirties. Roosevelt was a larger-than-life character, destined to dominate any room he walked into. The British Liberal John Morley once exclaimed that he had seen 'two tremendous works of nature in America – the Niagara Falls and Mr Roosevelt'.[3]

Having fired the two top officials in the New York Police Department within three weeks of taking office as commissioner, Roosevelt turned his attention to the officers on the beat. To root out endemic corruption he needed to address the frontline as well as the head office. Jacob Riis, a journalist who had become a friend, urged Roosevelt to accompany him on some unannounced nightwalks. Riis knew the city, paving stone by paving stone. Larger than life though Roosevelt was, hidden under a floppy hat and a big overcoat he became indistinguishable from the rest of New York nightlife. He found patrolmen sleeping, enjoying meals and in one case chatting to a prostitute who recommended to the unfortunate officer that the way to deal with the inquisitive stranger in the large overcoat was to 'fan him to death'.

The next morning, these officers and a group of others were summoned to the commissioner's office for a severe dressing down. Roosevelt loved it: 'these midnight rambles are great fun,' he wrote to his sister. The newspapers loved it too. As far away as San Antonio in Texas, it was reported in the *Daily Light* that 'Police Commissioner Roosevelt finds that he can secure more information in one night than he would in a year in broad daylight.'[4]

In short, he learned a lot, as no doubt did the patrolmen of New York City. Irreversibility depends on changing the facts on the ground, and there is no alternative but to check. If you can't always do it yourself, remember that, unlike in Roosevelt's day, everyone has a camera now. Idris Jala, head of Pemandu, sometimes sends his staff out to check that a piece of road or a bus shelter promised by the relevant department is actually there in reality.

OBSESSION AND THE ELEGANCE OF YOUR BEHAVIOUR

Not all learning comes from visits or even from the flow of data on outcomes. Nor is it the case that only the outcomes matter and the processes can be left to themselves. As Andrew Adonis points out, for the things that really matter micro-management is not a sin, it's a necessity.

In the Delivery Unit, once we were established, we had the flow of data and visibility of the relevant departments' delivery plans. We also had the dialogue that led up to the stocktakes and the stocktakes themselves. For a while we thought that was enough information for us to check on our impact. Then our deputy director, Peter Thomas, persuaded me that he should be allowed to tour the headquarters of several top-performing American companies. He came back passionate about a new insight: we weren't learning enough to ensure success. Yes, we knew in broad terms what progress was being made on wait times or railway performance, for example, but we knew little about the processes we had put in place to encourage improved delivery – and anyway in 2003 the data itself was hardly overwhelmingly encouraging. There were some good stories, but the whole programme of priorities in the summer of 2003 did not look on track, never mind irreversible.

Overcoming my initial reluctance, Peter insisted we had to identify the elements that we believed would make the Delivery Unit successful and then check whether we had them in place. He was persistent to the point of being irritating – one of his sterling qualities, incidentally – and what he developed, and we as a management team then adopted, became very important to us. We decided in effect to apply deliverology to our own processes. To ensure our future success, we agreed we had to have four elements in place:

1. *Great people* in our team
2. *Great processes* such as stocktakes and monthly meetings
3. *Great relationships* with key players in government
4. *Great outcomes* – were the goals we had set being achieved?

The key point here is that we understood that success on the fourth point would be a consequence of success on the first three. To put it in jargon, the first three were lead indicators. If we put in place the first three, which we controlled entirely, the fourth would follow. We took these four elements, put them into the kind of balanced scorecard advocated by Robert Kaplan, and every six months rated ourselves (inevitably) on a four-point scale (see Fig. 27).

We carried out this rating thoroughly. We commissioned independent people to interview ministers and officials in departments about their view of us and the quality of our relationship with them. When any member of staff left, we carried out an exit interview. We put one of our team in charge of each process so that, in addition to driving progress on whichever target they were responsible for, they had a responsibility periodically to review that process – a monthly note, for

PMDU Balanced Scorecard

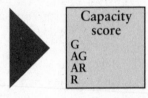

Figure 27

example – and see whether we could make it better still. Thomas's point was that we had to get our house in order; and if we did we would enhance our leverage.

The effect of all this was revolutionary. We were no longer leaving anything to chance. As great sportspeople do, we controlled at the level of detail everything we could control. (Maybe this is why the press referred to me as 'the control freak's control freak'.) In the light of Britain's later phenomenal success in cycling, I prefer to think that we were close to developing what Sir David Brailsford, former head of UK cycling, calls the aggregation of marginal gains. This is what he says:

> People often associate marginal gains with pure technology, but it is far more than that. It is about nutrition, ergonomics, psychology. It is about making sure the riders get a good night's sleep by transporting their own bed and pillow to each hotel. It is about using the most effective massage gel. Each improvement may seem trivial, but the cumulative effect can be huge.[5]

So huge, in fact, that Britain dominated the cycling events at the London Olympics (winning more gold medals in cycling than Australia won in the entire Games). Some of Britain's rivals even worried that the

British bikes had rounder wheels! Meanwhile, Team Sky, also managed by Brailsford, provided two consecutive (British) winners of the Tour de France.

In the Delivery Unit, we were on the way to becoming as obsessive as Dave Brailsford. As Nassim Nicholas Taleb puts it with only slightly less obsession than Brailsford:

> Your last recourse against randomness is how you act – if you can't control outcomes, you can control the elegance of your behaviour.[6]

This kind of obsession with your own processes at a level of detail unlocks the door to irreversibility. Next time someone tells you that leaders should focus on the big picture and leave the detail to subordinates, show them the door.

> **RULE 46**
> LEARN THE
> LEARNABLE AND
> CONTROL THE
> CONTROLLABLE
> (obsessively)

BUILDING CAPACITY

Nassim Nicholas Taleb's book *Antifragile* describes how organizations can become more than resilient; they can develop so that they don't just survive shocks, they benefit from them. Curiously, his two main examples of governments which succeeded in this respect are the Ottoman Empire and Switzerland, neither of which is an ideal example for modern governments. The former because it declined and fell, and the latter because it is consciously established as an exception. Even so, Nassim Nicholas Taleb's brilliant book makes numerous telling points, one of which happily introduces this section. In seeking to reduce its risk, he says, 'Government too often transfers risk from the collective to the unfit.'[7] It is a devastating statement, all the more so for being recognizably true. The implication is that to ensure anti-fragility in a system it is necessary to ensure it is 'fit' or, to put it more technically, has in place the capacity to deliver.

In chapter 2, the concept of the 'guiding coalition' was introduced – the small group of seven to ten people in key positions who share a deep understanding of the goal and how it is to be achieved. In this chapter, we have met an example of this in practice: Dalton McGuinty's Education Results Team, which included not just the premier himself, the education minister and key officials from both the premier's office and the education department, but also an outsider, Michael Fullan, who was appointed adviser on education to the premier. Fullan was and is one of the world's leading thinkers and writers about reforming education systems, as well as being a patriotic Canadian and a citizen of Toronto. As an adviser to McGuinty, he contributed powerfully in three ways. First, he brought to the guiding coalition insights from around the world; he was a kind of living, walking, talking engine of international benchmarking. Second, he was a bridge or translator between government and the teaching profession. McGuinty took power after years of conflict between government and teachers, so trust on both sides was at a low ebb. While neither side trusted the other at the outset, both trusted Fullan. Third, his knowledge and his relationships enabled him to assist McGuinty and his education ministers in thinking about the next steps. Remember Andrew Adonis's last rule (see p. 223), always have a plan for the future? Michael Fullan made sure they always did.

The Fullan role could be replicated in a variety of ways, but something like it is required because the guiding coalition, while necessary, is not enough. The guiding coalition has to reach out and build relationships in the system – and these need to become deeper and more extensive over time if irreversibility is to be ensured. The expression Fullan and I use to describe this process is 'ever-widening circles of leadership', illustrated in Figure 28.

Beyond the guiding coalition are the system leaders, the top officials who manage the system, perhaps in a government department or in key agencies or regional bodies. Beyond them are the unit leaders – such as local police chiefs, hospital managers, school principals or headteachers; and beyond them, the workforce. All these serve the users of the service and ultimately the citizens. The guiding coalition needs constantly to foster leadership commitment in each of the concentric circles, while at the same time representing and communicating with the outer circle, the citizens. If the approach to delivery is

Ever-widening Circles of Leadership

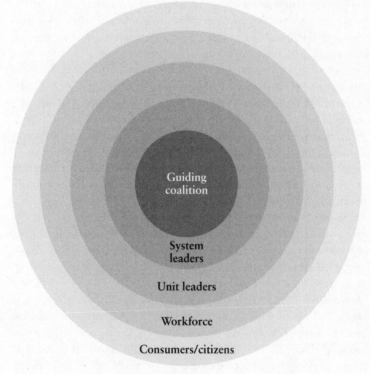

Figure 28

working, the number of committed and capable leaders in each of the circles should be increasing all the time. You can track this.

The lesson of the previous chapter's examination of resistance needs to be remembered – rather than winning hearts and minds and then making the change, the right approach is to win hearts and minds *by* making the change. Because behaviour comes before belief, and competence before confidence, fostering these widening circles of leadership cannot be divorced from building the skills and capacity of the workforce; indeed, the two have to be integrated. In effect, they are the same thing. Get this right and irreversibility is well on the way.

There are three levels to it. The third is the most important and the one that governments almost always miss (though often they also miss the first two). The first level is *awareness raising*: ensuring that the people involved in delivering a major change – civil servants, police or nurses, for example – are aware of what is coming, why it is coming and what it is likely to mean in practical terms. This has to be convincing in the sense that they have to believe it really is going to happen; otherwise, as someone once said to me, they think change is like London buses – you can miss one because another will be along in a minute. To ensure it is convincing and that it reaches all those who need to know, it is necessary to use multiple communication channels, not just the management cascade, which is notoriously inefficient on its own.

The second level is *formal training*, which may apply to specific segments or the entire workforce and provides the skills necessary to adopt whatever the change may be. Here governments make two classic errors. The first is to assume it is not necessary and that awareness-raising will be enough. There may occasionally be a significant change which does not demand any new skills from the workforce, but that is rare. The second mistake is to think that, for a complex new skill, a one-off training session at the beginning will be enough. However good, it almost never is, because with any skill, until you try using it you don't know what questions to ask. The moral is that this kind of formal training needs to be on the model of train-do-train-do etc. Much better to spread three days over a six-month period than to do all three in a block at the outset. The training also needs to be of the highest quality, otherwise it will breed cynicism in an inevitably sceptical workforce.

The third level of capacity-building is to *embed it* in the way the system operates. This is crucial to irreversibility (and anti-fragility). It is also fundamental to unleashing greatness. The best way for a nurse to follow through in practice on the learning related to a major change is to learn from his or her peers and line managers in context, rather than at a training centre. The best way for a police officer to learn how to follow up a mugging is to do so from a coach who not only knows how but has personally done it; much more convincing than a trainer who has never been on the beat. The model organization in this respect, in my experience, is BRAC, the Bangladeshi non-governmental organization. They embed continuous learning in all their major programmes, whether it is chicken farming, women's empowerment or education.

I have seen it first hand in their education programme. BRAC educate 10 per cent or more of the primary-age children in Bangladesh. Almost all of their pupils have for one reason or another dropped out of the (very poor) government system. BRAC take these children through to completion of primary school in four years instead of the five allowed in the government sector. In spite of spending a year less, the BRAC children massively outperform the children in the government sector. This is partly because BRAC have a well-worked-out model of good primary education, but above all it is because they train their teachers to be excellent. Almost all BRAC primary schools are one-room schoolhouses with thirty to forty children and just one teacher, which makes their success all the more impressive. Furthermore, these teachers are almost always young women from the local community who have just graduated from high school.

These young women receive no more than three or four weeks of training before they start teaching. That is enough to get them going, but what brings about the quality and the remarkable consistency from one school to another is the fact that these teachers are visited weekly by a trained coach who watches them in action and offers specific advice. These coaches were invariably BRAC teachers previously, which means they are able to demonstrate with the children the point they want to make. Then, once a month, the teachers meet in a cluster of a dozen or so at a nearby training centre and spend a day learning specific new skills, both from the trainer and from each other. For these training sessions, they sit on the floor with a pile of materials in front of them just as the children do in their classes. To put it in technical language, the training itself models the pedagogy required in the classroom.

You can visit one school after another and find the BRAC model being delivered again and again by teachers who most of the time are working alone. Remarkable. And the children not only learn, but are joyful. More remarkable still.

Once capacity-building is embedded in the day-to-day work, once peers learn systematically from each other and have the opportunity regularly to see excellence in practice, you have the chance to unleash greatness. What BRAC and many other successful organizations do is easy to describe and looks effortless, but is in fact extremely sophisticated, which is why it remains relatively rare. Too often individual public sector professionals or other staff rarely get feedback, rarely see excellence and rarely demand the highest standards of all their peers. This is the crux of the relationship between capacity and culture. Seen from the point of view of a government seeking to deliver results, this is one of the most sophisticated challenges there is. And here there really is no quick fix. Michael Fullan, as so often, captures what is required in a simple phrase: the learning is the work, and the work is the learning.

> **RULE 47**
> INVEST DEEPLY AND CONTINUOUSLY IN SKILL AND CAPABILITY
> (commitment will follow)

Twenty years on, the horror of Rwanda's genocide in 1994 remains hard to comprehend; in a small country, up to a million people were slaughtered and millions more displaced. The scale of the tragedy pushed the vast majority of those who survived into poverty and left the government and its system in utter disarray. In 1995, four in five civil servants in Rwanda had not even completed secondary school.

A few years later, President Kagame and his government embarked on 'Vision 2020' to try to rebuild their country. A major aspect of this was building the government's capacity. 'Capacity-building' is a key word in development-speak, the language spoken by providers of international aid. Much of capacity-building has been provided over the past twenty years or so around the world, some of it by 'fly-in, fly-out' consultants and some of it by sending officials in need of it to courses in other countries. The overall effect of this kind of capacity-building has been limited, and the Rwandan government knew it. 'The problem was that these fly-in, fly-out consultants just weren't leaving capacity here in the country,' commented Vivian Kayitesi of the Rwandan Development Board. Another Rwandan, Anita

Kayirangwa, was similarly critical of courses abroad: 'You send some-one to another country to train, and what they're learning isn't applicable at home. For example, they may be learning to use soft-ware that is not even used in their home office.'[8]

In collaboration with Tony Blair's Africa Governance Initiative (AGI), the Rwandan government designed a much more effective approach to capacity-building which took account of the lessons set out in the previous section, and has proved far more effective. It was based on a five-step process, the first two of which (about priorities and organization) have already been established earlier. The other three are:

1. *Assess capacity gaps*
   Analyse the relevant organizations and decide precisely where and how their capacity needs to be strengthened.

2. *Design a package of support*
   Design a tailored package of support to build the required capacity.

3. *Mobilize support*
   Mobilize the international community to find and where necessary provide the support.

In delivering the programme, which was broadly successful, vital lessons were learned. First, capacity-building needs to be provided at three levels – the individual, the institutional and the organizational. Miss any one of these and the capacity to deliver will not be in place. Second, the 'nuts and bolts' as the AGI puts it – HR systems and financial management systems, for instance – matter as much as, if not more than, general themes such as leadership. Third, focus on solving problems. The AGI and its Rwandan counterpart ensured the capacity-building was real; it helped to solve the actual problems that were preventing delivery as well as build people's skills.

In short, capacity-building is essential and should be powerful and engaging, as in this case. The tragedy is that in many countries, because the experience has been so poor over so long, the very phrase 'capacity-building' prompts stifled yawns – sometimes not even stifled.

Of course, Rwanda still has major problems. As much as 50 per cent of its government activity is donor-supported – it has been a darling of donors over the past decade – which leaves its progress a long way from irreversibility. In addition, there are risks that the government will slip into authoritarianism, as William Easterly has pointed out. Time will tell. In the meantime, the lessons from the country's Strategic Capacity Building Initiative remain pertinent and relevant to many other countries.

THE POLITICS OF IRREVERSIBILITY

There is a politics to irreversibility too. Just when you are pursuing the science of delivery to perfection and marching towards irreversibility, along comes an election and in comes a different government with a different agenda. In a trice, gone! Worse still, while your major change might have been a matter of vigorous debate in a campaign, it is also quite possible that it wasn't, that the government whose agenda you've been pursuing lost not on these reforms, but on something else altogether – a foreign conflict, economic competence, time for a change, a new charismatic leader of an opposition party, or all of the above.

There is an underlying point here: this is what happens in democracies. Just as it throws up all kinds of weird and wonderful representatives of the people, so it also sometimes flattens a good reform or reform programme by accident. The question to consider, therefore, while a reform agenda is being pursued, is, what can you do to make it more likely that the agenda will continue to be pursued after the next election, whatever happens? Or, to reverse the point, what can you do to minimize the political risk to your agenda?

One political scientist who has given this question careful consideration in his thoughtful and provocative book *Nation of Devils* is Stein Ringen of Yale and Oxford. Ringen defines government clearly and narrowly as the politicians who hold executive office – the cabinet in the UK, for instance. He makes a clear distinction between government and the officials or bureaucracies which theoretically serve them. His point is that the government is made up of a very small number of people trying to make very big changes in countries which, though varying in size, are – apart from the occasional Luxembourg – very large things. He argues:

The puzzle is this: if, say, twenty people are to rule 60 million, those twenty are when all is said and done, helpless. They are in power, but governing involves thousands and thousands of civil servants, officials and workers in a myriad of ministries, departments, directorates and other agencies. Indeed, it involves everyone who lives in the country, both those who are engaged in the apparatus of governance and everyone else who allows themselves to be governed. A minister cannot so much as set up a meeting without getting a secretary to arrange it.[9]

Ringen is in effect making the case for a science of delivery and reinforcing the rationale for this book. He goes on to lay out the difficulties of getting bureaucracies to do what you want, and the challenges of dealing with opposition and the various vested interests. He then comes to his profoundly important conclusion:

To get others to take you seriously, you start by showing them your power. But once it is established that you are a governor with the power to command, your ambition to be effective bids you to pull back from the use of the power you have in your hands . . . if you unleash it except in the last resort, you will get the power of others against you and fail in what you want to achieve. The prudent governor should leave power latent as much as possible and turn to persuasion.[10]

In other words, use power with restraint and try to bring people with you. Working for compliance gets you only so far; ultimately, he argues, 'Ministers must inform and educate their people, and touch their souls and stimulate their will.'[11] This is a high bar but, if it can be achieved, it almost guarantees irreversibility; after all, it is unlikely that any political party could be elected by promising to reverse something that has touched people's souls.

The question remains, though, *how* to do this or even get close to it in the messy, conflicted reality of many modern societies, especially given electoral cycles which tend to be no longer than four or five years. Here are some options.

First, as Ringen points out, the way you act – using power with restraint, being open, levelling with people even if the message is difficult or unpopular, all these count individually and above all cumulatively. They combine to create an overall impression, and that impression provides the context in which people judge a programme or decide what commitment to make to it or not. We all know there are some politicians we respond to and some we don't, and that this is a different point from whether we agree with them or not. In Pakistan, even his political opponents acknowledge that Shahbaz Sharif is seriously committed to the future of his province. To refer back to chapter 6, both Achilles and Odysseus have their parts to play, but for irreversibility Pericles is more important than either.

Second, the argument referred to (in chapter 3) about (in Blair's terms) moving from 'flogging the system' to 'a self-sustaining, self-improving system' is clearly central. The former approach depends on government; the latter by definition much less so and is therefore closer to irreversibility.

Third, in some countries the democratic process has developed a consensual tradition. It is not that the parties don't compete over ideas or personalities; rather that they expect to work together, sometimes in coalition and sometimes simply because that is the way the political culture expects them to behave. This is often true, for example, in the way Germany goes about fundamental reform, even when it doesn't have a grand coalition of the two largest parties. The result is often slower, more deliberate change, but also change with much better prospects of lasting longer and becoming irreversible.

Stein Ringen's underlying belief is that the Scandinavian countries, including his native Norway, are the paragons of good governance and move forward in consensual fashion. I agree that in consensual democracies such as Norway, the chances of irreversibility are higher, assuming there is systematic implementation. I am less convinced by the implication of Ringen's argument that if only other countries – his book is mainly about Britain and America – adopted the Norwegian approach, all would be well. To exaggerate slightly, his case is that Britain and America are badly governed, and the solution is for them to become like Norway. Somehow, I don't see that happening, because of the deep, combative political cultures in those places, though as always there is plenty to learn from Norway (and other well-governed countries). Still less is Norway a model that many developing countries and emerging democracies can simply adopt.

Fourth, therefore, the politics of irreversibility in conflictual democracies such as Britain, the US and Australia needs attention. Surprisingly, perhaps, it is possible. Essentially, the answer is simple – you push the reform far enough and deep enough for the opposition either to adopt it enthusiastically or at the very least decide it would be more effort to unwind it than to sustain it. One key factor in opposition thinking will of course be how popular the change is by the time the election comes round.

Here are two classic examples from the UK. Tony Blair, while in opposition, embraced the trade union reforms that Margaret Thatcher had put in place, because he believed they were popular and effective. He did so in spite of much of his own party, in part because he did not believe Labour would be electable if it proposed to overturn them but also because he believed they were right. A decade or so later, Michael Gove, while in opposition, expressed enthusiasm for the academies policy that Andrew Adonis had led and promised to expand their number if the Conservatives were elected. That has now become irreversible along with the trade union legislation.

In America, welfare reform, including Workfare, which required those receiving welfare to work for it, was adopted by some states in the US in the early 1990s and was generally strongly supported by Republicans. The (Democrat) Clinton administration then adopted the approach as the policy of the federal government. The effect was to make 'a hand up not a handout' a broadly shared policy across much of the United States. Similarly, standards-based school reform in the US – involving setting higher standards for students and testing students to see whether these standards have been achieved – originated in a number of states, mainly in the south, but ultimately became widespread and a shared agenda of (moderate) Republicans and Democrats. Successive US secretaries of education – the wonderfully named Margaret Spellings under Republican President George W. Bush and then Arne Duncan under Democratic President Obama – have put the weight of the federal government behind this agenda.

Building support at individual state level for this policy often involved a coalition of business and civil rights activists, who wanted better performance for children of all backgrounds. Some of the best state governors, such as Jim Hunt in North Carolina in the 1980s and 90s, proved adept at mobilizing this coalition and ensuring that both

Republicans and Democrats across the state supported the direction of travel. In fact, Texas and North Carolina, two of the most improved states in school performance in the 1990s, pursued a decade of reform through both Republican and Democrat administrations.

One underlying point in all these approaches is that the degree of popular support is vital. If a reform is popular, it is much harder to reverse. This is particularly the case if there are a large number of direct beneficiaries. The sale of council houses to their tenants was not just popular. Crucially, it also gave those who took the opportunity to purchase a very strong stake in then ensuring the policy was not reversed. Similarly, one of the reasons Nigel Lawson and his colleagues in the Thatcher administration were so keen to encourage small investors as well as institutions to buy shares in the newly privatized industries (see chapter 3) was that they thus created a powerful, well-motivated constituency of support for the policy. It is one thing for a government to renationalize an industry owned by 'fat cats' in the City; quite another to attempt it if millions of ordinary Joes (or as the advertisement of the time had it, Sids) are shareholders too.

In short, irreversibility depends on legitimacy and public support, another reason why it is important both to implement well and to communicate effectively as you do so.

In the search for irreversibility, it is possible to turn deadlines that look like a threat into an opportunity. An election, say. Often what happens when an election hoves into view is that, first, the campaign takes over so no one pays attention to delivery any more and, second, the incumbent government starts to play safe, to reduce risk, to close things down. Both responses are likely to have a negative effect on delivery.

The deadline of an election, though, is also an opportunity. I always said to my staff in the Delivery Unit that our job was not to help Blair get re-elected – he had other people much more capable of doing that than we were. Our job was to deliver outcomes for the citizens and get good value for every tax pound. That meant that, as it appeared on the horizon, the election of 2005 was not an acceptable distraction. On the contrary, I urged that we maintain or increase the momentum and make the most of having in place experienced teams of ministers and officials who, more than three years into a Parliament, knew what they were doing. We should do everything we could to continue to improve performance. After the election, what would be the state of affairs? No one knew. So make the most of the short term.

In this vein, I wrote a note to Blair on 13 October 2004 setting out what I wanted him to tell the cabinet as they began to think electorally.

- In some areas we've made huge progress and I don't want to lose it now by taking our eye off the ball. In others, real drive in the next two to three months will deliver the results we've worked for over the past three years.
- I want everything done between now and December to ensure successful delivery of this Parliament's objectives. This is your top priority for the next two months. In Delivery Unit terms you should be trying to shift as many traffic lights to green as possible by Christmas.
- It is vital that planning for implementation of the five-year strategies [which had been published in July 2004] proceeds with urgency and radical ambition in the next few months . . .
- In summary, it is very important that as the pre-election climate heats up in the next few months, you ensure your department doesn't get distracted from the central task of delivery both short and medium term.

Sometimes officials stand aside from politics somewhat disingenuously. They say that elections are nothing to do with them. It is true that neutral civil servants should not be seeking to help a governing party to win an election, but it is not true that the elections are irrelevant to their work. If the electoral cycles can be used to the advantage of citizens by getting more delivered and better value for taxpayers' money, go for it. Similarly, it is irresponsible to believe, as so many civil servants do, that in the run-up to an election everything should be allowed to slow down. Political decision-making

> **RULE 48**
> THINK THROUGH THE POLITICS OF IRREVERSIBILITY
> (anticipate the future)

may be temporarily suspended, but public money is still being spent, services are still being used – and patients, students and passengers are still hoping, perhaps expecting, to be served well. There should therefore be no let-up in the search for irreversibility.

PLAN FOR THE FUTURE

The final element of securing irreversibility is always to plan further ahead. 'Plan for the future,' said Andrew Adonis; 'You're never done,' said Dalton McGuinty. For very long periods of human history, there was a steady state punctuated by moments of drama or change. In our era, that is reversed – there is permanent change at pace punctuated by moments of steadiness. In other words, if you don't set out to change the future, it'll change you. So planning ahead is a necessary ingredient of seeing the current agenda through to irreversibility.

I had the opportunity to meet Shahbaz Sharif in June 2013, shortly after he had been re-elected as chief minister of Punjab. He was exhausted by the successive demands of an election campaign and reconstituting a government, which included assisting his brother, who had been swept into office as prime minister of Pakistan. There were maybe seven or eight of us in the meeting. Myself and my team, along with the chief minister and a couple of his most senior officials. On the plane journey, I had prepared eight ambitious goals that the chief minister might want to set for the end of his new five-year term. He liked them but, flushed with victory, wanted to be even more ambitious and more urgent. The officials were raising sceptical eyebrows in response, but when one of them intervened to say that what the CM was now proposing was impossible, the CM batted his admonition away. (It reminded me of a comment an official made to me in the heady months after Blair's election victory in 1997: 'I've understood,' he said. 'You want it all and you want it now.' That was about how it felt.)

But actually the goals didn't satisfy Shahbaz Sharif even as he amended them, until he hit on a way of encapsulating them in a sentence: 'I want to be like Malaysia.' Now that, by 2018, is seriously ambitious, but it is also an aspiration to capture the imagination of the citizens of Punjab. Malaysia may not be perfect, but it is a well-functioning Islamic democracy that has achieved middle-income status and is heading on up. Its education system and its public services generally are well ahead of Punjab's but are not so far ahead as to be off the charts.

With the aspiration clear, we have set out with the new team of officials to plan the next five years. We've set hard-edged and ambitious goals for 2018 and the system is gearing up to make progress towards them. And increasingly the drive towards the aspiration is coming from the Punjab officials rather than from my team. A plan for the future and growing capacity to deliver it – steps on the way to irreversibility.

DRIFT

On 12 November 1936, in the House of Commons Winston Churchill rose to propose an amendment which warned the (Conservative) government of the dangers posed to Europe by the Nazi rearmament of Germany. The government was genuinely worried about this important strategic development, but it was also conscious that the First World War had finished only eighteen years earlier; as a result there was little appetite in the country for an arms race, still less for conflict. The problem was the government didn't have a plan or a direction. It was a very British government led by a very British prime minister, Stanley Baldwin, and they were pursuing the very British approach of muddling through while hoping something would turn up.

Churchill was of the same party but out of office and out of favour. These were his wilderness years and he was obsessed with German rearmament. He had a clear plan for the future – in response Britain should rearm, not because he wanted war, but because he knew the famous maxim, 'If you want peace, prepare for war.' After arguing from the facts, Churchill came to a peroration which has justly become famous. The First Lord of the Admiralty, he said, had promised that the government was always reviewing the position.

Everything, he assured us, is entirely fluid. I am sure that that is true. Anyone can see what the position is. The government simply cannot make up their minds, or they cannot get the Prime Minister to make up his mind. So they go on in a strange paradox, decided only to be undecided, resolved to be irresolute, adamant for drift, solid for fluidity, all powerful to be impotent. So we go on preparing more months and years – precious perhaps vital to the greatness of Britain – for the locusts to eat.[12]

Baldwin, in his late sixties at this time, had been round the block more than once, and probably shrugged it off as one more rhetorical flourish from a politician who had long since had his day. But events bore out Churchill's fears rather than Baldwin's hopes, and Churchill's finest hour lay ahead. The speech stands as an incomparable critique of drift. For those committed to leading any great enterprise of public reform or transformation, the words should be committed to memory. Drift is the enemy of irreversibility, which depends on there being a vision of the future and momentum towards it.

In government such visions always have a hard edge. They cost money, often rather a lot of it. And the raising, oversight and allocation of government money are central to the realizing of a vision and to achieving irreversible change and therefore to the science of delivery; all the more so in an era of austerity. It is to this subject that the final chapter is devoted.

> **RULE 49**
> DRIFT IS THE ENEMY OF DELIVERY
> (momentum is its friend)

8

(Other People's) Money

'Let Pharaoh do this,' asserted Joseph, having interpreted the Pharaoh's dream.

> Let Pharaoh look out a man discreet and wise, and set him over the land of Egypt ... and let him appoint officers over the land and take up the fifth part of the land of Egypt in the seven plenteous years. And let them gather all the food of those good years that come, and lay up corn, under the hand of Pharaoh, and let them keep food in the cities. And that food shall be for store to the land against the seven years of famine, which shall be in the land of Egypt; that the land shall perish not through the famine.[1]

Pharaoh took this advice, and put Joseph, aged just thirty, in charge. He rewarded him with a precious ring, fine linen and gave him use of 'the second chariot which he had'.

Joseph 'went throughout all the land of Egypt. And in the seven plenteous years the earth brought forth by handfuls ... And Joseph gathered corn as the sand of the sea, very much, until he left numbering, for it was without number.' Then, as predicted, the famine years came; 'and dearth was in all lands; but in all the land of Egypt there was bread ... And all the countries came into Egypt to Joseph for to buy corn ...'[2]

There is great wisdom in the ancient texts. (The story of Yusuf appears in the Quran too.) Pharaoh's dream as interpreted by Joseph – what we would now call a Treasury Forecast – suggested that, contrary to contemporary assertions, boom and bust had not ended. After seven years, the boom would be followed by bust. Joseph advises strongly, therefore, that instead of spending as if there were no tomorrow, you should save 20 per cent ('the fifth part') of each year's revenue so that when the bust comes you have the resilience to get through it.

In other words, draw a trajectory for gathered corn, which will result in a store of at least 140 per cent of the baseline, a good year. Then strengthen the delivery chain; put 'a man discreet and wise' in charge of delivery and, for the next link in the chain, 'let him appoint officers over the land'.

Pharaoh was no fool. He saw that the wisest advice came from Joseph, so made him responsible. Joseph didn't hang around in the palace wearing his new finery; he got out there, just like Theodore Roosevelt. He built a data system and started counting the grain (or had someone like Tony O'Connor count it for him). He stopped counting only when he had more grain stored than he knew what to do with, because it was 'without number'. In delivery terms, he was well ahead of trajectory.

When the years of dearth came, not only could Joseph feed all Egyptians, people from other countries beat a path to his door too, including eventually, as the story ends, his own father. Even then, Joseph didn't lose his shrewdness – the Bible tells us that he 'sold' the grain to the Egyptians. He didn't want them to become dependent on a welfare cheque. He also sold the corn to the other countries, no doubt at a high price, 'because the famine was so sore in all the lands', thus building up Egypt's foreign exchange reserves.

The wisdom of the Pharaoh and Joseph therefore ensured Egypt's resilience through a crisis in the global economy. In fact, Nassim Nicholas Taleb might argue that Egypt didn't just survive the recession, it thrived, and thus demonstrated anti-fragility. (What would Egyptians give now for such stewardship and governance?)

The moral is clear: when the tax revenue rolls in in the boom years, don't spend it all at once. And as the downturn looms, be prepared. Why, thousands of years after the story of Joseph was written for us all to learn from, do governments find it so hard to apply these lessons? It might be argued that the electoral cycle confounds long-term thinking; Joseph, after all, planned fourteen years ahead. I'm not sure this is convincing, though, especially after the economic trauma of the past decade. My guess is that citizens would be impressed by a leader who argued that, as the recovery strengthens, not only are we going to pay off the debt, we are also going to invest in our own future resilience. This might not be the easiest message for the campaign trail, but surely it should not be beyond today's political leaders to find the words to express the fundamental concept of stewardship.

Neither Pharaoh nor Joseph refers to government money. The more you think about it, the more the phrase is problematic. It implies a bottomless pit of resource that can be allocated on a whim. The truth is that governments do not have money of their own; all they have is your money and mine, taken from us to meet the demands of the public (also you and me). Strictly speaking, governments have two sources of money: taxation, which they take from the present generation; or borrowing, which is in effect a tax liability on a future generation. Either way, it is a good discipline when in government to remember that the money you spend is other people's money.*

The content of the previous chapters is well established, even if only relatively few governments have applied it systematically. The content of this chapter is emerging, not established – an aspiration rather than a demonstrable reality. Surprising really, given how long we've known the story of Joseph.

BUDGETS

Mitch Daniels perhaps came closest to proving the case made here. When he took office as governor of Indiana in January 2005, the state's economy was suffering and the budget deficit he inherited was over $600 million. When he left office eight years later, he was able to look back on seven consecutive years of budget surplus, all the more remarkable for the fact that his second term was overshadowed by the worst recession in post-war US history.

The finances were not the only problem. The state had seventy-four departments, agencies, boards and commissions, working largely in

---

* The only exceptions to this rule are those thirty or so oil-rich nations which fund government from the proceeds of oil and tend to spend large amounts very wastefully indeed; and they too are in effect spending the future wealth of their nations.

silos, often with overlapping responsibilities and no clarity about what specifically they were supposed to be delivering. The Indiana Department of Transportation, for instance, was responsible for some toll roads where the toll was 15¢ while the cost of collecting each toll was 34¢! At the Bureau of Motor Vehicles, where people stood in line for far too long, some employees were still stuffing public dollars into desk drawers. The Pew Trust, which rates the efficiency of state authorities, gave Indiana a C grade, below the US average.

Daniels had campaigned on a platform of getting public expenditure and the deficit under control and took the view that he had to move fast. Drawing on contacts he had made in the course of his years in business and in federal government, during the transition period he had built a team of like-minded people – his guiding coalition, in the terms of this book.

The day after his inauguration, he set to work. In a letter to all public employees, after affirming his commitment to public service, he quickly made his point:

> Please understand: things are going to be different. From now on, Indiana state government will be about results. We will ask of every department, What are our goals here? What will we measure to determine whether we are achieving them or not and whether we are getting steadily better at it?[3]

This was a clear statement that the science of delivery would be applied. Immediately afterwards, Daniels reformed the muddled process for managing budgets. Building on his experience as head of the Office of Management and Budget under George W. Bush, he established a new central budget office, Indiana's own OMB, and gave its chief cabinet rank. 'Having a very empowered budget office was very important,' he later told Michael Scharff of Princeton.[4]

Within this OMB he set up the Government Efficiency and Financial Planning Unit, which was a next-of-kin to the delivery units described in this book. Daniels's unit combined a delivery agenda with a fiscal agenda. Cris Johnston, a partner from an accountancy/consulting firm, was appointed to lead it. It established goals for each department, systems for monitoring progress and then used the results to decide departmental or agency budget allocations.

The new unit had collaborative target-setting conversations with the departments and agencies. Cleverly they linked budget allocation not so much to demonstrable success, especially in the early days, but to a willingness to establish data systems and start measuring progress. As Adam Horst put it, an important consideration in allocating funding was 'how well the department embraced the idea of measuring agency performance ... Over time, they got the message that if they couldn't show they were efficient and effective and measuring, we would be less inclined to fund them.'[5]

Meanwhile, Governor Daniels used routine monthly cabinet meetings to check on progress towards the major goals. His own office collaborated with the new unit to submit summaries of progress to the government every two weeks. The governor had the personal discipline – not evident in all leading politicians – to commit to and stick to the routines he established.

Moreover, in contrast to the Blair administration, where the mantra was 'Investment for Reform', Daniels pursued reform alongside major cuts in expenditure. In this sense he anticipated the reckoning to come when the financial crisis hit in 2008. He ended collective bargaining on his first day in office. He outsourced swathes of services and there were layoffs too. However, for those who stayed, there were benefits. Daniels introduced significant rewards for performance, including, towards the end of his time in office, giving each state employee an extra $1,000 as a reward for their part in turning a major deficit into a substantial surplus. The key to progress with state employees was simple – the introduction of basic management. Everyone was more accountable; poor performers were removed; successes were rewarded.[6]

The drive for outcomes and efficiency worked. By 2012, Pew was describing Indiana as 'the most improved state in the country'.[7] Results were improved too. The average wait time for a driver's licence was under nine minutes, down from over forty, for example. The governor's approval rating was 63 per cent in April 2012, unusually high in a year when politicians around the world, after years of economic gloom, were perceived poorly. Interestingly too, in spite of the cuts and the end of collective bargaining (or perhaps because of them), state employees were better paid and more strongly motivated than they had been.

Daniels had not avoided controversy, far from it. In addition to his hard line on state employees, he had also raised taxes in his early days to the chagrin of some of his political allies. And by the end of his eight years, in spite of the progress, he wasn't satisfied. 'We believed strongly that culture was an impediment to success and that it required changing if Indiana were ever to move ahead at somewhere near the pace of change in the world,' said one of his key advisers.[8] Daniels agreed that that was a multi-year task, not yet irreversible by the time he had to stand down as his term limit required.

What Mitch Daniels showed is that you can improve performance significantly while controlling or even reducing costs. This is surely the task for government around the world in the twenty-first century. People never enjoy paying taxes, but are generally willing to do so if they see that they and their fellow citizens get a good return on their investment. Most people are sufficiently broad-minded too that they are willing to pay for some services or functions that they themselves don't necessarily need: care for the elderly, education for children and welfare, at least as a temporary measure for people between jobs, for instance. However, unlike in the mid-twentieth century, when the welfare state was new and, after the predations of the 1930s and the devastation of war, people were willing to pay up and take it on trust that the government would do its best, in the early twenty-first century they want to see outcomes, to see the evidence that their money is used well.

As people's work and capital have become more mobile, competition between countries in effect limits what can be collected in tax. Yes, some countries, in Scandinavia for example, continue a tradition of high tax for quality services, but such settlements are unlikely to arise in future, and in some high-tax countries such as France, the settlement is coming under sustained pressure from the globalized economy.

Corporate taxation, a major source of revenue for governments in the twentieth century, is also proving ever more difficult to collect as companies themselves become globalized. Some corporations may be blatantly manipulating the various tax systems to avoid paying up, but the problem goes deeper than that. In a globalized economy, it is not clear whether a company should be taxed where its owners reside, where its goods or services are produced or where its goods or services are consumed. Existing tax systems are still based on a twentieth-century model which assumes a national base and a physical product; neither assumption is true any longer.

This downward pressure on the ability to collect tax coincides with a need to pay off debt, which many governments accumulated to frightening levels during the global recession. Some of this debt arose from inefficiency, but much of it resulted from acting necessarily to stave off a meltdown in the global economy and the misery that would have accompanied it.

Now add into the mix a growing expectation among citizens for quality services from government. The take-it-or-leave-it public service that was accepted as good enough by grateful citizens is a thing of the past. They want quality and evidence of quality. And, while taxpayers are willing to take a broad view, their willingness to keep paying taxes will erode if the services they *do* use – schools or social services, say – are of poor quality.

So the context for the science of delivery in the next decade is one in which the government faces a triple bind:
1. Downward pressure on the ability to raise taxes.
2. A debt burden which needs to be reduced.
3. Growing demand for improved quality of services.

The challenge is therefore, in a word, productivity, the productivity of public services. Where Mitch Daniels has led, others will have to follow. Certainly we in the Prime Minister's Delivery Unit began to think hard about these issues back in 2004–5. Maybe, we were thinking, the Blair mantra of 'Investment for Reform' had passed its sell-by date. Maybe we'd get more reform for less cost by tightening our grip on the public finances. If at that point we weren't ready

> **RULE 50**
> 'MORE FOR LESS' TRUMPS 'INVESTMENT FOR REFORM' (and may deliver more)

to cut public expenditure, at least we could control the rate of increase.

That was then. Before the financial crisis. Before the ballooning of public debt. Before the era of austerity. What was then a speculative case now seems to me to be the very essence of the challenge of how best to spend other people's money. 'More for Less' trumps 'Investment for Reform'.

To reinforce this case, it was possible back when I was in No. 10 to consider the value for money of health service expenditure, as the resources available to it increased at 8 or 9 per cent per annum. While significant improvements in healthcare were evident, it was clear too that they were not being brought about as efficiently as they might have been. Choice and competition certainly helped, but some of the new national contracts – such as the deal done with general practitioners – were excessively generous: too much investment for too little reform. My team and I wrote a note to the prime minister setting this out, but while the Blair government innovated in the way it drove performance, its innovations in controlling cost did not keep up.

It's not that there weren't innovations; it's just that in the end they didn't go far enough. In 1998, in his first Comprehensive Spending Review, Gordon Brown introduced the notion of Public Service Agreements which the Treasury formally agreed with government departments. These set targets for the outcomes that the departments would deliver in return for the funding the Treasury allocated. The basic idea was both radical and excellent, but at first there were far too many targets and some of them were poorly designed and unmeasurable. The idea was refined in future spending reviews. A second innovation was that spending would be allocated for a three-year period, not just one, with the spending review process on a two-year cycle. This meant that each spending review picked up and refined the last year of the previous spending review while allocating funding for a further two. Furthermore, departments were allowed to shift money between years, as were individual service units such as hospitals and schools. This was a major advance, often overlooked. These changes set the context in which the original Delivery Unit was established in 2001. In partnership with the Treasury, it took the discipline of managing public expenditure further by reducing the number and improving the quality of targets and most of all by putting in place a process of driving delivery rather than just allocating the money and hoping for the best.

When, in 2002–3, I met the IMF team that visited annually to review the British economy, I asked them for advice on which countries to learn from about how to manage delivery and public expenditure more effectively. They were very clear in their response: 'This is the frontier.' We had important elements it is true; PSAs, three-year budgets and a systematic approach to delivery. In addition, citizens could check progress against the targets on the Treasury website (though it wasn't always up to date).

The two gaping holes were first that we didn't vigorously control cost, the Treasury's public expenditure officials having become policy wonks rather than bean-counters; and second that, while we managed for outcomes, we did not manage public sector productivity. To put this in different terms, we were not able to compare even within departments, never mind across departmental boundaries, the cost per outcome. That seemed to us an impossible task, but during those same years two leading practitioners of public service reform in the US faced up to it, undaunted.

While the British government was bringing about these improvements in the management of public expenditure, on the other side of the Atlantic two Americans were developing an altogether more radical approach to the same issues, and working with states such as Washington to put it into practice. In the aftermath of the dotcom crash of 2001 – which barely registered an effect on UK public expenditure – many US cities and states found themselves facing a fiscal crisis. Against this backdrop, David Osborne, who in the previous decade had been one of Vice-President Al Gore's favourite thinkers on the subject of reinventing government, and Peter Hutchinson wrote *The Price Government: Getting the Results We Need in an Age of Permanent of Fiscal Crisis*. It was relevant then, but now, in the age of austerity, its time has surely come.

They set out five key challenges that any government should address in shaping a budget:

1. *Get a grip on the problem*: looking at the problem in what they describe as a 'clear-headed' way. Is it about income, borrowing or spending, or a combination of all three?
2. *Set the price of government*: how much in total would the government like to spend and how much are the citizens willing to pay?
3. *Set the priorities of government*: among the many possible priorities, where should the government focus its energy and investment?
4. *Allocate available resources across the priorities*: at this point, hard choices have to be made because the overall total (what we in the Blair administration called 'The Envelope') has already been set. The priorities guide the choices, but that doesn't make them easy. It is always difficult in practice to redirect resources from lower to higher priorities, but if you are not willing to do that you are not really prioritizing.
5. *Develop a purchasing plan for each result*: this is the most radical part of the model. Once the allocations are decided, instead of simply passing the funding on to the relevant existing services, Osborne and Hutchinson propose the development of a purchasing plan by a Results Team for each priority area. They quote the then governor of Washington State, Gary Locke, putting the point succinctly: 'We asked them to forget the loyalties they have to the agencies they represent. Be like citizens. Tell us where to put the money, so we get the best results. Tell us what programs can be consolidated. Tell us what programs don't make a large enough difference in getting the results we want.'[9] The Results Teams then produce what I would call a Delivery Plan for each major outcome. Because the assumptions of the status quo have been directly challenged, the result is an outbreak of creativity.

Note here Governor Locke's suggestion to 'Be like citizens'. This is the way to think about other people's money. With this perspective in place, they rigorously examined the existing agencies and their budgets – what would they buy or continue to buy? What would they like to buy if they had more money? What would they eliminate first if they had less? And what would they eliminate anyway?

Osborne and Hutchinson propose a number of means, within this framework, of getting better value for money, including 'divesting to invest', 'consolidation', 'rewarding performance' and streamlining administrative systems so that they enhance accountability and reduce bureaucracy.

What they suggest is not unlike what Mitch Daniels actually did so successfully. When I reflect on our own approach in the Blair administration, I see parallels too. An analysis of 'the problem' was undertaken and an overall 'envelope' for public expenditure was fixed by Blair and Brown, but the setting of priorities fell short of the Osborne and Hutchinson model. Blair and Brown had different and competing priorities, and the cabinet as a whole did not debate the issue thoroughly. Moreover, unlike the final stages of the Osborne and Hutchinson model, departments tended to be less radical in the preparation of 'purchasing plans' and in rethinking the budgets of existing agencies. I think this is where the problem of having too much money, or at least too fast a rate of increase, meant we collectively lacked rigour and creativity. The situation did not force us to rethink the status quo; too often we were simply able to add to it. The Cameron government has been much more vigorous in taking an axe to existing budgets, but ironically much less clear about defining priorities and outcomes. Maybe one day a British government will put the whole thing together . . .

Here is an approach to budgeting that is conceptually clear as well as radical and practical; the question arises then, why is it so rarely used? The answer is that it is very difficult to do well. Challenging existing budgets means challenging well-entrenched interests. Public sector workforces are usually well organized and usually, too, they are advocates of the status quo or at best incremental change. Even within government, among the politicians as well as the bureaucrats, establishing shared priorities, questioning current practices and taking courageous decisions can cause divisions and conflict. In these circumstances, rather than apply the bold, clean-slate approach Osborne and Hutchinson propose, it is easier to muddle through a year at a time. This may not solve the fundamental problem, but it postpones the day of reckoning for another year. In any case, as Osborne and Hutchinson point out, there are a number of 'deadly deceptions' – use of accounting tricks, borrowing, selling off assets or delaying maintenance, among others – which can help massage your budget into something like respectability, at least in the short term, leaving you to breathe a sigh of relief and, like the Charles Dickens character Micawber, hope that in the meantime something will turn up. It didn't work for him (until he emigrated and started over) and, in an age of austerity, it won't work for governments either.

> **RULE 51**
> PERIODICALLY ADOPT A BOLD, CLEAN-SLATE APPROACH TO BUDGETING (to liberate resources)

At the moment the incentives at every level in the system run counter to the practices Osborne and Hutchinson advocate and we should want to see. The machismo of ministers is measured by how big their budget is and how much more they can add to it in a spending round. There are no prizes for offering up a failing programme and its budget, still less an adequate one that isn't a top priority. The whole negotiation between a spending minister and his or her department all too often becomes a charade – 'smoke and mirrors' as they used to say in Whitehall. Or, in another unappealing phrase, when under pressure to deliver evidence of being tough on costs, officials would recommend offering up a 'bleeding stump' – a programme that you pretended to be willing to cut, knowing that the finance minister or the prime minister could not countenance giving it up.

If the incentives for ministers are misaligned, they are no better for officials. Of course, officials understandably want to impress their ministers, so tend to share their incentives, but there is more to it than this. Generally speaking, civil service pay scales and management practices reward civil servants who manage large budgets or large numbers of people or both – the bigger the organization you run, the more respected you are. While on the face of it this seems obvious, in truth it runs directly counter to what is required for an era of austerity when, surely, the efforts of civil servants who lead small, effective teams, cut programmes, control costs and reduce numbers of people should be highlighted and rewarded.

Then there are the public servants – police officers, teachers, nurses and so on – who, as we've seen, also constantly demand increased pay, better conditions, reduced workload or more support. If these are denied, we are told in a frequent refrain, 'morale' will be worse than ever. In April 2014, the BBC News website included a quote typical of the genre. Christine Blower, general secretary of one of England's teachers' unions, was quoted justifying a threat of strike action by saying that Education Secretary Michael Gove should engage with the union on 'education policies, on workload and accountability, teacher pay including performance related pay and his unfair pension changes ... If the strike happens it will be Michael Gove's fault ... Teacher morale is at a dangerously low ebb.' In short, the union didn't like the policies of the elected government and would strike to protest against them. The education department's response was to point out that 'the vast majority of our teachers and school leaders are hard-working dedicated professionals ... teaching has never been more attractive, more popular or more rewarding. A record number of top graduates are now applying to become teachers ...' In other words, the union's leadership were speaking for an unrepresentative minority. This exchange might have been played out in dozens of languages across dozens of countries – and the point to note is that it is entirely about inputs.

The claims of spending ministers to have serious budgets, the relevance of senior officials who can manage large numbers of people and budgets in the billions, and the morale, latent skill and commitment of public sector workforces are undeniably important. Indeed, they are essential ingredients of delivering for citizens. So how do we square the circle of ensuring these features are in place while at the same time not incentivizing their steady incremental growth, that constant accretion that absorbs so much public money?

The answer is that as long as the debate is focused purely on the inputs – the amount of money spent – it will always be flawed. A major theme of the science of delivery is a shift to outcomes – the results that government and public services actually deliver. This is a major advance but on its own is not sufficient either. The original PMDU was given the task of ensuring some ambitious outcomes were delivered and, thanks to the efforts of government departments and millions of public sector professionals and workers, progress was indeed achieved. However, this progress was made during a period of rapid growth in public expenditure – arguably too rapid – and no attempt was made to ensure the results were delivered while restraining the costs. This is where the debate now needs to go. The way to square the circle is to focus not just on the inputs nor just on the outcomes, but on both simultaneously. It is time for the public services to come to terms with public sector productivity.

PUBLIC SECTOR PRODUCTIVITY

The vexed question of the productivity of public services has a long academic history. It involves extensive examination of economic theory and some major technical complexity. In the market sector, inputs and outputs can be reasonably easily computed because the outputs have a price and inputs have a cost. This is not to say that the measurement of productivity in the market sector is without its complexity, but for practical purposes most of the time it is straightforward. In the public sector – where the service is free at the point of use or where the price is fixed by government rather than the invisible hand of the market – the measurement of productivity becomes much harder.

Adding to this complexity is what value to put on quality – how well a teacher teaches a lesson has a major impact on student outcomes, but it is hard to put a number to it. Or again, the thoughtfulness and responsiveness of a care worker who visits an elderly person in their home makes a huge difference to the person visited, but is hard to measure. To take the complexity one step further, the quality of surgery may make a difference to whether the patient needs further surgery in future. If the first operation is effective, it may reduce the need for future operations – that is surely a gain in productivity, but could easily be accounted as a loss. Preventative measures – such as promoting the use of suncream to reduce skin cancer in future – pose similar questions to those interested in public sector productivity.

Then there are those vital public services whose sole aim is that nothing happens – the measure of success of a counter-terrorism organization is that nothing happens. Similarly, in relation to protection against floods, the ultimate measure of success for the British Environment Agency would be that no one is flooded. But there is no bottomless pit of other people's money. Resources are constrained. What is the right amount to spend to protect the public against floods? And how would you account for the outcome?

Richard Murray of the Swedish Agency for Public Management suggests:

> In part this can be explained by general difficulties in measuring the output of services . . . But in part it must be explained by a completely different perspective [from that of economists] on public services . . . Resource for the production of public services has not been regarded as input into a production process but *as an end in itself* [my italics] . . .[10]

In short, for practical purposes, the input is the output.

Tony Atkinson, the Oxford academic asked by the UK Treasury to report on public sector productivity, put it even more succinctly. Having explored the challenges rather more thoroughly than I have here, he suggests that 'In the face of these difficulties, some might wish to return to the earlier convention that output = input.'[11] To his credit, he rejects this counsel of despair, but his simple little equation explains eloquently why around the world we have the problems described above, with spending ministers and officials and with public sector workforces. Many governments faced with these difficulties still leave productivity in the 'too difficult' box and continue to operate on the output = input basis in spite of its obvious inadequacy. This suits public sector workforces, whose pay, conditions and pensions form the bulk of the 'input' and whose accountability depends on moving away from output = input.

Atkinson, urged on by the UK Treasury (and the European Commission), argued for something better, namely measuring what is achieved by spending on public services because 'we cannot simply assume that outputs equal inputs in such a major part of the economy'.[12]

Atkinson goes on to argue that the UK Office for National Statistics should seek to take account of quality in the public services even though 'Quality has many dimensions and some will prove elusive . . .'[13] He adds that 'If quality adjustments cannot be comprehensive, they should be representative of the range of dimensions.'[14] Furthermore, he sets out the challenge of taking this view; no single number can capture the full complexity of the desired outcomes.[15]

Those words, 'no single number', are the key here. Instinctively we all know – without mastering either economics or statistics – that you can't reduce something complex to a single number, which is why in the *Hitchhiker's Guide to the Galaxy* we find the notion ludicrous that the meaning of life is 42. Relying on outputs = inputs is manifestly absurd and, especially in an era of austerity, unacceptable; we need to move on and seek to measure the output of government services, including quality as well as quantity. This is difficult to do and we will need more than one number to make sense of something so complex.

There is one further problem. The Atkinson Review was commissioned by the Office for National Statistics, whose job is to publish a mass of data on extremely important aspects of the country. By definition, once this data appears, it is already out of date, sometimes significantly so.

Of course, it is important to analyse productivity retrospectively to see the patterns and trends. The accumulation of this kind of analysis will inform public policy over time. What it won't do is provide a basis from which those responsible for a specific programme day-to-day can drive improved productivity – i.e. improved outcomes for the same or less funding – nor will it help governments have an informed conversation about which of a number of different ways to invest public money is likely to be most productive.

To do this, we need an approach which is predictive (it will tell us what is likely to happen), pragmatic (we can cut through the complexities of theoretical debate and have something do-able) and, above all, provides a common language for those within and outside government who want to have an intelligent conversation about productivity and what to do in a practical way to enhance it.

For that, we must turn to Harvard professor Mark H. Moore, whose classic *Creating Public Value* (published in 1995) has stood the test of time. Moore's book sees the world from the perspective of public sector managers – his examples range from refuse collection to management of parks and drug rehabilitation. From our point of view, what makes his account so helpful is that everyone we meet in the book is tasked to deliver a service of some kind to citizens. This gives his work a powerful dose of day-to-day practice to go with the strong theoretical perspective. As he himself says, his aim is to help 'practitioners actually facing the problems'.[16] The proper definition of management success, he argues, is 'to increase the public value produced by public sector organisations in both the short and the long run'.[17]

Moore goes on to set out what he calls 'a managerial view of public value'. First, he argues that value is in part a matter of perceptions – if citizens think a service is good, then that is positive. Second, he points out that the dialogue between citizens and government enables society to identify what it values. This will be different in different places and at different times. Third, therefore, public managers need to strengthen the institutions they lead. Delivering in the short-term at the expense of long-term capacity of the institution or service is not necessarily progress. Fourth, the citizens, not just the users of a service, need ultimately to be convinced because the money being spent is their money. Fifth, this means that citizens need a convincing account of how public service leaders intend to allocate their resources. And finally, public service leaders need to be adaptable and able to respond to changing circumstances.

Moore's definition of public value and his advice on its implications for public managers take us a step on the way from the Atkinson Review towards something that is both predictive and pragmatic – and something that will not just have one number summarizing this complex area – but it doesn't quite get us to where we need to be. As Moore himself explains, 'even though [the] conceptual definition of success for public managers is clear, how to measure it is not ... Moreover ... much of the effectiveness of managerial interventions may depend on the small details of execution as well as on conception.'[18]

The question is whether we can take Moore's analysis and push it that critical stage further. In essence Moore's argument is that public value is created when the following are in place:

- Outcomes are delivered.
- The institution or service concerned is well managed, resilient and capable of delivering in the long-run as well as in the short-run. We could summarize this by saying public managers are responsible for 'pragmatic stewardship' as well as outcomes.
- The beneficiaries of the service and the citizens/taxpayers perceive it to be effective and run broadly in accordance with society's values.
- The resources allocated to it are being used efficiently in pursuit of the authorized goals.

If these are the elements of public value, it should be possible to create a review framework which would help public managers and officials or indeed government ministers to think through systematically what it would take to drive public value.

In a report for the Massachusetts Business Alliance for Education, published in March 2014, my colleagues and I attempted something along these lines. Making the case that this chapter has made throughout, we argued that if Massachusetts aspires to have the best education system in the world then, among other things, it needs to become more effective at managing productivity. There is support for this view from no less a figure than US Secretary of Education Arne Duncan, who put it bluntly:

> It's time to stop treating the problem of educational productivity as a grinding, eat-your-broccoli exercise. It's time to start treating it as an opportunity for innovation and accelerating progress.[19]

Exactly. And Duncan's point applies to public services in general, not just to education.

We were wary, however, of urging a focus on productivity without spelling out how it might become operational so, drawing on Mark Moore and the kind of practical thinking elsewhere in this book, we set out a framework for productive reviews. Table 18 summarizes it.

It looks neat, but how would you use it?

Framework for Productivity Reviews

A. Results	B. Citizen commitment	C. Organizational health		
1. Ambition of outcomes	1. Public confidence	1. Effective processes		Overall productivity
2. Progress on outcomes	2. Student motivation	2. Staff attitude/capacity	=	
3. Lead indicators	3. Parental participation	3. Strong relationships		
÷ D. Inputs				
1. Adequacy of funding	2. Efficiency	3. Transparency		

Table 18

A Framework for Productivity Reviews

The first part examines the results or outcomes the system aspires to, the degree of ambition, the progress made towards the goals and, where it is too early to tell, what can be learned from lead indicators. At its simplest, a measure of productivity would take these outcome measures and 'divide' them by the inputs and reach a measure, but the productivity of public systems is not that simple.

The second part of the framework measures the views of citizens, students and parents. A public system also needs to generate public confidence, partly because that will help ensure its longevity, but also because public confidence is itself a desirable outcome. In education, if students are motivated and parents actively supportive, then that will affect the academic outcomes positively. In health, if people work out and eat well, again outcomes will be better. Public systems therefore need survey data to enable comparisons of citizen and user attitudes. Even without productivity reviews, such data would be powerful and valuable.

The third part of the framework is designed to ensure that those who have stewardship of the system at each level think not just about the present and the delivery of results this year and next, but also consider the long-term well-being of the system – its resilience and capacity to anticipate and manage change over time. This resilience comes from having in place effective processes, such as budgeting or contracting, from having staff with the right attitudes and capacity, and from having great relationships within the system. This part of the framework would require valid and reliable surveys of staff attitudes and motivation, which would in any case have intrinsic merit.

The fourth part of the framework examines inputs. Are these adequate? Are they used efficiently? Can the citizen follow the money through the system in a transparent way? To make the review feasible, key financial data would have to be made available and be comparable across local units, such as districts, not just at an aggregate level, but also on specifics such as the costs of pensions and benefits. Much of this data is available in government systems around the world, but it is not always used systematically, and is often presented poorly, making it hard to use.

It should be immediately clear that the framework picks up the four points above we drew out from Mark Moore's analysis, including separating the beneficiaries (in a school system, the students and parents) from what Moore calls the owners, the public. A framework of this kind is potentially valuable, but how could it be applied in practice? I would suggest a pragmatic approach such as that described for delivery capacity reviews in chapter 2. The outcome of a review would be traffic lights judgements on each of the four parts of the framework.

How useful would this be? Critics would say that it would fall well short of the mathematical precision beloved of economists and scientists and from this perspective therefore fail to provide a satisfying answer to the productivity question. To which my answer is, that is precisely the point. Remember Atkinson's warning that one number could never capture something so complex? Remember Mark Moore's point that in spite of the insight his book provides, it does not offer a means of measuring public value? It is worth remembering too the warning of Louise Horner and Will Hutton, that 'Public value ... entails responsiveness to refined (that is considered, informed) public preferences, which means that the public value will change over time.'[20] And, finally, don't forget that out there are some seriously good economists working theoretically and experimentally to try to crack this public sector equivalent of Fermat's Last Theorem. One day, they might tell us the answer or answers, but supposing it takes a while (as indeed it did with Fermat's theorem), what then? My reply to the critics of the approach outlined here is *it's all we've got*. And at the very least, unless we start attempting something practical we will not make any progress.

Evidently doing just one productivity review on the basis described above, while it would no doubt yield something of value, would not tell us a lot, but imagine five, ten, a hundred or more? Imagine the ability to compare across services, admittedly imperfectly, the ambition of outcomes, the use of lead indicators, the degree of public confidence or the approach to transparency. Surely this would provide rich insights from which those leading public organizations – whether politically or officially – could learn lessons and then apply them. For example, it would help government avoid 'resource imprisonment' (trapping money in failing programmes) and achieve 'resource fluidity' (moving money towards priorities and successes).[21] In the process we would have achieved another of our goals: the establishment of a common language about public sector productivity that would take it out of the field of theoretical economics and place it firmly in the hands of practitioners. The debate that would ensue could change the nature of the conversation between a spending minister and a finance minister; it could change the way civil servants are evaluated and rewarded, and it could change the nature of the dialogue between governments and the public sector workforce. These are more than marginal gains.

And it has to be worth a try because the current alternative is the intellectually bankrupt output = input. Who could possibly defend that in an era of austerity?

Let's now imagine how a government could combine the various elements we have discussed in this chapter – setting goals, setting budgets and measuring productivity – into a sequence or cycle that would bring order to the management of other people's money as Mitch Daniels did so effectively.

Constitutions and laws affect the budget process in each country, so it is not possible to set out a definitive approach. The Public Expenditure Cycle (Table 19) is intended to be a conceptually clear approach that pulls all the crucial elements together in a new way that could then be adapted and refined for specific purposes in a given country. I've allocated times of the year to each step not because they are necessarily right for each country – clearly not – but to give a sense of how the process might unfold.

A two-year cycle of this kind has a great deal going for it. It allows

Public Expenditure Cycle

Year 1	
Spring	• Cabinet debate on government priorities, following public 'conversation' or consultation over six months before
	• The overall framework for public expenditure in the next cycle proposed by finance ministry, debated and agreed by cabinet, thus identifying priorities
Summer	• Departmental proposals developed within this context, including identifying clear outcomes/targets, programmes that might be cut and areas where the approach to delivery might be changed
	• Separate, related process applied to cross-cutting themes (such as tackling drug abuse or problem families)
Autumn	• Departments finalize negotiation with finance ministry and settle
	• New overall settlement agreed by cabinet and published
	• Departments begin work on a 'purchasing plan'
Year 2	
Spring/Summer	• Purchasing plans finalized and formally approved
	• Focus on setting up to deliver and starting on delivery
Autumn	• Review of progress so far, including productivity reviews and lessons learned
	• Public conversation begins again
	• Lessons of review applied
Year 3	
Spring	• Cycle begins again

Table 19

time to refine and define priorities and to rethink how to approach delivery as in Osborne and Hutchinson's purchasing plans. It also ensures there is an entire year devoted to finalizing planning and then implementing, without the distraction of a spending round. By contrast, a one-year cycle is an endless negotiation, with all the key players focused inward on each other's tactics rather than outward on what is being delivered. To illustrate this point, I remember in the late 1990s driving with US Education Secretary Dick Riley – a former governor of South Carolina and a tough, experienced operator with a wonderfully gentle demeanour – from the education department to the White House, where I had been invited to see Bill Clinton sign that year's budget, which he did surrounded by police officers and teachers, who were the main beneficiaries. On the way back to the education department, just minutes after the budget had been signed, Riley made a call to an important congressman. He told me it was the first step in negotiating the following year's budget.

> **RULE 52**
> MAKE PUBLIC SECTOR PRODUCTIVITY CENTRAL (a two-year budget cycle will make a big difference)

FINANCE MINISTERS

However much emphasis the government as a whole places on the productivity of public expenditure, in the end the person who has to eat, sleep and breathe it is the finance minister. Even if every finance minister adopted the processes described above – and few have done so yet – there is another major problem which is simply this: finance ministers are extremely busy people who have a huge burden of responsibility. In 2014 I had the privilege of spending a few days with half a dozen African ministers of finance, when my main contribution was to discuss with them delivery and productivity as part of the management of public finances. Clearly, this was an important part of their job and they were certainly interested. It was striking though, when we asked them to list their ambitions and priorities, how this was just one of many. Here are some of the others:

Raising economic growth and making it inclusive.

Eliminating corruption.

Maintaining macro-economic stability and sustainable debt.

Restructuring the National Treasury.

Improving the standard of living for the people.

Reducing poverty.

Reducing social vulnerability.

Putting in place proper macro-economic and fiscal policies.
Mobilizing adequate domestic resources.
Implementing new tax measures.
Attaining single-digit inflation.
No one could argue that any of these are unimportant or relatively insignificant!

Often in African countries the finance minister is a technocrat, perhaps with an economics or business degree from a (US) university and the experience of a spell at the World Bank. This makes sense at one level because the tasks of ensuring macro-economic stability, such as cutting inflation and managing debt, clearly require significant technical knowledge; at another level it is a problem because these tasks are intensely political, both inside with cabinet colleagues and outside with the people.

This became apparent when we asked the ministers what the biggest barriers to their success were. Reflecting on their challenges inside government, they pointed to:
Emerging unbudgeted needs.
Many priorities to implement.
Timely implementation of requirements from other sector ministries.
Political buy-in with weak capacity in Parliament.
Political interference.

Donors weren't always helpful either. One finance minister expressed frustration with 'bureaucracy and long processes in mobilising international resources'. Another referred simply to 'conditionalities'. If internal politics was complicated, externally it was harder still. One minister referred to the difficulty of winning 'people's support in implementation of new measures of tax', and the 'inadequate domestic resources' available. Another referred to 'corporate cartels [who] avoid taxes', 'high interest rates', the 'slow pace of implementation' and 'corruption'. Still another to 'vested interests'.

These are by no means the only challenges they face. There are also the big public–private partnership deals – such as a dam in an environmentally important location – for which the finance ministry, on behalf of the government, is usually the centre of expertise. These can become explosive issues. We took the ministers through the case study of the Chilean government, Endesa (a large company) and the proposed Ralco Dam on the Biobío river. The basic conflict was between the citizens of Santiago, the capital, whose energy needs were increasing rapidly along with the city's growing wealth, and the Pehuenche indigenous people whose land, hundreds of miles from Santiago, would be flooded once the dam was constructed. Most of the Pehuenche settled, but famously five 'nanas', or grannies, held out and in the end, after a massive local and international campaign, Endesa gave up.[22]

This context is worth spelling out for finance ministers because in these circumstances it is difficult – perhaps impossible – for them to give the time and attention to public sector productivity that is required, however much people such as myself might advocate it. It is also worth pointing out that some of what these ministers are held to account for – indeed are holding themselves to account for – such as macro-economic stability, is hugely affected by matters far beyond their control. The Zambian minister of finance, just to take one case, has very limited influence over the price of copper (which will be heavily determined by the growth rate in China); yet this is central to all his projections for the Zambian economy. Still less could he or any of his colleagues in Africa be held to account for the sub-prime lending crisis in the US which prompted the near-meltdown of the global economy in 2008. So the pressures on these pivotal figures in governments are huge; they have an array of vital responsibilities, for some of which they are at the mercy of global economic affairs.

Nor is this the case just for finance ministers in the developing world. Take Alistair Darling, who was Britain's Chancellor of the Exchequer from 2007 to 2010, through the most demanding period of global economic turmoil the world had seen since the early 1930s. Alistair is a truly unflappable individual. In a succession of roles, among them Secretary of State for Transport, he was one of the unsung heroes of the Blair years; calm, methodical, undemonstrative and intelligent, he got things done, such as making the trains run on time (or at least run on time more often). He could calm down any ministry after a crisis.

A year into his term as Chancellor of the Exchequer, the global economy, and therefore the British banks, found themselves in very serious trouble. This is how Alistair Darling saw it:

> I don't believe in panicking before it's absolutely necessary but I came close to considering it on the morning of 7 October 2008 . . . We took off from RAF Northolt on a small chartered jet. A sunrise never felt so bleak. I knew the London markets were about to open and that they would react badly to the leaked news, however wrong it was. Iceland and its banking system were close to collapse and one of its banks would probably fail that day. In Ireland the day before they had, without warning, underwritten all the savings in their banks, causing disarray for everyone else in Europe. Three weeks earlier, in the United States, the collapse of Lehman Brothers, one of the country's oldest banks, had pushed the rest of Wall Street to the edge. We were looking over the precipice.[23]

Here you see a finance minister from one of the world's top economies sensing that he had (almost) lost control. And if Alistair Darling can't control events, then you can be reasonably confident no one else could. How much more must a finance minister in a weaker country feel at the mercy of events, especially if they have large loans from the World Bank and the IMF, whose regular delegations dictate to them what they should and shouldn't do?

All of this surely strengthens the case for the establishment of a delivery function, along the lines of the various models advocated in chapter 2. Then, as these massive global events or local conflicts, as with Endesa, swirl around finance ministries, at least there is one authoritative part of the government machine constantly focused on delivering results and improving public sector productivity. A finance minister also needs someone hard-edged on the team – someone for whom popularity is not an important consideration.

Anything but likeable, his biographer, Thomas Penn, calls him (in *Winter King*): 'an avaricious Machiavellian king who inspired not love but fear';[24] Francis Bacon called him a 'dark prince'; and Shakespeare decided he couldn't face writing a play about him. Yet measured on the test 'Did the monarch leave the country better than he found it?', Henry VII may well be as good a monarch as England ever had. He seized the kingdom in a battle in 1485 and over the twenty-four years of his reign put an end to the decades of civil war that had riven England. He founded a dynasty, the Tudors, that in turn founded a strong state. Most importantly, he brought peace, put the unruly barons in their place and got a grip on the country's finances. He left a huge surplus, rare among the monarchs of his time, and it was not his fault that his son and more famous (or infamous) successor, Henry VIII, squandered it while divorcing or beheading a succession of wives.

Getting a grip on the finances at the turn of the sixteenth century was no mean feat. Henry VII may very well have been paranoid, but he had more reason than most to be so. There were plenty of important people, at home and abroad, out to get him. Henry's solution was to build around him a close-knit team – a guiding coalition we might call them – who were totally loyal and who were most definitely not from among the high nobility, all of whom had agendas of their own and could not be trusted.

One key member of this team was Edmund Dudley, an intelligent, well-connected and ambitious rising star who had specialized in understanding the law pertaining to the king's prerogatives. 'Sharp, silver-tongued and intellectually curious' is how Thomas Penn describes him.[25] In 1504, Henry VII made him Speaker of Parliament (kings could do that back then) and soon afterwards put him on the payroll in the palace. From then on, Henry and Edmund Dudley were often to be found sitting together – imagine them by candlelight in the cavernous palace – sifting through accounts and, drawing on Dudley's specialist knowledge, finding ways to screw as much money for the state coffers as possible from the only three sources available – the nobility, the merchants of the City of London and the Church. As long as he had Henry's support, Dudley had no anxiety about upsetting any of the leaders of these constituencies. He may even have enjoyed it. The state's coffers filled. You can almost imagine Henry and his loyal servant (like those football fans from Millwall in south London in later generations), singing 'No one likes us, we don't care.' Even as Henry aged, the state was getting stronger, if not more cheerful.

Before anyone says anything, I am not recommending the return of a Machiavellian prince or the paranoia of Henry VII. And I am not recommending the ethics of the sixteenth century either, when it was simply assumed that Dudley would enrich his family as well as the state.

I am recommending, though, that a leader who wants to deliver in a time of austerity needs the modern equivalent, following modern ethics, of Edmund Dudley: someone who can go through the accounts line by line; someone who knows the law and how it operates; someone who is intensely loyal; someone with no desire for adulation. It is possible to imagine this role being played in some governments by a top civil servant, but the right kind of politician would be better still. Not every politician wants to be a public figure; there are some who prefer the kind of behind-the-scenes role that Edmund Dudley performed and are more effective at mastering the detail than painting the big picture.

I chose Edmund Dudley as the emblematic case knowing it to be both slightly creepy and a caricature. The point is, though, that the effective management of finances and the allocation of funds to the priorities requires someone capable not just of repeatedly saying 'No', but of picking holes in numerous plausible proposals for spending money on a good cause. That is someone with a sharp brain, an attention to detail and a thick skin. So the not unreasonable question for anyone seeking to deliver public sector productivity is 'Who is your Edmund Dudley?' As we've seen, Herbert Mayhew Lord, Calvin Coolidge's Budget Director, was a twentieth-century exemplar.

Plausible candidates may be put off by one final detail of Dudley's life. Shortly after Henry VIII succeeded his father in 1509, he discovered that an easy way to improve what we might now call his poll ratings among the nobility, the merchants and the bishops was to have Edmund Dudley beheaded.

RULE 53
ANSWER THE QUESTION: 'WHO IS YOUR EDMUND DUDLEY?' (there is more to delivery than being loved)

RULE 54
FINANCE MINISTERS ARE UNDER HUGE PRESSURE (another reason for a delivery function)

*

To conclude the chapter, it's worth emphasizing that no one ever said this was going to be easy. No government has yet quite put together the combination of a drive for delivery, the mastery of public sector productivity and the efficient management of the public finances. Governor Mitch Daniels came close. It was important to Indiana then. It is vital to the world now. It is not an exaggeration to suggest that, unless governments master this critical combination, the success of both the global economy and accountable government will be at stake. Any country that is able to apply systematically the wisdom of Joseph in the ancient texts will be set up to thrive in the twenty-first century.

Conclusion: The Future of Delivery

Sohail Raza has a beaming smile and an infectious laugh. When he speaks, he speaks fast; in his enthusiasm, the words tumble over each other as in a torrent. He moved from the private sector in Lahore to help establish the data collection system for the Punjab Education Roadmap (described in chapter 4). My friend and colleague Katelyn Donnelly and Sohail worked through how to collect the data efficiently, what the targets might be for each district and for the province as a whole, and then produced trajectories for each district for each of the targets. These targets and trajectories became fundamental to the progress that has been made.

But by then Sohail had moved on. As if designing and implementing a data system for Punjab, with 60,000 schools and 25 million children wasn't tough enough, he agreed to move to Peshawar and do the same for the old North-West Frontier Province now called Khyber Pakhtunkhwa. True, it had about half as many schools and children, but in every other respect this was a much tougher place to work. In the south of the province there is desert heat; in the north, huge mountains where the Hindu Kush and Himalayas meet. Simply getting to the schools at all in some locations at some times of year is a major challenge.

To make matters worse, Khyber Pakhtunkhwa is the province most affected by endemic conflict and terrorism. Its long border with Afghanistan and its infamous tribal areas have been an unruly and unruled base for conflict of various kinds since the mid-nineteenth century. In 2009, the first year I visited Pakistan, the Taliban advanced as far as the Swat valley, one of the districts of Khyber Pakhtunkhwa. Girls' schools were closed or destroyed. The Taliban invasion had reached to just eighty miles or so from the country's nuclear-armed capital, Islamabad. Since then the situation has improved somewhat, but terrorism in Khyber Pakhtunkhwa is still endemic, creating misery for some and uncertainty for many.

These are not the easiest of circumstances in which to establish a data collection process for a school system, involving monthly visits to almost 30,000 schools, some of them very remote. But Sohail was undaunted. For two years (a period which involved, in May 2013, an election and change of government in the province), he developed a plan drove it forward and painstakingly helped it jump every bureaucratic hurdle that was put in its way. Some hurdles it had to jump twice because the new government understandably wanted to ensure it was not inheriting a boondoggle from the outgoing administration it had deposed. Meanwhile, in Khyber Pakhtunkhwa, unlike Punjab, the revolving door for officials still applied, at least until recently. Some only lasted a few months in post before being whirled away. Each time, Sohail found himself starting over.

With Sisyphean persistence, he explained once again to each new top official in Khyber Pakhtunkhwa what he believed was necessary and eventually, unlike Sisyphus, he rolled his boulder to the top of the hill. He won approval for the Information Monitoring Unit, struck up a friendship with the official designated to lead it, recruited the 500 data monitors, trained all of them, and secured, through the proper procurement process, motorbikes so that each of them could make the fifteen school visits a week on which the data collection system would depend.

In March 2014, their first month in operation, the newly trained data monitors managed to collect data from 88 per cent of the schools in spite of harassment from militants in some places and heavy snowfall blocking the valleys in others. The data collectors are determined people devoted to Sohail, as he explained to me. 'I trained them personally,' he laughs, 'they are my friends. I love them.' In May 2014, data was collected from 96 per cent of the schools. The results of this new approach are already apparent; absenteeism of teachers has dropped significantly. So far, so similar to the Punjab approach. But Sohail is an innovator and an entrepreneur too. In addition to everything else he'd done, he contracted software developers to gather all the data as it came in each day and then present it on a dashboard. In April 2014 the dashboard was shown to Khyber Pakhtunkhwa's chief minister, Pervez Khattak. He praised his education department (and the UK's Department for International Development) for their contribution and said the new system would enable him to track down 'ghost schools and proxy teachers'.[1] Now he can find out at any time of day (or night for that matter) not just the performance of his school system last month on teacher presence, student attendance and the provision of facilities, but also what the data shows about individual districts or even schools. He can break it down by gender and type of school too.

The next stage for the development of this data collection system and dashboard will be to make it public. Chief Minister Khattak rapidly realized that by making this data publicly available he could unlock citizen pressure for improvement of the shockingly poor school system – which he believes is an embarrassment to his province. The message for other parts of the public services, such as health, is clear: transparency is to corruption what daylight is to a vampire.

In some of the least propitious circumstances imaginable, Sohail Raza has done something remarkable: not just made sure data is collected systematically, important though that is, but also anticipated two developments which are likely to transform approaches to delivery in the next decade: big data and transparency.

This brief concluding chapter has two main points. The first is to summarize some developments in the nature of government that will help to shape the science of delivery in the next decade. The second is to show how these reinforce the central argument of this book. In fact, the combination of these developments with the science of delivery could be transformative and deliver precisely those better outcomes at lower cost that citizens across the world are increasingly likely to demand. So, what are these developments?

DATA AND TRANSPARENCY

Sohail Raza's innovations in Khyber Pakhtunkhwa are just one example of what is happening globally. The digital revolution is creating a data revolution – the era of Big Data has arrived and is shaping everything from sport and shopping to government and public services.

> **RULE 55**
> BIG DATA AND TRANSPARENCY ARE COMING (prepare to make the most of them)

Expect to see more and more data made public and the rise of social and other enterprises that crunch the numbers government publishes and reach new conclusions. In an era where joggers and

Using Data

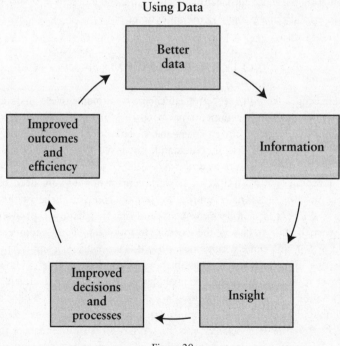

Figure 29

cyclists the world over are already monitoring every inch of ground they cover, expect citizens to take (and be expected to take) ever greater responsibility for their own health and well-being. Judge Damon Keith's observation that 'democracies die behind closed doors'[2] looks increasingly prescient.

PRIVACY

As the data explosion occurs there will be growing concern about privacy, especially when extensive data about individuals comes into the possession of governments. In the era of Wikileaks and lost flash drives, many people simply don't trust governments (or corporations) with their data. The problem is that the data explosion is happening so fast that there isn't time to write the rules of the game before the game changes. Paradoxically, governments will have to strengthen transparency and privacy at the same time.

CITIZEN ENGAGEMENT

Increasingly we will see better educated, wealthier citizens making more demands on government. As Governor Martin O'Malley puts it, 'The next horizon is citizen engagement.' They will expect to be participants in the services they demand, not just recipients. They will expect to exercise choice as well as voice. They will be more assertive as consumers and as citizens. Governments will therefore need to become more responsive and agile. Jeremy Heimans believes that there will be '21st century movements and ventures that use the power of participation to change the world'. He and Henry Timms compare old power with this emerging new power. Old power, they say, is held by a few and is 'closed, inaccessible and leader-driven', whereas new power is made by many and is 'open, participatory and peer-driven'.[3]

I doubt that new power will replace old power. The future will be a combination of the two. Certainly governments will have to adapt how they approach delivery and, as services shift from adequate to good to great, participatory processes will become ever more important. For example, a July 2014 paper from the think tank Reform on 'The Expert Citizen' suggests that a combination of redesigned buildings and communities with active, better-informed citizens could reduce the burden on the police.

DIGITAL GOVERNMENT

As increasing numbers of people experience daily, much of government is going online. Consulting company BCG discovered that there are online services in all areas, from parks and sporting facilities to health, housing, tax and transport. They also found that people's frustration was greatest with the services they considered most important. Even so, they did not want to turn the clock back. They like the direction and want it delivered better. To satisfy citizens, whole services, not just demands for information, need to go online. It may be some comfort to government officials to learn that BCG did not find that government was any worse at this transition than the business sector.[4]

Digital government transforms the prospects for data and transparency. Take OpenGov, a US platform on which 150 US local governments analyse more than $50 billion of annual expenditure:

> Governments use OpenGov *internally* to create custom reports, help operations manage the budget, keep senior executives and legislators maximally informed, and help with important workflows from the budgeting process to internal audits. And they use it *externally* to publish interactive budgets, share this information with the community, and even achieve revenue goals by disseminating important financial data around tax or bond measures.[5]

COMPETITIONS

Arne Duncan, Barack Obama's education secretary, pulled off a masterstroke – he ran a competition called Race to the Top. States would compete for funds to reform their education systems. To enter they had to meet certain requirements – introduce data systems, or lift any cap they might have had on the number of charter schools. The prize money was quite substantial, so twenty or thirty states changed their laws to enable them to enter, though only a dozen actually won.

In other words, running the competition enabled Arne Duncan not just to promote innovation, but also to influence policy right across the country. In the terms of chapter 8, he got more output for his money.

Competitions, run transparently, are likely to become a widespread means for government to innovate and advance an agenda, especially where the way forward is not entirely clear.

MARKETS AND GOVERNMENT

William Easterly's book *The Tyranny of Experts* is a *tour de force*; his central argument is that the most important role of government is to secure individual economic and political rights and create well-regulated markets. Beyond that, how much government does should be a matter of political choice. Easterly points out that Adam Smith thought that only government could solve some problems, such as a malfunctioning market or one where public goods are required (such as schools or roads) which do not provide enough of a private return.

He argues forcefully that limiting government to these basic functions and leaving markets to do the rest is the route to economic growth. Certainly he believes this approach will be far more effective over the long run than the combination of experts and autocracy which he argues has underpinned the approach to development in the aid community.

While there will be outliers, such as the Scandinavian countries, I expect the future will see markets becoming steadily more important in meeting the needs and aspirations of citizens, with governments becoming smaller but needing to become more effective.

Thus, contrary to some ill-informed commentary, the choice is not between markets and government, but between effective combinations of the two. Theodore Roosevelt, a powerful president deeply committed to markets, put it this way, as he ended his term: 'The danger to

American democracy lies not in the least in the concentration of administrative power in competent and accountable hands. It lies in having the power insufficiently concentrated so that no one can be held accountable for its use.'[6]

In short, as the boundaries of markets are extended, governments will need to become more competent and more accountable. The science of delivery will become more important than ever.

> **RULE 56**
> SUCCESSFUL MARKETS AND EFFECTIVE GOVERNMENT GO TOGETHER (avoid the false dichotomy)

ENTREPRENEURSHIP

Entrepreneurship used to be seen as the preserve of the business sector, in contrast to the public sector, which was seen as 'risk-averse'. Two shifts over the past generation have made this analysis obsolete. One is the rise of successful social enterprises, some of which are now providing vital services. The other is the spread of entrepreneurial thinking from the business sector into the social and public sectors. As Mitchell Weiss comments, the phrase 'government entrepreneur' is not necessarily an oxymoron.[7] Increasingly, he goes on to argue, entrepreneurship can and should be taught to leaders in all sectors.

Indeed, if students from all sectors learn entrepreneurship together, they may well develop mutual understanding and opportunities to collaborate. The key ingredients of successful entrepreneurship are – to summarize Weiss – test early, test often, don't grow too fast or too soon, collaborate with like-minded people across sector boundaries, and have a compelling narrative of what you intend to do and why. This should be common ground in any sector. The British government, for example, claims 'A hundred new British

> **RULE 57**
> PUBLIC AND SOCIAL ENTREPRENEURSHIP WILL BECOME INCREASINGLY IMPORTANT TO DELIVERING OUTCOMES (encourage it)

businesses have been spun out from the public sector and are delivering nearly £1.5 billion of public services.'[8]

This way of thinking is already spreading in government circles. Boundaries are blurring. Increasingly, citizens are focused on the outcomes and the cost; they are generally open-minded about who provides and how, as long as they get the desired results at a reasonable price.

THE IMPLICATIONS FOR THE SCIENCE OF DELIVERY

These trends are likely to change the nature of government radically over the next decade or so, but they will not replace the need for a science of delivery; far from it. They will reinforce it, because the distilled essence of the science of delivery is that it is a set of processes that enables governments to deliver ambitious goals by learning effectively as they go, and refining as necessary.

The science of delivery itself is still in its infancy. The more it is applied, the deeper our knowledge of it will become. We should leave the last word, therefore, to one of its acknowledged masters.

Idris Jala, whom we have met several times before in this book, is a classic example of a government entrepreneur. Interviewed by Deepa Iyer of the Woodrow Wilson School of Public and International Affairs, he set out his thinking, which brings together the trends for the future mentioned in this conclusion and the accounts of delivery described throughout this book. He emphasized clear priorities, good data, regular progress updates, delivery chains and a delivery unit with a small, lean team. He also warned that, however good the delivery unit might be, it is the ministers and ministries who must ultimately deliver. The delivery unit itself can only be a catalyst. He listed the principles on which his approach is based – set ambitious goals (he calls it 'the game of the impossible'); choose good indicators; ensure people shift from talking to acting; adapt the reform approach as the situation changes; and build ever stronger coalitions.

The science of delivery, important though it is to the future of government, is not a complete science and never will be. The soap opera factors of politics and government will never be eliminated. This is a cause for celebration – human judgement in all its fallibility will ultimately reign supreme. However much we know and however much power we wield, there will always be the unexpected development to throw us off course. For those with power, hubris is always a risk. Pride comes before a fall, in government above all. Idris Jala puts it thus:

> The [last] principle is ... divine intervention ... You could ask who controls the world and some people say it is God, some people say it is Fate ... there are lots of things outside of our control ... the beauty of understanding this is the following; we become humble ... Vulnerability is to my mind a virtue. If you feel vulnerable ... you know the world is not at your feet.[9]

Idris Jala's final point reinforces my own concluding message: you might adopt in full the science of delivery and still fall short. Even so, we should do our best to apply what we do know, confident that doing so will, in most places, most of the time, make a big difference to the outcomes government delivers for citizens. This will strengthen both markets and government. If with due humility the knowledge of how to run a government becomes more widely shared, then surely the world will become a better place.

Appendix: The 57 Rules

1. PRIORITIES

1. HAVE AN AGENDA (even if, like Lord Salisbury, it is to do nothing)
2. DECIDE ON YOUR PRIORITIES (really decide)
3. BE UNREASONABLE (sometimes) AND USE THE MAP OF DELIVERY
4. SET A SMALL NUMBER OF WELL-DESIGNED TARGETS (but don't call them targets if you don't want to!)
5. APPLY THE SCIENCE TO TARGET-SETTING (but don't depend on it)
6. CHECK FOR PERVERSE OR UNINTENDED CONSEQUENCES (they may not happen)
7. CONSULT WITHOUT CONCEDING ON AMBITION (opposition is inevitable)
8. TARGETS ARE IMPORTANT BUT NOT THE POINT (state and restate the story about the moral purpose)

2. ORGANIZATION

9. REVIEW THE CAPACITY OF YOUR SYSTEM TO DELIVER THE AGREED GOALS (and do it quickly)
10. SET UP A DELIVERY UNIT (call it what you like, but separate it from strategy and policy)
11. THE DELIVERY UNIT NEEDS TO BE SMALL AND WELL LED (and excellent at building relationships)
12. CREATE A GUIDING COALITION FOR EACH PRIORITY (to increase clarity and speed)
13. BUILD THE CAPACITY TO DELIVER YOUR AGENDA (civil service reform for its own sake can be an energy drain)

3. STRATEGY

14. WORK FROM PRINCIPLES TO STRATEGY TO POLICY (and put a stake through the heart of initiatives)
15. TRUST AND ALTRUISM IS POPULAR BUT DOESN'T WORK (other than in unusual circumstances)
16. THE HIERARCHY AND TARGETS APPROACH WILL GET YOU FROM AWFUL TO ADEQUATE (if executed well)
17. CHOICE IS BECOMING INCREASINGLY IMPORTANT IN PUBLIC SYSTEMS (it's a good in itself)
18. TRANSPARENT PUBLIC RANKING WORKS (don't flinch)
19. CONTRACTING OUT SERVICES BREAKS MONOPOLIES (but don't think it relieves you from management responsibilities)
20. WELL-DESIGNED PRIVATIZATION CAN IMPROVE EFFICIENCY (it can also lead to smaller, more effective government)
21. A WELL-DESIGNED VOUCHER SCHEME EMPOWERS THE BENEFICIARIES (and can promote equity)
22. GOVERNMENT SHOULD TAKE ITS STEWARDSHIP RESPONSIBILITY SERIOUSLY; THAT INCLUDES STRATEGY, REGULATION AND THE SUPPLY OF SKILLED PROFESSIONALS

4. PLANNING

23. UNDERSTAND IN YOUR HEAD (and feel in your heart) THE GAP BETWEEN YOUR ASPIRATION AND THE UNVARNISHED REALITY
24. UNDERSTAND THE POTENTIAL DRIVERS OF CHANGE (and base your plan on them)
25. PREPARE A PLAN TO IMPLEMENT YOUR STRATEGY THAT IS GOOD ENOUGH TO GET STARTED (and don't make concessions for a quiet life)
26. STRENGTHEN THE DELIVERY CHAIN (don't think you can get away without doing so)
27. NEVER GO ANYWHERE WITHOUT A TRAJECTORY (you'll learn better, faster and deeper)
28. COLLECT DATA, ASK THE RIGHT QUESTIONS AND PRESENT THE ANSWERS BEAUTIFULLY (and don't forget integrity)

29. DATA MAKES A JOB DO-ABLE (until then, all you can do is make excuses and hope for the best)

5. ROUTINES

30. DON'T BE SPOOKED BY THE DEAFENING SILENCE (but keep listening)
31. ANTICIPATE THE IMPLEMENTATION DIP (and demonstrate the leadership required to get through it)
32. DEAL WITH CRISES (but don't use them as an excuse)
33. GOVERNMENT BY ROUTINE BEATS GOVERNMENT BY SPASM (it's not even close)
34. PREPARE MONTHLY NOTES FOR THE LEADER (and make them 'deeply interesting')
35. ROUTINE MEETINGS OR STOCKTAKES CREATE FALSE DEADLINES (and solve problems before they become crises)
36. A FULL-SCALE REVIEW OF THE PROGRAMME AT LEAST ONCE A YEAR PROVIDES DEEP LEARNING (which can be acted on immediately)
37. UNDERSTAND THE WOOD AND THE TREES (and the view beyond)

6. PROBLEM-SOLVING

38. CATEGORIZE PROBLEMS BY THEIR INTENSITY (and act accordingly)
39. DIAGNOSE PROBLEMS PRECISELY (and act accordingly)
40. TAKE ALL THE EXCUSES OFF THE TABLE
41. LEARN ACTIVELY FROM EXPERIENCE (failure is a great teacher)
42. NEGOTIATE ON THE BASIS OF PRINCIPLE (but don't depend on it)
43. GUARD AGAINST FOLLY (it has been common throughout history)

7. IRREVERSIBILITY

44. THERE IS NO SUBSTITUTE FOR SUSTAINED, DISCIPLINED POLITICAL LEADERSHIP
45. PERSIST (but don't expect the credit)

46. LEARN THE LEARNABLE AND CONTROL THE CONTROL-LABLE (obsessively)
47. INVEST DEEPLY AND CONTINUOUSLY IN SKILL AND CAPABILITY (commitment will follow)
48. THINK THROUGH THE POLITICS OF IRREVERSIBILITY (anticipate the future)
49. DRIFT IS THE ENEMY OF DELIVERY (momentum is its friend)

8. (OTHER PEOPLE'S) MONEY

50. 'MORE FOR LESS' TRUMPS 'INVESTMENT FOR REFORM' (and may deliver more)
51. PERIODICALLY ADOPT A BOLD, CLEAN-SLATE APPROACH TO BUDGETING (to liberate resources)
52. MAKE PUBLIC SECTOR PRODUCTIVITY CENTRAL (a two-year budget cycle will make a big difference)
53. ANSWER THE QUESTION: 'WHO IS YOUR EDMUND DUDLEY?' (there is more to delivery than being loved)
54. FINANCE MINISTERS ARE UNDER HUGE PRESSURE (another reason for a delivery function)

CONCLUSION: THE FUTURE OF DELIVERY

55. BIG DATA AND TRANSPARENCY ARE COMING (prepare to make the most of them)
56. SUCCESSFUL MARKETS AND EFFECTIVE GOVERNMENT GO TOGETHER (avoid the false dichotomy)
57. PUBLIC AND SOCIAL ENTREPRENEURSHIP WILL BECOME INCREASINGLY IMPORTANT TO DELIVERING OUTCOMES (encourage it)

Notes

PREFACE

1. Gold, p. 9
2. Quoted in Goodwin, p. 564
3. Quoted in Fukuyama (2014), p. 152
4. *Sunday Telegraph*, 19 October 2014

INTRODUCTION: THE MISSING SCIENCE OF DELIVERY

1. *Economist*, 4 November 2010
2. Quoted in Barber (2008), p. 71
3. Bok, p. 2
4. Kim, p. 6
5. McKinsey, pp. 64–5
6. Drèze and Sen, p. ix
7. Ibid., p. xi
8. *Economist*, 18 October 2014
9. Easterly, p. 254
10. Kapuściński, quoted in Mishra, pp. 304–5
11. Fukuyama (2014), p. 6
12. *The Times*, 8 October 2014

I. PRIORITIES

1. Barber (2008), p. 124
2. Taliaferro, p. 185
3. Shlaes, p. 9
4. Ibid.

5. Speech, 3 July 1948
6. Barber (2008), p. 49
7. Ibid., pp. 80–81
8. Pasternak, p. 424
9. *The Times*, 1 August 2003
10. *Evening Standard*, 27 February 2014
11. Blair, p. 338

2. ORGANIZATION

1. Barber (2008), p. 32
2. Blair, p. 124
3. Ibid., p. 207
4. Ibid., p. 283
5. Doz and Kosonen, p. 6
6. Blair, pp. 338–9
7. Iyer, p. 8
8. Ibid.
9. All quotes from Mulgan (2014)
10. Technical Note No. IDB-TN-563, p. 10
11. Ibid., pp. 41–2
12. Ibid., p. 31
13. See Mulgan (2014)
14. Technical Note No. IDB-TN-563, p. vii
15. Sugden, p. 849
16. Brainy Quotes website
17. See Steinberg, p. 106
18. Emmet Regan, unpublished MBA dissertation, Warwick University

3. STRATEGY

1. See, for example, Bevan and Wilson
2. Le Grand (2003), p. 8
3. Bevan and Wilson, pp. 250–51
4. Ibid., p. 246
5. Pink, p. xi
6. Bevan and Wilson, p. 246
7. Personal conversation with Governor O'Malley
8. Quoted in Bevan and Hamblin, p. 166

9. Ibid., p. 168
10. Lawson, p. 120
11. Garman, p. 3
12. Sahlgren, p. 18
13. Liu and Hanauer, p. 11
14. Fukuyama (2014), pp. 3–23
15. Guha, pp. 299–300
16. Ibid., p. 299
17. Ibid., p. 335
18. Ibid., p. 300

4. PLANNING

1. Smith, pp. 344–5
2. Ibid., p. 353
3. Brainy Quotes website
4. Ellis, pp. 149, 157
5. Kotter
6. Ellis, p. 157
7. Ringen, p. 4
8. Iyer, p. 3
9. Ibid.
10. Ibid., p. 4
11. Powell, p. 29
12. 'The Character of War', Oxford University lecture, 2010
13. Wiggins, pp. 100–105
14 *Sunday Telegraph*, 6 January 2002
15. Quoted in Freedman, p. 104

5. ROUTINES

1. Wainwright
2. Russakoff
3. Ibid.
4. *Huffington Post*, 3 October 2014
5. *Education Week*, 9 July 2014
6. Gawande (2008), p. 29
7. Duhigg, p. xix
8. Ibid., p. 98

9. Ibid., p.100
10. Barber (2008), p. 309
11. Ibid., p. 228
12. Andrew, p. 291
13. Ibid., p.193
14. Ibid., p. 192
15. Reich, pp. 74–5
16. King and Crewe, p. 386
17. Shlaes, p. 254
18. Ibid., pp. 261, 428
19. Iyer, p. 7
20. *New York Times*, 1 December 2013
21. *The Times*, 23 July 2004

6. PROBLEM-SOLVING

1. Macfarlane, p. 129
2. Cavendish, p. 15
3. Quoted in Pink, p. 198
4. Scharff (2012), p. 2
5. Ibid., p. 5
6. Ibid., p. 11
7. Ibid.
8. Freedman (2013), pp. 33, 37
9. Rogers
10. Parker and Miller, p. 6
11. Tuchman, p. 6
12. Ibid., pp. 2–3
13. Ibid., p. 3
14. Ibid., p. 4
15. Ibid., p. 6
16. McNamara, pp. 267–8
17. Quoted in ibid., p. 299

7. IRREVERSIBILITY

1. Adonis, p. 37
2. Quoted in Smith, p. 293
3. Quoted in Goodwin, p. 5

4. Ibid., p. 208
5. David Brailsford website
6. Nassim Nicholas Taleb website
7. Taleb, location 1520
8. Africa Governance Initiative, pp. 9–10
9. Ringen, p. 64
10. Ibid., p. 72
11. Ibid., p. 73
12. Hansard, Debate on the Address, 12 November 1936

8. (OTHER PEOPLE'S) MONEY

1. King James Bible, p. 60
2. Ibid., p. 61
3. Scharff (2013), p. 5
4. Ibid.
5. Ibid., pp. 7–8
6. Ibid., p. 10
7. Ibid., p. 13
8. Ibid., pp. 14–15
9. Osborne and Hutchinson, pp. 6–12
10. Richard Murray, *A Review of the Atkinson Review* (2005), p. 2
11. *Atkinson Review*, p. 182
12. Ibid.
13. Ibid., p. 183
14. Ibid.
15. Ibid.
16. Moore, p. 11
17. Ibid., p. 10
18. Ibid.
19. Barber and Day, p. 112
20. Benington and Moore, p. 125
21. Doz and Kosonen, pp. 7–8
22. Harvard Business School Case, 7 May 2009, *Endesa Chile: Raising the Ralco Dam*
23. Darling, pp. 1–2
24. Penn, p. xix
25. Ibid., p. 158

CONCLUSION: THE FUTURE OF DELIVERY

1. *The News* (Pakistan), 19 April 2014
2. Quoted in Bingham, p. 151
3. Heimans and Timms
4. Carrasco and Goss, pp. 3–4
5. B. S. Srinavasan, http://a16z.com/2014/09/24/opengov/, p. 2
6. Quoted in Goodwin, p. 564
7. *Harvard Business Review* blog, 28 March 2014
8. Press release, 23 July 2014
9. Iyer, pp. 9–10

Bibliography

Acemoglu, D. and Robinson, J. (2012), *Why Nations Fail: The Origins of Power, Prosperity and Poverty*, London, Profile Books

Adonis, A. (2012), *Education, Education, Education: Reforming England's Schools*, London, Biteback

Africa Governance Initiative (2013), *Two Steps at a Time: Rwanda's Strategic Capacity Building Initiative*, London, AGI

Andrew, C. (2009), *The Defence of the Realm: The Authorized History of MI5*, London, Allen Lane

Andrews, L. (2014), *Ministering to Education: A Reformer Reports*, Cardigan, Parthian

Andrews, M., Pritchett, L. and Woolcock, M. (2012), *Escaping Capability Traps Through Problem-Driven Iterative Adaptation (PDIA)*, CGD Working Paper 299, Washington DC, Center for Global Development

Auditor General for Wales (2005), *NHS Waiting Times for Wales*, vol. 1: *The Scale of the Problem* and vol. 2: *Tackling the Problem*

Barber, M. (1996), '"A Heaven-Sent Opportunity": James Callaghan and the Ruskin Speech', London, *Times Educational Supplement*

— (1997), *The Learning Game: Arguments for an Education Revolution*, London, Indigo

— (2004), *Courage and the Lost Art of Bicycle Maintenance*, London, PMDU

— (2008), *Instruction to Deliver: Fighting to Transform Britain's Public Services*, London, Methuen

— (2013), *The Good News from Pakistan: How a Revolutionary New Approach to Education Reform in Punjab Shows the Way Forward for Pakistan and Development Aid Everywhere*, London, Reform

— and Day, S. (2014), *The New Opportunity to Lead: A Vision for Education in Massachusetts in the Next 20 Years*, Boston, Massachusetts Business Alliance for Education

— with Moffit, A. and Kihn, P. (2010), *Deliverology 101: A Field Guide for Educational Leaders*, California, Corwin

— and Mourshed, M. (2007), *How the World's Best Performing School Systems Come Out on Top*, Chicago, McKinsey Company

Benington, J. and Moore, Mark H. (2011), *Public Value: Theory and Practice*, London, Palgrave Macmillan

Bevan, G. and Hamblin, R. (2009), 'Hitting and Missing Targets by Ambulance Services for Emergency Calls: Effects of Different Systems of Performance Measurement within the UK', *Journal of the Royal Statistical Society*: Series A, vol. 172, no. 1, pp. 161–90.

— and Hood, C. (2006), *What's Measured is What Matters: Targets and Gaming in the English Public Healthcare System*, Public Administration

— and Wilson, D. (2013), 'Does "Naming and Shaming" Work for Schools and Hospitals? Lessons from Natural Experiments following Devolution in England and Wales', *Public Money and Management*, vol. 33, issue 4, pp. 245–52.

Bhagwati, J. and Panagariya, A. (2014), *Why Growth Matters: How Economic Growth in India Reduced Poverty and the Lessons for Other Developing Countries*, New York, Public Affairs

Bingham, T. (2011), *The Rule of Law*, London, Penguin

Blair, T. (2011), *A Journey*, London, Arrow

Blunkett, D. (2006), *The Blunkett Tapes: My Life in the Bear Pit*, London, Bloomsbury

Bobbitt, P. (2003), *The Shield of Achilles: War, Peace and the Course of History*, London, Penguin

— (2009), *Terror and Consent: The Wars for the Twenty-first Century*, London, Penguin

Bok, D. (2002), *The Trouble with Government*, paperback edition, Boston, Harvard University Press

Botsman, P. and Latham, M. (2001), *The Enabling State: Putting People Before Bureaucracy*, Australia, Pluto Press

Bratton, W. and Knobler, P. (1998), *Turnaround*, New York, Random House

Brooks, G. et al (1996), *Reading Performance at Nine*, Slough, National Foundation for Educational Research

Bryson, B. (1995), *Notes from a Small Island*, London, Doubleday

Butler, R. A. (1971), *The Art of the Possible*, London, Hamish Hamilton

Campbell, A. (2007), *The Blair Years*, London, Hutchinson

Carrasco, M. and Goss, P. (2014), *Digital Government: Turning the Rhetoric into Reality*, Boston Consulting Group

Cavendish, Mark (2014), *At Speed: My Life in the Fast Lane*, London, Ebury Press

Christensen, C., Allworth, J. and Dillon, K. (2012), *How Will You Measure Your Life?*, New York, HarperCollins

Clarke, C. (ed.) (2014), *The Too Difficult Box: The Big Issues Politicians Can't Crack*, London, Biteback

Collins, J. (2001), *Good to Great: Why Some Companies Make the Leap ... and Others Don't*, London, Random House

Collins, J. C. and Porras, J. I. (1996), *Built to Last: Successful Habits of Visionary Companies*, London, Century

Collins, P. and Byrne, L. (eds.) (2004), *Reinventing Government Again*, London, Social Market Foundation

Colville, J. (1985), *The Fringes of Power: Downing Street Diaries 1939–1955*, London, Weidenfeld & Nicolson

Connolly, S., Bevan, G. and Mays, N. (2011), *Funding and Performance of Healthcare Systems in the Four Countries of the UK Before and After Devolution*, London, Nuffield Trust

Dallek, R. (2007), *Nixon and Kissinger: Partners in Power*, London, Allen Lane

Darling, A. (2011), *Back from the Brink: 1000 Days at No. 11*, London, Atlantic

Davis, J. (2007), *Prime Ministers and Whitehall 1960–74*, London, Hambledon Continuum

Davis, S., Lukomnik, J. and Pitt-Watson, D. (2006), *The New Capitalists: How Citizen Investors Are Reshaping the Corporate Agenda*, Cambridge MA, Harvard Business School Press

de Madariaga, I. (1981), *Russia in the Age of Catherine the Great*, London, Phoenix

DiCerbo, K. and Behrens, J. (2014), *Impacts of the Digital Ocean on Education*, London, Pearson

Dixon, N. (1994), *On the Psychology of Military Incompetence*, London, Pimlico

Doz, Y. and Kosonen, M. (2014), *Governments for the Future: Building the Strategic and Agile State*, Helsinki, Sitra

Drèze, J. and Sen, A. (2013), *An Uncertain Glory: India and Its Contradictions*, London, Allen Lane

Duhigg, C. (2013), *The Power of Habit: Why We Do What We Do in Life and Business*, London, Random House

Dumas, V., Lafuente, M. and Parrado, S. (2013), *Strengthening the Center of Government for Results in Chile: The Experience of the Ministry of the*

Presidency and its President's Delivery Unit (2010–13), Washington, Inter-American Development Bank

Easterly, W. (2014), *The Tyranny of Experts: Economists, Dictators and the Forgotten Rights of the Poor*, New York, Basic Books

Ellis, J. (2013), *Revolutionary Summer: The Birth of American Independence*, New York, Alfred Knopf

Filmer, D., Hammer, J. and Pritchett, L. (2000), 'Weak Links in the Chain: A Diagnosis of Health Policy in Poor Countries', Washington, *World Bank Research Observer*, vol. 15, no. 2, August

Freedman, L. (2013), *Strategy: A History*, Oxford, Oxford University Press

Friedman, B. M. (2005), *The Moral Consequences of Economic Growth*, New York, Alfred Knopf

Friedman, M. (2005), *Trying Hard is Not Good Enough*, Victoria, Canada, Trafford Publishing

Friedman, T. (2006), *The World Is Flat: A Brief History of the Twenty-first Century*, London, Penguin

— and Mandelbaum, M. (2011), *That Used to Be Us: What Went Wrong with America and How it Can Come Back*, New York, Little, Brown

Fukuyama, F. (2011), *The Origins of Political Order: From Prehuman Times to the French Revolution*, London, Profile Books

— (2014), *Political Order and Political Decay: From the Industrial Revolution to the Globalisation of Democracy*, London, Profile Books

Garman, J. (2014), *Europe's Power: Re-energising a Progressive Climate and Energy Agenda*, London, Institute for Public Policy Research

Gawande, A. (2008), *Better: A Surgeon's Notes on Performance*, London, Profile Books

— (2010), *The Checklist Manifesto: How to Get Things Right*, London, Profile Books

Ghani, A. and Lockhart, C. (2009), *Fixing Failed States: A Framework for Rebuilding a Fractured World*, Oxford, Oxford University Press

Giuliani, R. (2002), *Leadership*, New York, Little, Brown

Gold, J. (2014), *International Delivery: Centres of Government and the Drive for Better Policy Implementation*, London, Institute for Government

Goodwin, D. K. (2013), *The Bully Pulpit: Theodore Roosevelt, William Howard Taft and the Golden Age of Journalism*, New York, Simon & Schuster

Guha, R. (2013), *Gandhi Before India*, London, Allen Lane

Halberstam, D. (1992), *The Best and the Brightest*, New York, Ballantine Books

Harding, R. (2014), 'World Bank: Man on a Mission', London, *Financial Times*, 7 April

Harris, J. and Rutter, J. (2014), *Centre Forward: Effective Support for the Prime Minister at the Centre of Government*, London, Institute for Government

Harvard Business Review (2013), *On Teams*, Boston, Harvard Business Review Press

Heifetz, R. (1994), *Leadership Without Easy Answers*, Boston, Harvard University Press

— and Linsky, M. (2002), *Leadership on the Line: Staying Alive Through the Dangers of Leading*, Boston, Harvard Business School Press

Heimans, J. and Timms, H. (2014), 'Understanding "New Power"', *Harvard Business Review*

Hennessy, P. (2000), *The Prime Minister: The Office and its Holders Since 1945*, London, Allen Lane

Hill, P. et al (2013), *Strife and Progress: Portfolio Strategies for Managing Urban Schools*, Washington, Brookings Institution Press

Holt, R. (2001), *Second Amongst Equals: Chancellors of the Exchequer and the British Economy*, London, Profile Books

Hunt, T. (2005), *Building Jerusalem: The Rise and Fall of the Victorian City*, New York, Metropolitan Books

Hyman, P. (2005), *1 Out of 10*, London, Vintage

Iyer, D. (2011), 'Interview with Idris Jala' for Innovations for Successful Societies, Woodrow Wilson School of Public and International Affairs and the Mamdouha S. Bobst Center for Peace and Justice, Princeton University

Jenkins, R. (1995), *Gladstone: A Biography*, London, Macmillan

— (2001), *Churchill: A Biography*, London, Macmillan

Jenkins, S. (2006), *Thatcher and Sons: A Revolution in Three Acts*, London, Allen Lane

Kaplan, R. (2014), 'Strategy Execution', presentation, Harvard Business School

Kelman, S. (2006), 'Improving Service Delivery Performance in the United Kingdom', *Journal of Comparative Policy Analysis*, vol. 8, no. 4, December

Kerchner, C. and Mitchell, D. (1988), *The Changing Idea of a Teachers' Union*, Lewes, Falmer Press

Kim, J. Y. et al (eds.) (2000), *Dying for Growth: Global Inequality and the Health of the Poor*, Cambridge MA, Common Courage Press

King, A. and Crewe, I. (2013), *The Blunders of Our Governments*, London, Oneworld

King James Bible (2011 edition), London, Collins

Kotter, J. (1996), *Leading Change: An Action Plan from the World's Foremost Expert on Business Leadership*, Boston, Harvard Business School Press

Lane, J. E. (2000), *The Public Sector: Concepts, Models and Approaches*, London, Sage Publications

Lawson, N. (2010), *The View from No. 11: Memoirs of a Tory Radical*, revised edition, London, Biteback

Lax, D. and Sebenius, J. (2006), *3-D Negotiation: Powerful Tools to Change the Game in Your Most Important Deals*, Boston, Harvard Business School Press

Le Grand, J. (2003), *Motivation, Agency and Public Policy: Of Knights and Knaves, Pawns and Queens*, New York, Oxford University Press

— (2007), *The Other Invisible Hand: Delivering Public Services through Choice and Competition*, Princeton, Princeton University Press

Lesley, E. (2014), *Mapping a Transformation Journey: A Strategy for Malaysia's Future, 2009–2010*, Innovations for Successful Societies, Woodrow Wilson School of Public and International Affairs and the Mamdouha S. Bobst Center for Peace and Justice, Princeton University

Liu, E. and Hanauer, N. (2011), *The Gardens of Democracy: A New American Story of Citizenship, the Economy and the Role of Government*, Seattle, Sasquatch Books

Macfarlane, R. (2013), *The Old Ways: A Journey on Foot*, London, Penguin

Major, J. (1999), *John Major: The Autobiography*, London, HarperCollins

Mandelson, P. (2002), *The Blair Revolution Revisited*, London, Politico's

Manna, P. and McGuinn, P. (eds.) (2013), *Education Governance for the Twenty-first Century*, Washington, Brookings Institution Press

Mayer-Schönberger, V. and Cukier, K. (2014), *Big Data: A Revolution That Will Transform How We Live, Work and Think*, New York, Mariner Books

McChesney, C., Covey, S. and Huling, J. (2012), *The Four Disciplines of Execution*, New York, Free Press

McGuinty, D., Speech 2010, personal communication with the author

McKinsey & Co (2013), *Voices on Society: The Art and Science of Delivery*, London, McKinsey and Company

McNamara, R. (1996), *In Retrospect: The Tragedy and Lessons of Vietnam*, New York, Vintage

Micklethwait, J. and Wooldridge, A. (2014), *The Fourth Revolution: The Global Race to Reinvent the State*, London, Penguin

Mishra, P. (2012), *From the Ruins of Empire: The Intellectuals Who Remade Asia*, New York, Farrar, Staus and Giroux

Moore, M. (1995), *Creating Public Value: Strategic Management in Government*, Boston, Harvard University Press

Morris, E. (2001), *Theodore Rex*, New York, Random House

Mourshed, M., Chijioke, C. and Barber, M. (2010), *How the World's Most Improved School Systems Keep Getting Better,* Chicago, McKinsey and Company

Mulgan, G. (2006), *Good and Bad Power: The Ideals and Betrayals of Government,* London, Allen Lane

— (2008), *The Art of Public Strategy: Mobilizing Power and Knowledge for the Common Good,* Oxford, Oxford University Press

— (2014), 'Rewiring the Brain: A Rough Blueprint for Reforming Centres of Government', London, NESTA

Naughtie, J. (2001), *The Rivals: The Intimate Story of a Political Marriage,* London, Fourth Estate

Nishtar, S. (2010), *Choked Pipes: Reforming Pakistan's Mixed Health System,* Oxford, Oxford University Press

Norris, E., Rutter, J. and Medland, J. (2013), *Making the Games: What Government Can Learn from London 2012,* London, Institute for Government

Olivier, R. (2002), *Inspirational Leadership: Henry V and the Muse of Fire,* London, Spiro Press

Osborne, D. and Gaebler, T. (1993), *Reinventing Government: How the Entrepreneurial Spirit is Transforming the Public Sector,* New York, Plume

Osborne, D. and Hutchinson, P. (2006), *The Price of Government: Getting the Results We Need in an Age of Permanent Fiscal Crisis,* New York, Basic Books

Page, E. C. and Jenkins, B. (2005), *Policy Bureaucracy: Government with a Cast of Thousands,* New York, Oxford University Press

Panchamia, N. and Thomas, P. (2014), *Public Service Agreements and the Prime Minister's Delivery Unit,* London, Institute for Government

Parker, L. and Miller, J. (2012), 'The Eleven Conversations', *Brunswick Review,* issue 6

Pasternak, B. (2011), *Doctor Zhivago,* London, Vintage

Penn, T. (2012), *Winter King: The Dawn of Tudor England,* London, Penguin

Pink, D. (2011), *Drive: The Surprising Truth About What Motivates Us,* Edinburgh, Canongate

Policy Profession Board (2013), *Twelve Actions to Professionalise Policy Making,* London, UK Civil Service

Powell, J. (2011), *The New Machiavelli: How to Wield Power in the Modern World,* London, Vintage

Propper, C., Sutton, M., Whitnall, C. and Windmeijer, F. (2010), 'Incentives and Targets in Hospital Care: Evidence from a Natural Experiment', *Journal of Public Economics,* vol. 94, issues 3–4, pp. 318–35

Ramsbotham, O., Woodhouse, T. and Miall, H. (2005), *Contemporary*

Conflict Resolution: The Prevention, Management and Transformation of Deadly Conflicts, 2nd edition, Cambridge, Polity Press

Regan, E. (2013), 'Hitting the Target or Missing the Point: What are the Drivers to Influence the Achievement of Key Targets in Governmental Performance Management Systems? An Examination of the Role of the Prime Minister's Delivery Unit in Relation to A&E Waiting Times (2001–2005)', dissertation for MBA at Warwick Business School

Reich, R. (1998), *Locked in the Cabinet*, New York, Vintage Books

Riddell, P. (2005), *The Unfulfilled Prime Minister: Tony Blair's Quest for a Legacy*, London, Politico's

Ringen, S. (2013), *Nation of Devils: Democratic Leadership and the Problem of Obedience*, Yale, Yale University Press

Rogers, Everett M. (1983), *Diffusion of Innovations*, New York, Free Press

Russakoff, D. (2014), 'Schooled', *New Yorker*, 19 May

Ryan, Alan (2013), *On Politics: A History of Political Thought from Herodotus to the Present*, London, Penguin

Sahlberg, P. (2011), *Finnish Lessons*, New York, Teachers College Press

Sahlgren, G. (2013), *Incentivising Excellence: School Choice and Education Quality*, London, Centre for Market Reform of Education

Scharff, M. (2012), *Delivering on a Presidential Agenda: Sierra Leone's Strategy and Policy Unit, 2010–2011*, Innovations for Successful Societies, Woodrow Wilson School of Public and International Affairs and the Mamdouha S. Bobst Center for Peace and Justice, Princeton University

— (2013), *A New Approach to Managing at the Center of Government: Governor Mitch Daniels and Indiana, 2005–2012*, Innovations for Successful Societies, Woodrow Wilson School of Public and International Affairs and the Mamdouha S. Bobst Center for Peace and Justice, Princeton University

Schlesinger, R. (2008), *White House Ghosts: Presidents and Their Speechwriters*, New York, Simon & Schuster

Seldon, A. (2005), *Blair*, London, Simon & Schuster

—, Snowden, P. and Collings, D. (2007), *Blair Unbound*, London, Simon & Schuster

Sellar, W. and Yeatman, R. (1998), *1066 and All That*, London, Methuen

Shlaes, A. (2013), *Coolidge*, New York, HarperCollins

Silver, N. (2012), *The Signal and the Noise: The Art and Science of Prediction*, London, Penguin

Smillie, I. (2009), *Freedom from Want: The Remarkable Success Story of BRAC, the Global Grassroots Organisation That's Winning the Fight Against Poverty*, Dhaka, Kumarian Press

Smith, J. E. (2012), *Eisenhower in War and Peace*, New York, Random House

State of Victoria (2005), *Growing Victoria Together*

Steinberg, J. (2011), *Bismarck: A Life*, Oxford, Oxford University Press

Stevenson, A. (2013), *The Public Sector: Managing the Unmanageable*, London, Kogan Page

Sugden, J. (2012), *Nelson: The Sword of Albion*, London, Bodley Head

Taleb, N. N. (2007), *The Black Swan: The Impact of the Highly Improbable*, London, Allen Lane

— (2012), *Antifragile: How to Live in a World We Don't Understand*, London, Allen Lane

Taliaferro, J. (2013), *All the Great Prizes: The Life of John Hay, from Lincoln to Roosevelt*, New York, Simon & Schuster

Thaler, R. and Sunstein, C. (2008), *Nudge: Improving Decisions About Health, Wealth and Happiness*, London, Penguin

Timmins, N. (1995), *The Five Giants: A Biography of the Welfare State*, London, HarperCollins

Trewhitt, K. et al (2014), *How to Run a Country: A Collection of Essays*, London, Reform

Tuchman, B. (1990), *The March of Folly: From Troy to Vietnam*, St Ives, Abacus

US Senate Committee on the Budget and Taskforce on Government Performance, Report, 29 October 2009

Wainwright, A. (2007), *The Southern Fells*, revised edition, London, Frances Lincoln

Wales Audit Office (2006), *Ambulance Services in Wales*

Weiss, M. (2014), 'Government Entrepreneur' is not an Oxymoron, Cambridge MA, Harvard Business Review Blog Network, 28 March 2014

Whelan, F. (2014), *The Learning Challenge*, self-published

Wiggins, B. (2012), *My Time*, London, Yellow Jersey Press

Williams, J. and Rossiter, A. (2004), *Choice: The Evidence*, London, Social Market Foundation

Wolmar, C. (2013), *To the Edge of the World: The Story of the Trans-Siberian Railway*, London, Atlantic Books

Acknowledgements

The preparation of this book drew heavily on conversations with many and varied friends and colleagues around the world, only a few of whom I can thank here. In particular, I have drawn on my experience of eight years working for the British government, four of them directly on delivering results for Tony Blair in No. 10 Downing Street. I have also drawn on my work since then in dozens of countries around the world, including the US, Chile, Colombia, Malaysia and Pakistan, all of which feature in these pages.

Many politicians and officials, writers and thinkers, colleagues and friends have contributed to my thinking.

I will always be grateful to Tony Blair for the opportunity he gave me in 2001 to set up and lead the Prime Minister's Delivery Unit. Our collaboration over the next four years was a remarkable experience and we discovered that together we had become innovators in the process of government. I also stayed in dialogue with Blair in the years since he stepped down and began, through his Africa Governance Initiative, for example, to assist other leaders of governments.

During my time in the Prime Minister's Delivery Unit, I worked with and learned from numerous ministers and officials in the UK. My team in the Delivery Unit was as talented and committed a group of people as you could ever wish to meet. Clara Swinson and Vanessa Nicholls have become top officials. Adrian Masters is one of the leaders of the National Health Service, and Peter Thomas, in a variety of roles, has helped shape the future of the British civil service. Tony O'Connor, mentioned a number of times in the text above, has led the Government Operational Research Society with distinction for over a decade and remains a good friend and powerful influence.

Kieran Brett has also gone on to greater things. Richard Page-Jones, Simon Day, Simon Rea and Leigh Sandals were colleagues then and have often been colleagues since as we've shared our knowledge and experience on four continents; their skill, insight, commitment and integrity are an inspiration.

I have stayed closely in contact with some of the ministers I got to know during the Blair years, and have kept learning from them: Andrew Adonis, David Blunkett, Charles Clarke, Tessa Jowell and David Miliband are among them.

I've also been privileged to be in touch with political leaders in the UK since Blair, including Gordon Brown, who has made such a commitment to education around the world since he left office. In the Cameron years, Michael Gove and Andrew Mitchell have always been open to dialogue about government, policy and delivery.

Former colleagues from No. 10 have remained a significant influence. Peter Hyman has set up and now runs an inspiring school while continuing to comment on politics and policy. Liz Lloyd and Gavin Kelly were excellent advisers to Blair and Brown respectively. Geoff Mulgan, Nick Pearce, Matthew Taylor and Phil Collins, all colleagues from that time, have become leading British intellectuals, and are a constant source of ideas. Jonathan Powell, a colleague in No. 10, has done wonderful work since, and written with clarity and wit about his time in Downing Street. Jeremy Heywood, now the cabinet secretary, is a peerless public servant and good friend. Nick Macpherson, then in charge of public spending and now permanent secretary of the Treasury, invented the gently mocking term 'deliverology' and stayed true to its tenets.

Across the world, I've had the opportunity to meet and sometimes work with a range of political leaders, some of whom appear in the book. Julia Gillard's ability to pursue a strategy while simultaneously thriving in the cut-throat political culture that is Australia was never less than impressive. Three leaders whose work features in these pages were unfailingly kind enough to give me time to discuss making government work and, more importantly, showed how to in their daily work: Najib Razak, prime minister of Malaysia, Dalton McGuinty, premier of Ontario, and Shahbaz Sharif, chief minister of Punjab, Pakistan. In US education I was privileged to be in dialogue with Arne Duncan, the education secretary; Joel Klein, for several rollercoaster years Chancellor of

New York City Schools; Paul Pastorek, State Superintendent in Louisiana; and Mitchell Chester, his equivalent in Massachusetts. I always enjoyed interacting with Antonio Villaraigosa when he was mayor of Los Angeles, and his chief of staff at the time, Robin Kramer. Melanie Walker, who leads the President's Delivery Unit at the World Bank, is exactly the kind of driven, inspired individual required for such a post, and always a source of ideas and information.

Around such politicians, there are always talented advisers or officials helping to make things happen; Idris Jala has done so for Najib Razak; Gerald Butts, Jamieson Steeve and Michael Fullan (the latter my collaborator on many ventures) did so for Dalton McGuinty; and now Aizaz Akhtar is doing so for Shahbaz Sharif. All these advisers are dedicated, talented people who, with the best kind of patriotism, devote themselves to their countries.

In the US, I had the opportunity in 2010 to found the Education Delivery Institute, which has been working with US states to assist in the delivery of successful education reform. Kathy Cox, its chief executive, Nick Rodriguez and Ellyn Artis are good friends and committed experts in delivery.

Over the past year, I've had the pleasure of working with the Harvard School of Public Health on a programme designed to assist ministers of health and ministers of finance in the developing world have a greater impact on outcomes. Julio Frenk, the dean of the school, and Michael Sinclair, the programme's dauntless leader and organizer, are great colleagues.

In addition to the Harvard School of Public Health, I'm grateful for opportunities to collaborate with or lecture at a number of universities around the world and always find interaction with students energizing and insightful. These include the Judge Business School at the University of Cambridge, Exeter University, the Harvard Graduate School of Education, the Lahore University of Management Sciences, the London School of Economics, the Blavatnik School of Government at the University of Oxford, Queen Mary University London, the Lee Kuan Yew School of Public Policy at the National University of Singapore and Stanford University. Sir Steve Smith, vice-chancellor of Exeter University, is one of the shrewdest observers of the modern world and a constant source of insight.

Since August 2009, I have visited Pakistan on more than forty occasions to assist the governments of Punjab and Khyber Pakhtunkhwa with education reform. In addition to Shahbaz Sharif, whom I have already mentioned, numerous officials in Punjab have stood out for their talent and determination in difficult circumstances. I'll mention just two: Aslam Kamboh, the Secretary – Schools from 2010 to 2013, and his successor, Abdul Jabar Shaheen. They are both outstanding public servants.

Both the British High Commission and the DFID have provided outstanding support for my work in Pakistan. By thanking successive High Commissioners – Sir Adam Thomson and Philip Barton – and successive DFID Heads of Mission – George Turkington and Richard Montgomery – I thank all the officials with whom I've had the pleasure to interact.

Throughout the time I've been working there, a succession of talented young people have been part of my team supporting the government of Punjab. They are too numerous to mention. Two of them I'll come to later. Here, let me thank Fenton Whelan, who provided insight and drive throughout the years I've been working there and who had the courage to join me on my first visit to Pakistan in August 2009.

For the six years after I left Downing Street, I was a partner at McKinsey and worked with numerous talented people around the world. McKinsey taught me that it prefers to work behind the scenes and stay out of the limelight, so here I'll just thank successive managing partners, Ian Davis and Dominic Barton, for putting up with me, and through them thank all the others with whom I collaborated.

Since then I've worked for Pearson, the education company, as Chief Education Advisor. Successive chief executives, Marjorie Scardino and John Fallon, have been good colleagues and friends and consistently supportive of my varied activities. Pearson's radical reorganization with its focus on demonstrating learning outcomes has been taking place at the same time as I have been writing this book and represents a classic delivery challenge. Colleagues in the Pearson Executive have tolerated it cheerfully when I've circulated a Power-Point slide based on this book as a means of suggesting the way forward for the company. The members of my team at Pearson over recent years have been talented, creative and diligent colleagues and great to work with.

Two colleagues in particular have become close friends and mentors to me, though neither is yet thirty. Katelyn Donnelly and Saad Rizvi joined my team in Punjab, Pakistan in January 2011 and were instrumental in establishing the Education Roadmap which has since made such a difference to millions of children. Later that year, Katelyn joined me at Pearson; Saad joined us too, early in 2012. Collaborating with them on work and writing has been a privilege. Their energy and iconoclasm, curiosity and creativity, their understanding of the twenty-first-century world, their constant stream of ideas (all of them exciting and most of them excellent), and their restless dissatisfaction with the way the world is are both a challenge and an inspiration. With these two and Richard Page-Jones, Simon Day, Simon Rea, Leigh Sandals and I have founded Delivery Associates, a small organization committed to assisting governments to deliver better results for citizens.

Denise Todd is another colleague who followed me from McKinsey to Pearson, where she is the business manager for my team. In addition to her meticulous work, she is a thoughtful friend, always willing to offer me good advice, even when sometimes I'd prefer not to hear it. Meanwhile, her organizational skills quite simply make my crazy working life possible. Georgina Cooke, a close friend of ours who would have loved to see the book come to fruition, sadly died during its writing. The question 'What would Georgina think?' enters my head regularly, especially when I have blundered. She always had a practical answer while seeing the funny side too. Kirsche Hunt, who now schedules my working life with unfailing good humour, deserves thanks too.

My good friends over decades, Robin Alfred, David Keeton and David Pitt-Watson provided numerous ideas and challenges during the course of our endless conversations. Alan Evans has also been a good mentor and source of insight over many years. I never have a conversation with David Puttnam without gathering at least one golden nugget of insight into the world. Meanwhile, Iqbal Khan is deeply thoughful on the future of government in Islamic countries. I am fortunate too to be involved in setting up the Boston Consulting

Group's Centre for Public Impact, which I co-chair. Adrian Brown at BCG is a good friend and thoughtful colleague. I have also enjoyed collaboration with Jitinder Kohli at Deloitte.

Nandini Ramamurthy and Rachelle Albern undertook important research which enabled me to find many more examples of interesting and effective practice in government, while at the same time helping me to round out others. Simon Rea read a draft from cover to cover and suggested numerous stylistic improvements. Peter Riddell, Chief Executive of the Institute for Government in London, also offered numerous helpful comments on the text.

Tanya Kreisky has been a collaborator on more writing and publishing projects for over twenty years than either of us cares to remember. What has made working with her on this book and others a pleasure is the combination of her consummate professionalism with a rare *joie de vivre*, which means every conversation with her, even when the pressure is on, is cheerful as well as practical. I would also like to thank Josephine Greywoode, Richard Duguid and Bela Cunha, all of whom were total professionals.

Last, but of course not least, there is the family. My three wonderful daughters, Naomi, Anja and Alys, mock me, laugh at me, bring me down to earth and tease me for my love of graphs. Each in their different ways is a joy to spend time with, as are my two sons-in-law, Guy and Morgan. My grandson, Jacob, born the year I left No. 10, would win an Olympic gold medal if there were one for talking and swimming at the same time, and persuaded me that I should give him the first copy of this book I receive from the publisher. Whether he'll enjoy it as much as the Horrible Histories remains to be seen.

Then there's Karen, whose love and friendship make life worth living. After thirty years together in Hackney, we've spent the past few years in Devon. While I've been writing this book, Karen has cast her magic spells and created our own small corner of paradise. To live with such an incredible person in such a beautiful place is endlessly restorative and a blessing beyond words. It is also a perfect setting for writing.

Needless to say, any errors or misjudgements in the pages above are mine alone.

Index